Access® 2013

ABSOLUTE BEGINNER'S GUIDE

Alison Balter

800 East 96th Street,
Indianapolis, Indiana 46240 USA

Access 2013 Absolute Beginner's Guide

ISBN-13: 978-0-7897-4871-3
ISBN-10: 0-7897-4871-1

The Library of Congress Cataloging-in-Publication Data is on file.

Printed in the United States of America

First Printing: April 2013

Trademarks

Warning and Disclaimer

Bulk Sales

Que Publishing offers excellent discounts on this book when ordered in quantity for bulk purchases or special sales. For more information, please contact

U.S. Corporate and Government Sales
1-800-382-3419
corpsales@pearsontechgroup.com

For sales outside of the U.S., please contact

International Sales
international@pearsoned.com

Editor-in-Chief
Greg Wiegand

Executive Editor
Loretta Yates

Development Editor
The Wordsmithery LLC

Managing Editor
Sandra Schroeder

Project Editor
Seth Kerney

Copy Editor
Apostrophe Editing Services

Indexer
Lisa Stumpf

Proofreader
Jess DeGabriele

Technical Editor
Ross Pimentel

Publishing Coordinator
Cindy Teeters

Book Designer
Anne Jones

Compositor
MPS Limited

Contents at a Glance

Table of Contents

About the Author

Alison Balter is the president of InfoTech Services Group, Inc., a computer consulting firm based in Newbury Park, California. Alison is a highly experienced independent trainer and consultant specializing in Windows applications training and development. During her 28 years in the computer industry, she has trained and consulted with many corporations and government agencies. Since Alison founded InfoTech Services Group, Inc. (formerly Marina Consulting Group) in 1990, its client base has expanded to include major corporations and government agencies such as Cisco, Shell Oil, Accenture, Northrop, the U.S. Drug Enforcement Administration, Prudential Insurance, Transamerica Insurance, Fox Broadcasting, the U.S. Navy, the University of Southern California , Massachusetts Institute of Technology, and others.

Alison is the author of more than 300 internationally marketed computer training videos and CD-ROMs, including 18 Access 2000 videos, 35 Access 2002 videos, 15 Access 2003 videos, 14 Access 2007 User Videos, and 18 Access 2007 Developer Videos. Alison travels throughout North America giving training seminars on Microsoft Access, Microsoft SQL Server, and Visual Basic for Applications.

Alison is also the author of 13 books published by Sams Publishing: *Alison Balter's Mastering Access 95 Development*, *Alison Balter's Mastering Access 97 Development*, *Alison Balter's Mastering Access 2000 Development*, *Alison Balter's Mastering Access 2002 Desktop Development*, *Alison Balter's Mastering Access 2002 Enterprise Development*, *Alison Balter's Mastering Microsoft Access Office 2003*, *Teach Yourself Microsoft Office Access 2003 in 24 Hours*, *Access Office 2003 in a Snap*, *Alison Balter's Mastering Access 2007 Development*, three e-books on Microsoft Access 2007, and *Teach Yourself SQL Express 2005 in 24 Hours*. Alison is a co-author of three Access books published by Sams Publishing: *Essential Access 95*, *Access 95 Unleashed*, *Access 97 Unleashed*, and *Using Microsoft Access 2010*.

An active participant in many user groups and other organizations, Alison is a past president of the Independent Computer Consultants Association of Los Angeles and of the Los Angeles Clipper Users' Group. She served as president of the Ventura County Professional Women's Network for 2 years.

Alison's firm, InfoTech Services Group, Inc., is available for consulting work and onsite training in Microsoft Access, Visual Studio .NET, and SQL Server, as well as for Windows Server 2008, Windows Vista, Windows XP, Windows 7, Windows 8, PC networking, and Microsoft Exchange Server. You can contact Alison by email at Alison@TechIsMyThing.com, or visit the InfoTech Services Group website at http://www.TechIsMyThing.com.

Dedication

Many people are important in my life, but there is no one as special as my husband Dan. I dedicate this book to Dan. Thank you for your ongoing support, for your dedication to me, for your unconditional love, and for your patience. Without you, I'm not sure how I would make it through life. Thank you for sticking with me through the good times and the bad! There's nobody I'd rather spend forever with than you.

I also want to thank God for giving me the gift of gab, a wonderful career, an incredible husband, two beautiful children, a spectacular area to live in, a very special home, and an awesome life. Through your grace, I am truly blessed.

Acknowledgments

Authoring books is not an easy task. Special thanks go to the following wonderful people who helped make this book possible and, more important, who give my life meaning:

Dan Balter (my incredible husband), for his ongoing support, love, encouragement, friendship, and, as usual, patience with me while I authored this book. Dan, words cannot adequately express the love and appreciation I feel for all that you are and all that you do for me. You treat me like a princess! Thank you for being the phenomenal person you are, and thank you for loving me for who I am and for supporting me during the difficult times. I enjoy not only sharing our career successes, but even more I enjoy sharing the lives of our beautiful children, Alexis and Brendan. I look forward to continuing to reach highs we never dreamed of.

Alexis Balter (my daughter and confidante), for giving life a special meaning. Your intelligence, drive, and excellence in all that you do are truly amazing. Alexis, I know that you will go far in life. I am so proud of you. Even in these difficult teenage years, your wisdom and inner beauty shine through. Finally, thanks for being my walking partner. I love the conversations that we have when we walk together.

Brendan Balter (my wonderful son and amazing athlete), for showing me the power of persistence. Brendan, you are relatively small, but, boy, are you mighty! I have never seen such tenacity and fortitude in a young person. You are able to tackle people twice your size just through your incredible spirit and your remarkable athletic ability. Your imagination and creativity are amazing! Thank you for your sweetness, your sensitivity, and your unconditional love. I really enjoy our times together, especially all the cuddling. Most of all, thank you for reminding me how important it is to have a sense of humor.

Charlotte and Bob Roman (Mom and Dad), for believing in me and sharing in both the good times and the bad. Mom and Dad, without your special love and support, I never would have become who I am today. Without all your help, I could never get everything done. Words can never express how much I appreciate all that you do!

Al Ludington, for giving me a life worth living. You somehow walk the fine line between being there and setting limits, between comforting me and confronting me. Words cannot express how much your unconditional love means to me. Thanks for always being there for me and for showing me that a beautiful mind is not such a bad thing after all.

Roz, Ron, and Charlie Carriere, for supporting my endeavors and for encouraging me to pursue my writing. It means a lot to know that you guys are proud of me for what I do. I enjoy our times together as a family. Charlie, I am very proud of you for all of your successes.

Herb and Maureen Balter (my honorary dad and mom), for being such a wonderful father-in-law and mother-in-law. Although our paths were rocky at the beginning, I want you to know how special you are to me. I appreciate your acceptance and your warmth. I also appreciate all you have done for Dan and me. I am grateful to have you in my life.

Reverend Molly, for advancing me spiritually in ways that I can't even describe. You are an amazing woman and are my mentor. I love you dearly. Thanks also to all my church friends: Ed, Zach, Brynn, Gail, Diana, Martha, Marti, Dominic, Sonny, Kathy, Kayeanne, Sonna, Betty, Melba, Bobbi, Ivette, Gary, Sheryl, John, Rick, Janie, Sherry, Cory, Opal, Suemary, Susan, Beth, Peter, Shannon, Karon, Stacy, Juan, Lucy, Sylvia, David, Maria, Steve, Susie, Evelyn, and everyone I am forgetting to mention, for all your love and support.

Dr. William Cipriano for helping to add balance to my life and for being a good listener. I appreciate your time and your dedication.

Grace Hollow for being such a wonderful friend. Grace, I *love* our long walks and conversations. I feel that I can tell you absolutely everything. You are unbelievably dear to me!

Tracy Williams for being a special light in my life. Tracy, I appreciate our relationship at church and as friends. Thanks for introducing me to ToastMasters and for supporting my life endeavors!

Ivette Saiz for your friendship and support. I love spending time with you at church and socially. I only wish that we could see each other more.

Stacy and Juan Ros for your friendship, and for being godparents to Alexis and Brendan. Stacy, thanks for all your spiritual support and for your friendship. You are an awesome leader for our kids. Juan, thanks for being a wonderful friend to me and to Dan.

Paula Williams for your support and inspiration. Paula, you are a wonderful friend and I love having you in my life. I admire and appreciate you.

Sue Lopez, for her friendship. Sue, thank you for your unconditional love, and for all the great times that we have had together.

Greg Stuart for your incredible support as my business and life coach. Greg, you have made a major impact on my life. It seems that whatever goals I set with you come to fruition. You are a great inspiration to me.

All my friends at BNI for supporting me every Monday, and for sharing in my joy about writing so many books: Pam, Debbie, Steve, Terri, Jeremy, Phil, Veronica, Bill, Kathleen, Shari, Fred, Greg, Jim, Jennie, Aaron, Benny, Joyce, Mike, Jared, Tom M., and Tom D.

Ross Pimentel, for being so understanding as I completed this book. I so much enjoy working with you, and have fun on both on our programming ventures, and at our lunches. Thank you also for your contribution to this book. I appreciate your willingness to jump in and be my technical editor. You gave it your all, and it shows. You're awesome! Give my love to Hanna for all her patience while you were busy helping me to support all my endeavors.

Philip and Sharyn Ochoa for giving me the opportunity to work at such a special company. I appreciate all the work, as well as the friendships that I have been able to make. Thanks for all your faith in me.

Chris Sabihon, Kassandra Dinwiddie, and Tim Gale for being clients that have uniquely touched my life. Each of you has made a difference in my life in your own exceptional way. Chris, you have changed my spiritual life forever and will always occupy a special place in my heart. Kassandra, you are a blast to work with. You are so bright. I am so glad that we got to know each other in person. Tim, I appreciate the work with USC, and I have enjoyed getting to know you over the past months.

Loretta Yates, for making my book-writing experience such a positive one. Loretta, I can't tell you how much I have enjoyed working with you over the past several years. You are easy to work with, and I enjoy the personal relationship that we have developed as well. I look forward to working together for years to come.

We Want to Hear from You!

As the reader of this book, *you* are our most important critic and commentator. We value your opinion and want to know what we're doing right, what we could do better, what areas you'd like to see us publish in, and any other words of wisdom you're willing to pass our way.

We welcome your comments. You can email or write to let us know what you did or didn't like about this book—as well as what we can do to make our books better.

Please note that we cannot help you with technical problems related to the topic of this book.

When you write, please be sure to include this book's title and author as well as your name, email address, and phone number. We will carefully review your comments and share them with the author and editors who worked on the book.

Email: feedback@quepublishing.com
Mail: Que Publishing

ATTN: Reader Feedback
800 East 96th Street
Indianapolis, IN 46240 USA

Reader Services

Visit our website and register this book at **quepublishing.com/register** for convenient access to any updates, downloads, or errata that might be available for this book.

INTRODUCTION

Who Should Read This Book

This book is for anyone comfortable using a personal computer who needs to collect and manipulate information. Experience with Microsoft Access 2013 or an earlier version of Access is helpful, but not necessary. This book takes you from the basic techniques on how to use Microsoft Access 2013 to a strong intermediate level. After reading this book, you should be comfortable creating and working with databases and the objects that they contain.

How This Book Is Organized

This book starts by covering the basics of working with Microsoft Access. You learn the basics of working with databases, tables, queries, forms, and reports. After learning the basics, you are ready to move to more advanced features, where you learn how to build your own databases and tables and how to relate the tables within your database. You are then ready to embark on a journey through power query, form, and report techniques. During the home stretch, you learn about three exciting aspects of Access 2013. You learn how to create macros, how to share data with other applications, and how to build a database that runs in a browser. Finally, you see how to put everything that you learned together and build a complete application.

Requirements, Editions, and Features

Microsoft hasn't dramatically increased the hardware requirements for Access 2013 compared to those for earlier versions of Access. Access 2013 runs on existing hardware as well as or even better than earlier versions of Access.

To be sure you can run Access 2013, here's a look at the basic hardware and operating system requirements:

- 1GHz or faster x86 or x64-bit processor

- 1GB of RAM (32 bit); 2GB of RAM (64 bit)

- 3GB available hard disk space

- 1024 × 576 resolution monitor

- Windows Server 2008 R2 (32 bit or 64 bit), Windows Server 2012, Windows 7, Windows 8, or later operating systems

Now take a peek at some of the techniques for using Access 2013 that you'll learn about:

- **Overview**—Chapter 1, "Why Use Microsoft Access," begins by teaching you about relational databases and what Microsoft Access 2013 offers. You preview the database components and see the types of things you can do with Microsoft Access. .

- **Getting started**—Chapter 2, "Getting Started with Microsoft Access," covers the process of creating your own database, both with and without a template. You learn how to view database objects, and how to perform important tasks such as how to open and close databases.

- **Table basics**—Chapter 3, "Tables: The Repository for Your Data," shows you how easy it is to work with data in Access. You learn how to add, edit, and delete table data. You also learn how to search for and filter data.

- **Retrieving the data you need**—Chapter 4, "Using Queries to Retrieve the Data You Need," shows you all the basics of working with queries. You learn techniques such as how to select fields, apply criteria, and order the query result.

- **Displaying data with forms**—Chapter 5, "Using Forms to Display and Modify Information," shows you how to manipulate table data from within a form.

You learn how to add, edit, and delete data and how to search and filter form data.

- **Creating forms**—Chapter 6, "Creating Your Own Forms," shows you how to build forms using the AutoForm feature and the wizards. You learn about three important types of forms: Navigation, Split, and Multiple Item.

- **Printing data with reports**—Chapter 7, "Using Reports to Print Information," first shows you how to open, view, and print an existing report. You learn important techniques such as how to zoom, move from page to page, and view multiple pages.

- **Creating Reports**—Chapter 8, "Building Your Own Reports," shows you how to use the AutoReport feature and the wizards to build your own reports. You even learn how to design mailing labels!

- **Building tables**—Chapter 9, "Creating Your Own Tables," covers the process of creating new tables. In this chapter, you learn important techniques such as how to select the best field type and how to work with field properties.

- **Relating the data in your database**—Chapter 10, "Relating the Information in Your Database," shows you how to relate the tables that you build. After this chapter provides you with a crash course on database design, you learn how to establish relationships and how to enforce referential integrity.

- **More about queries**—Chapter 11, "Enhancing the Queries That You Build," enhances what you learned about queries in Chapter 4. In this chapter, you learn how to build queries based on multiple tables. You also learn how to modify the datasheet view of a query and how to work with criteria in text, number, and date fields.

- **Advanced query techniques**—Chapter 12, "Advanced Query Techniques," shows you how to add calculations to the queries that you build, how to run parameter queries when you don't know the criteria at design time, and how to use action queries to update your table data. You also learn how and why to work with outer joins.

- **Working with forms**—Chapter 13, "Building Powerful Forms," enhances what you learned about forms in Chapters 5 and 6. In this chapter, you learn how to work with form controls, how to apply conditional formatting, and how to modify form and control properties.

- **Advanced form techniques**—Chapter 14, "Advanced Form Techniques," shows you how to work with combo boxes and the Command Button Wizard and how to build forms based on more than one table. You also learn how to work with subforms.

- **Working with reports**—Chapter 15, "Building Powerful Reports," enhances what you learned about reports in Chapters 7 and 8. In this chapter you learn how to work with report bands, work with controls, build multitable reports, and work with subreports.

- **Advanced report techniques**—Chapter 16, "Advanced Report Techniques," shows you how to add sorting and groupings to the reports that you build. You learn how to work with group header and footer properties and how to take advantage of report properties.

- **Using macros to automate your database**—Chapter 17, "Automating Your Database with Macros," shows you how to automate the databases that you build. In this chapter, you learn important techniques such as how to create and run macros, how to control the flow of the macros that you build, and how to create submacros. You also learn how to take advantage of embedded macros.

- **Advanced macro concepts**—Chapter 18, "Advanced Macro Techniques," shows you how to use data macros and drill through macros. You learn how to work with variables and error handling, and finally, you learn how to take advantage of a special macro: AutoExec.

- **Sharing data with other applications**—One of Access's greatest strengths is its capability to share data with other applications. In Chapter 19, "Sharing Data with Other Applications," you learn how to export data to and import data from Excel, text files, and other Access databases. You learn how to link to data in other databases, and how to use a powerful tool called the Linked Table Manager to manage the links that you create. As a special bonus, you learn how to link to data in a SQL Server database so that you can take advantage of Access's strong capability to participate in a client/server environment.

- **Running your application in a web browser**—Chapter 20, "Working with Web Databases," shows you how to take your database to the web. In this chapter, you learn about web databases and what they are. You learn how to build and modify web forms. Finally, you witness your completed application running in a web browser.

- **A complete application**—Chapter 21, "Putting it All Together," shows you how to build a database, complete with all the necessary elements. You learn how to design the tables, queries, forms, reports, and macros that compose your completed database.

Whether it's the new and exciting macro environment, or the ability to easily take Access data to the web, it won't take long for you to get to know this new and exciting version of Microsoft Access. Access 2013 is fast, stable, and extremely packed with new and thrilling features. *The Absolute Beginners Guild to Access 2013* is your personal guide to learning how to use Access 2013 and how to get the most out of what it has to offer.

Using This Book

This book enables you to customize your own learning experience. The step-by-step instructions give you a solid foundation in using Access 2013.

Here's a quick look at a few structural features designed to help you get the most out of this book.

- **Chapter objectives**—At the beginning of each chapter is a brief summary of topics addressed in that chapter. The objectives enable you to quickly see what is covered in the chapter.

- **The Absolute Minimum**—Each chapter ends with a section called "The Absolute Minimum." Rather than just providing a review of what you just learned, this section consolidates the key points in the chapter and often adds a few ideas not covered in the body of the chapter.

IN THIS CHAPTER

- So what exactly is a relational database?
- What sorts of things can I use Microsoft Access for?
- What composes an Access database?

1

WHY USE MICROSOFT ACCESS?

In this chapter, you learn what a relational database is. You then explore all the types of objects available in Microsoft Access. You are exposed to tables, relationships, queries, forms, reports, and modules. You then discover some of the exciting things you can do with Access. With that information under your belt, you will be ready to dive into the exciting world of working with Microsoft Access.

What Is a Relational Database?

The term database means different things to different people. For many years, in the world of the older database technologies, database was used to describe a collection of fields and records. Access refers to this type of collection as a *table*. In Access terms, a *database* is a collection of all the tables, queries, forms, reports, macros, and modules that compose a complete system. *Relational* refers to concepts based on set theory. These concepts are covered in Chapter 10, "Relating the Information in Your Database."

What Types of Things Can I Do with Microsoft Access?

Access offers a variety of features for different database needs. You can use it to develop five general types of applications:

- Personal applications
- Small-business applications
- Departmental applications
- Corporation-wide applications
- Front-end applications for enterprisewide client/server databases
- Web applications
- Access as a development platform for personal applications

At a basic level, you can use Access to develop simple, personal database-management systems. Some people automate everything from their wine collections to their home finances. The one thing to be careful of is that Access is deceptively easy to use. Its wonderful built-in wizards make Access look like a product that anyone can use. After answering a series of questions, you have finished application switchboards that enable you to easily navigate around your application, data-entry screens, reports, and the underlying tables that support them. Actually, when Microsoft first released Access, many people asked whether the author was concerned that her business as a computer programmer and trainer would diminish because Access seemed to let absolutely anyone write a database application. Although it's true that you can produce the simplest of Access applications without any thought for design and without any customization, most applications require at least some design and customization.

If you're an end user and don't want to spend too much time learning the intricacies of Access, you'll be satisfied with Access as long as you're happy with a wizard-generated personal application. After reading this text, you can make some modifications to what the wizards have generated, and no problems should occur. It's when you want to substantially customize a personal application without the proper knowledge base that problems can happen.

Access as a Development Platform for Small-Business Applications

Access is an excellent platform for developing an application that can run a small business. Its wizards let you quickly and easily build the application's foundation. The ability to create macros and to build code modules allows power users and developers to create code libraries of reusable functions, and the ability to add code behind forms and reports allows them to create powerful custom forms and reports.

The main limitation of using Access for developing a custom small-business application is the time and money involved in the development process. Many people use Access wizards to begin the development process but find they need to customize their applications in ways they can't accomplish on their own. Small-business owners often experience this problem on an even greater scale than personal users. The demands of a small-business application are usually much higher than those of a personal application. Many doctors, attorneys, and other professionals have called the author after they reached a dead end in the development process. They're always dismayed at how much money it will cost to make their application usable. An example is a doctor who built a series of forms and reports to automate her office. All went well until it came time to produce patient billings, enter payments, and produce receivable reports. Although at first glance these processes seem simple, on further examination the doctor realized that the wizard-produced reports and forms did not provide the sophistication necessary for her billing process. Unfortunately, the doctor did not have the time or programming skills to add the necessary features. So, in using Access as a tool to develop small-business applications, you must be realistic about the time and money involved in developing anything but the simplest of applications.

Access as a Development Platform for Departmental Applications

Access is perfect for developing applications for departments in large corporations. Most departments in large corporations have the development budgets to produce well-designed applications.

Fortunately, most departments also usually have a PC guru who is more than happy to help design forms and reports. This gives the department a sense of ownership because it has contributed to the development of its application. If complex form, report design, or coding is necessary, large corporations usually have on-site resources available that can provide the necessary assistance. If the support is not available within the corporation, most corporations are willing to outsource to obtain the necessary expertise.

Access as a Development Platform for Corporation-Wide Applications

Although Access might be best suited for departmental applications, you can also use it to produce applications that you distribute throughout an organization. How successful this endeavor is depends on the corporation. There's a limit to the number of users who can concurrently share an Access application while maintaining acceptable performance, and there's also a limit to the number of records that each table can contain without a significant performance drop. These numbers vary depending on factors such as the following:

- How much traffic already exists on the network.

- How much RAM and how many processors the server has.

- How the server is already being used. For example, are applications such as Microsoft Office being loaded from the server or from local workstations?

- What types of tasks the users of the application are performing. For example, are they querying, entering data, running reports, and so on?

- Where Access and Access applications are run from (the server or the workstation).

- What network operating system is in place.

The author's general rule of thumb for an Access application that's not client/server-based is that poor performance generally results with more than 10 to 15 concurrent users and more than 100,000 records. Remember that these numbers vary immensely depending on the factors mentioned and on what you and the other users of the application define as acceptable performance. If you go beyond these limits, you should consider using Access as a front end to a client/server database such as Microsoft SQL Server—that is, you can use Access to create forms and reports while storing tables and possibly queries on the database server.

Access as a Front End for Enterprisewide Client/Server Applications

A client/server database, such as Microsoft SQL Server or Oracle, processes queries on the server machine and returns results to the workstation. The server software can't display data to the user, so this is where Access comes to the rescue. Acting as a front end, Access can display the data retrieved from the database server in reports, datasheets, or forms. If the user updates the data in an Access form, the workstation sends the update to the back-end database. You can accomplish this process either by linking to these external databases so that they appear to both you and the user as Access tables or by using techniques to access client/server data directly.

Access as a Tool to Develop Web Applications

Introduced with Access 2010 was the ability for you to use Access to build web applications, which are applications that can run in a browser. Access's web capabilities have been greatly enhanced in Access 2013. Chapter 20, "Working with Web Databases," cover the intricacies of designing and building a web database.

A Preview of the Database Components

As mentioned previously, tables, queries, forms, reports, macros, and modules combine to compose an Access database. Each of these objects has a special function. The following sections take you on a tour of the objects that make up an Access database. The examples use the sample Northwind database to illustrate the use of each object. If you want to follow along, you can create the Northwind database as covered in Chapter 2, "Getting Started with Microsoft Access." You can log in as any user, which will take you to the Home form. Close the Home form to follow along.

Tables: A Repository for Data

Tables are the starting point for an application. Whether data is stored in an Access database or you reference external data (such as data in an Excel spreadsheet) by using linked tables, all the other objects in a database either directly or indirectly reference tables.

To view all the tables that are contained in an open database, you select Tables from the list of objects available in the database (see Figure 1.1). A list of available tables appears (see Figure 1.2).

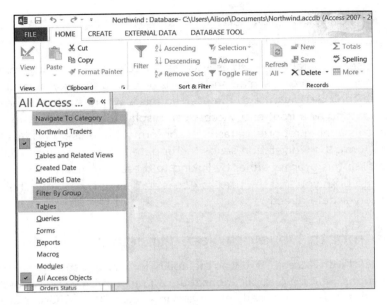

FIGURE 1.1

To view the tables in a database, select Tables from the list of available objects.

FIGURE 1.2

You can view the tables contained in a database.

To view the data in a table, double-click the name of the table you want to view. (You can also right-click the table and then select Open.) Access displays the table's data in a datasheet that includes all the table's fields and records (see Figure 1.3). You can modify many of the datasheet's attributes and even search for and filter data from within the datasheet; these techniques are covered later in this chapter.

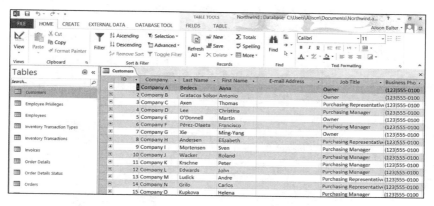

FIGURE 1.3

A table's datasheet contains fields and records.

If the table is related to another table (such as the Northwind database's Customers and Orders tables), you can also expand and collapse the subdatasheet to view data stored in child tables (see Figure 1.4).

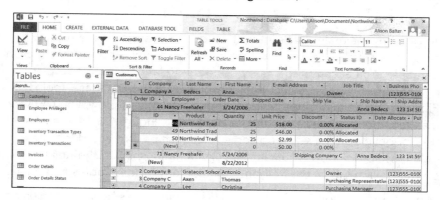

FIGURE 1.4

Datasheet view of the Customers table in the Northwind database.

As an Access user, you often want to view the table's design, which is the blueprint or template for the table. To view a table's design (see Figure 1.5), right-click the table name in the Navigation Pane, and then select Design View. In Design view, you can view or modify all the field names, data types, and field and table properties. Access gives you the power and flexibility you need to customize the design of tables. Chapter 3, "Tables: The Repository for Your Data," and Chapter 9, "Creating Your Own Tables," cover these topics.

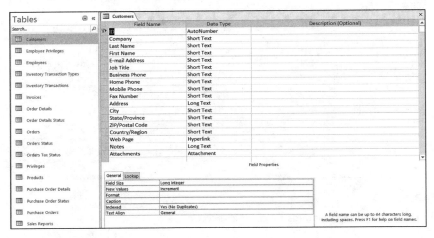

FIGURE 1.5

The design of the Customers table.

Relationships: Tying the Tables Together

To properly maintain data's integrity and ease the process to work with other objects in a database, you must define relationships among the tables in a database. You accomplish this by using the Relationships window. To view the Relationships window, select Relationships from the Database Tools tab of the Ribbon. The Relationships window appears. In this window, you can view and maintain the relationships in the database (see Figure 1.6). If you or a fellow user or developer have set up some relationships, but you don't see any in the Relationships window, you can select All Relationships in the Relationships group on the Design tab of the Ribbon to unhide any hidden tables and relationships.

Many of the relationships in Figure 1.6 have join lines between tables and show a number 1 on one side of the join and an infinity symbol on the other. This indicates a one-to-many relationship between the tables. If you double-click a join line, the Edit Relationships dialog box opens (see Figure 1.7). In this dialog box,

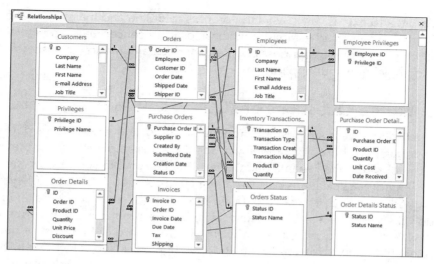

FIGURE 1.6

The Relationships tab, where you view and maintain the relationships in a database.

you can specify the exact nature of the relationship between tables. The relationship between the Customers and Orders tables in Figure 1.7, for example, is a one-to-many relationship with referential integrity enforced. This means that the user cannot add orders for customers who don't exist. Notice in Figure 1.7 that the Cascade Update Related Fields check box is not selected. This means that if the user cannot update the CustomerID field. Because Cascade Delete Related Records is not checked in Figure 1.7, the user cannot delete from the Customers table customers who have corresponding orders in the Orders table.

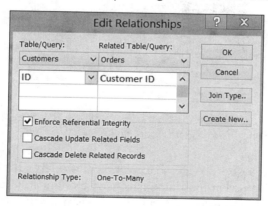

FIGURE 1.7

The Edit Relationships dialog box, which enables you to specify the nature of the relationships between tables.

Chapter 10 extensively covers the process to define and maintain relationships. For now, you should establish relationships both conceptually and literally as early in the design process as possible. Relationships are integral to successfully design and implement your application.

Queries: Stored Questions or Actions You Apply to Data

Queries in Access are powerful and multifaceted. A query retrieves data from your database based on criteria you specify. An example is a query that retrieves all employees who live in Florida. Select queries enable you to view, summarize, and perform calculations on the data in tables. Action queries enable you to add to, update, and delete table data. To run a query, first close the Relationship window if you still have it open. Next select Queries from the Objects list and then double-click the query you want to run. Or you can click in the list of queries to select the query you want to run and then right-click and select Open. When you run a Select query, a datasheet appears, containing all the fields specified in the query and all the records meeting the query's criteria (see Figure 1.8). When you run an Action (Append, Update, Delete, or Make Table) query, Access runs the specified action, such as making a new table or appending data to an existing table. In general, you can update the data in a query result because the result of a query is actually a dynamic set of records, called a *dynaset*, based on the tables' data. A dynaset is a subset of data on which you can base a form or report.

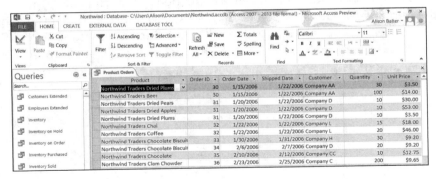

FIGURE 1.8

The result of running the Product Orders query.

When you store a query, Access stores only the query's definition, layout, or formatting properties in the database. Access offers an intuitive, user-friendly tool that helps you design queries: the Query Design window (see Figure 1.9). To open this window, select Queries from the Objects list in the Navigation Pane, choose the query you want to modify, right-click, and select Design View.

The query pictured in Figure 1.9 selects data from the Customers table. It displays the Company, Job Title, Work Phone, Home Phone, and Mobile Phone from the Customers table. Chapter 4, "Using Queries to Retrieve the Data You Need," Chapter 11, "Enhancing the Queries That You Build," and Chapter 12, "Advanced Query Techniques," cover the process of designing queries. Because queries are the foundation for most forms and reports, they are covered throughout this book as they apply to other objects in the database.

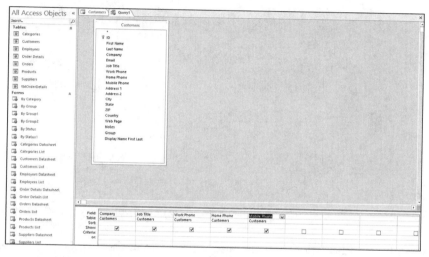

FIGURE 1.9

The design of a query that selects data from the Customers table.

Forms: A Means to Display, Modify, and Add Data

Although you can enter and modify data in a table's Datasheet view, you can't control the user's actions very well, nor can you do much to facilitate the data-entry process. This is where forms come in. Access forms can have many traits, and they're flexible and powerful.

To view a form, you select Forms from the Objects list. Then you double-click the form you want to view or right-click in the list of forms to select the form you want to view and then click Open. Figure 1.10 illustrates a form in Form view. This Customer Details form is actually two forms in one: one main form and one subform. The main form displays information from the Customers table, and the subform displays information from the Orders table (a table related to the Customers table). As the user moves from customer to customer, the form displays the orders associated with that customer. When the user clicks to select an order, the form displays the entire order.

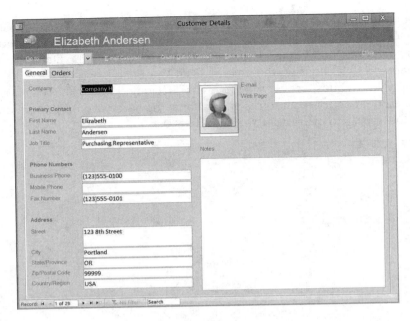

FIGURE 1.10

The Customer Details form, which includes customer, order, and order detail information.

Like tables and queries, you can also view forms in Design view. The Design view provides tools you may use to edit the layout of your form. To view the design of a form, you select Forms from the Objects list, choose the form whose design you want to modify, and then right-click and select Design View. Figure 1.11 shows the Customer Details form in Design view. Chapter 5, "Using Forms to Display and Modify Information," Chapter 13, "Building Powerful Forms," and Chapter 14, "Advanced Form Techniques," cover forms in more detail.

Reports: Turning Data into Information

Forms enable you to enter and edit information, but with reports, you can display information, usually to a printer. Figure 1.12 shows a report in Preview mode. To preview any report, select Reports from the Objects list. Double-click the report you want to preview or right-click the report want to preview from the list of reports in the Navigation Pane, and then click Open. Notice the report in Figure 1.12. It shows the Monthly Sales Report which outputs the sales by product for a month. If you attempt to run this report, Access loads the Sales Reports Dialog form. Here you select how you want to view the sales, the sales period, and the year, quarter, or month as appropriate. For the example, I selected Sales by Product, Monthly Sales, 2006 for the year, and June for the month. Like forms, reports can be elaborate and exciting, and they can contain valuable information.

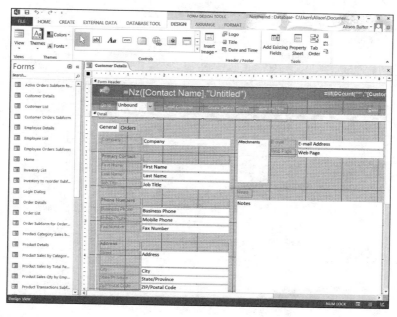

FIGURE 1.11

The design of the Customer Details form.

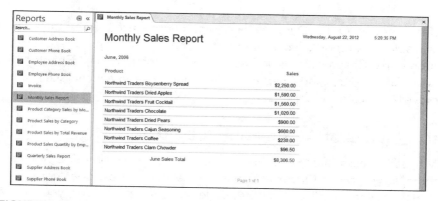

FIGURE 1.12

A preview of the Monthly Sales report.

As you may have guessed, you can view reports in Design view, as shown in Figure 1.13. To view the design of a report, select Reports from the Objects list, select the report you want to view, and then right-click and select Design View. Figure 1.13 illustrates a report with many sections; in the figure, which shows the Design view of the Invoice report, you can see the Page Header, Order ID Header,

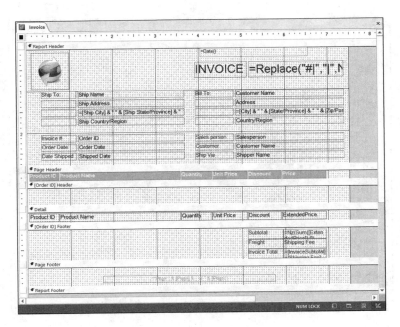

FIGURE 1.13

Design view of the Invoice report.

Detail section, Order ID Footer, and Page Footer (just a few of the many sections available on a report). Just as a form can contain subforms, a report can contain subreports. Chapter 7, "Using Reports to Print Information," Chapter 15, "Building Powerful Reports," and Chapter 16, "Advanced Report Techniques," cover the process of designing reports.

Macros: A Means of Automating a System

Macros in Access aren't like the macros in other Office products. You can't record them, as you can in Microsoft Word or Excel, and Access does not save them as Visual Basic for Applications (VBA) code. With Access macros, you can perform most of the tasks that you can manually perform from the keyboard, Ribbon, and QuickAccess toolbar. Macros enable you to build logic in to your application flow.

To run a macro, select Macros from the Objects list, and then double-click the macro you want to run. Or you can right-click the macro and click Run. Access then executes the actions in the macro. To view a macro's design, you select Macros from the Objects list, select the macro you want to modify, right-click, and select Design View to open the Macro Design window (see Figure 1.14). The macro pictured in Figure 1.14 opens the form called Startup Screen, and then opens the form called Login Dialog. Chapter 17, "Automating Your Database with

Macros," and Chapter 18, "Advanced Macro Techniques," cover the process of building and working with macros.

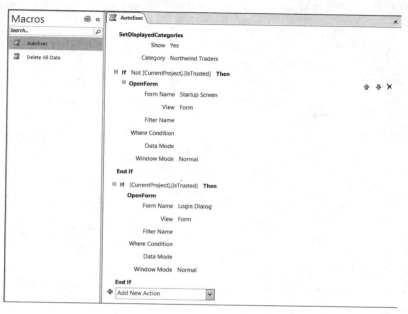

FIGURE 1.14

The design of a macro that opens two forms.

Modules: The Foundation of the Application Development Process

Modules, the foundation of any complex Access application, enable you to create libraries of functions that you can use throughout an application. You usually include subroutines and functions in the modules that you build. A function always returns a value; a subroutine does not. By using code modules, you can do just about anything with an Access application. Figure 1.15 shows an example of a module called PurchaseOrders. You can double-click the module in the Navigation Pane to access the module code. This will take you to the Visual Basic Editor (VBE) where you can view and modify the programming code. To return to the Access environment, click the View Microsoft Access toolbar button, or use the Alt-F11 keystroke combination.

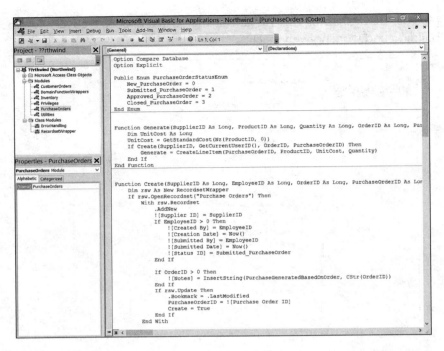

FIGURE 1.15

The PurchaseOrders module in Design view, showing the General Declarations section and the Generate and Create functions.

THE ABSOLUTE MINIMUM

With this chapter under your belt, you should now have a clear understanding of what a database is and how you can benefit from using Microsoft Access. Access is a wonderful tool to manage any type of data. As you learned in the chapter, you can use it for anything from managing your exercise history to gathering data over the Internet.

Access databases are composed of tables and other objects. The tables contain columns and rows. The columns are called *fields*, and the rows are called records. Each field contains specific information about a *record*. For example, the City field contains the city associated with a customer.

As you saw, Access is a relational database. Quite simply stated, this means that the tables in an Access database usually relate to one another. For example, the Customers table relates to the Orders table in that each order is associated with an existing customer. If you take advantage of referential integrity between tables, you cannot add an order unless it is associated with an existing customer.

After you create tables and relate them, you need to insert, edit, and delete table data. You can accomplish this using Access forms, which can be rich in design and features.

Whereas you modify table data using forms, you view table data using reports. Reports are designed to be viewed on the screen or sent to a printer.

Forms and reports are often based on queries. Select queries return specific rows and columns of data. You can designate criteria so that you get just the data that you need. Whereas select queries return data, action queries modify data. Action queries include insert, update, delete, and make table queries.

Finally, macros and modules enable you to automate the applications that you build. Using macros and modules you can automate tasks that you would usually perform on the keyboard. You can also use macros and modules to validate data. For example, you can use a macro, or programming code, to ensure that if a credit card is selected as the type of payment, that the user enters a credit card number.

All the concepts in this chapter are developed throughout the book. Now that you have an idea what Access is all about, you can jump in and start using it.

IN THIS CHAPTER

- How can you create a database from a template?
- How can you view existing tables, queries, forms, and reports?
- How can you create a database from scratch?
- How can you open an existing database?
- How can you close a database?
- How can you exit Access?

GETTING STARTED WITH MICROSOFT ACCESS

In this chapter, you learn how to create your own databases. You learn how to view existing database objects in the databases that you create. Finally, you learn how to open and close existing databases, and how to exit Access when you finish working with it.

Creating a Database from a Template

Database templates help you to quickly and easily create Access databases. Microsoft provides a plethora of database templates that you can use to build new databases. These templates are categorized into Assets, Business, Contacts, Employee, Inventory, Project, and Sales. To create a database from a template:

1. On the Ribbon, click the File tab.

2. In the list of menu items, click New.

3. Click within the Search online templates text box, and type a search word or click to select the category of templates you want to view. Depending on the speed of your internet connection there may be a delay before Access displays the available templates. In Figure 2.1, the Business category is selected.

4. Single-click to select the database template that you want to use. The Create database dialog appears. See Figure 2.2 where the Desktop Northwind 2007 Sample database is selected.

5. Enter a filename for the database.

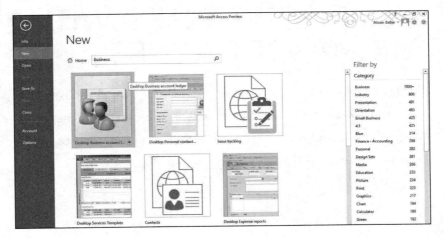

FIGURE 2.1

Access provides categories of templates that you can easily use.

6. Click the folder to select a location for the database.

7. Click Create to complete the process. Access creates and opens the database.

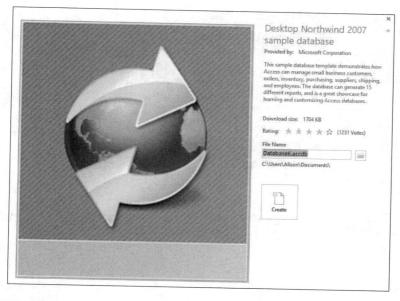

FIGURE 2.2

Use the Create Database dialog to specify the name and location of the database.

CAUTION   If you double-click a database template in step 4, rather than single-clicking, Access bypasses the Save As process and saves the new database in the My Documents folder with a default name.

Viewing Database Objects

In Chapter 1, "Why Use Microsoft Access?," you learned about the various database components available. Now that you've created a template, you are ready to explore the objects within it. You can learn how to view the tables, queries, forms, and reports that make up the database.

Viewing Database Tables

As you learned in Chapter 1, tables are the foundation of the database. You base everything else in your database on your database tables. To view the data in an existing table, follow these steps:

1. Make sure that the Navigation Pane is visible (see Figure 2.3). If it is not, press your F11 function key on your keyboard.

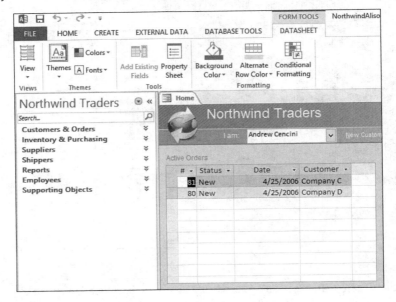

FIGURE 2.3

Use your F11 function key to open the Navigation Pane.

2. Click the Navigation Pane title bar, and change the Category to Object Type (see Figure 2.4). The results of this change appear in Figure 2.5.

FIGURE 2.4

Changing the Navigation Pane Category to Object Type.

FIGURE 2.5

Viewing the Navigation Pane by Object Type.

3. If necessary, click to expand the list of tables.

4. Double-click to view the data in the wanted table, or right-click the table and select Open. The table appears in Datasheet view (see Figure 2.6).

FIGURE 2.6

Double-click to view the table data.

Viewing Queries

The process of viewing queries is similar to that of viewing tables. Follow these steps:

1. Make sure that the Navigation Pane is visible.

2. Make sure the list of queries is visible. If not, click to expand the list.

3. Double-click to view the data in the wanted query, or right-click the query and select Open. The result of running the query appears in Datasheet view.

Viewing Forms

To view the data in an existing form, follow these steps:

1. Make sure that the Navigation Pane is visible.

2. Make sure the list of forms is visible. If not, click to expand the list.

3. Double-click to view the data in the wanted form, or right-click the form and select Open. The result of opening the Northwind Customer Details form appears in Figure 2.7.

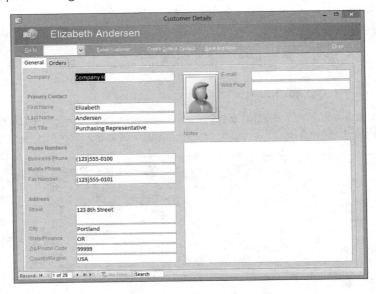

FIGURE 2.7

Double-click to view the wanted form.

Viewing Reports

To preview the data in an existing form, follow these steps:

1. Make sure that the Navigation Pane is visible.

2. Make sure the list of reports is visible. If not, click to expand the list.

3. Double-click to view the wanted report, or right-click the report and select Open. The result of opening the Top Ten Biggest Orders report appears in Figure 2.8.

FIGURE 2.8

Double-click to view the wanted report.

Creating a Database from Scratch

Sometimes you must perform a task for which no template meets your specific needs. In this situation, it is best to create the database from scratch. You must understand that you need to create all the necessary tables, queries, forms, reports, and macros required by the database. Fortunately, most of the remainder of this book focuses on the skills necessary to accomplish this task. Whereas Chapters 3 through 5 focus on working with existing objects, Chapters 6 through 22 cover everything that you need to know to build your own database objects.

To create a database from scratch, follow these steps:

1. On the Ribbon, click to select the File tab.

2. In the list of menu items, click New.

3. Click to select Blank Desktop Database. The Blank Desktop Database dialog appears.

4. Provide a database name.

5. Select a database location.

6. Click Create. Access creates a blank database and places you in the Datasheet view of a new table (see Figure 2.9). You must now create all the tables, queries, forms, reports, and macros that will compose the database.

FIGURE 2.9

Access creates the database and places you in datasheet view of a table.

Opening an Existing Database

Now that you know how to create your own databases, you must know how to open and work with an existing database. Follow these steps:

1. On the ribbon, click to select the File tab.

2. In the list of menu items, click Open. The screen appears as shown in Figure 2.10.

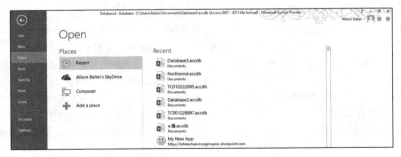

FIGURE 2.10

Opening an existing database.

3. Select the place where the file is located. If you select Computer, you can see recent locations on your computer, or click Browse to browse files on your computer.

4. Click to select the file you want to work with, and click Open.

Closing a Database

You can close a database in several ways:

- Open another database. This process closes the currently open database.
- Click the File menu and select Close.
- Exit Access using the close (x) button at the top right corner of the application window.

Regardless of the method that you choose, Access prompts you to save any changes that have not yet been saved.

Exiting Access

To exit Access you can do any of the following:

- Select Close from the Control menu on the upper-left corner of the application window.
- Use the Alt-F4 keystroke combination.
- Click the Close button (x) on the upper-right corner of the application window.

 NOTE Regardless of how you exit Access, you will receive a prompt to save each database object that you have modified but have not yet saved.

As with closing a database, Access prompts you to save any changes that have not yet been saved.

THE ABSOLUTE MINIMUM

When creating databases, you can use a template or create a database from scratch. Templates help you to quickly and easily create a database designed to perform a commonly performed task. For example, Access comes with business templates that do anything from managing contacts, to asset tracking, to managing expense reports. There are many templates available to you.

If you have a specialized need, you can forgo the templates and build a database from scratch. Whereas the templates come with predefined tables, forms, reports, and other objects, you must build the components of a database that you design from scratch.

Remember that you can have only one database open at a time in each instance of Access that you run on your computer. When you open another database or create a new database, Access closes the current database. Access prompts you to save any unsaved objects.

IN THIS CHAPTER

- How can I view and navigate through table data?
- What do I need to know about editing table data?
- How can I search for and replace table data?
- What's a filter, and how can I benefit from using it?

3

TABLES: THE REPOSITORY FOR YOUR DATA

In this chapter, you learn how to work with the tables in your database. You begin by opening a table. You learn how to navigate through its data. If a table is large, it's beneficial to search through its data, replacing table values that meet specific criteria. For example, you may want to locate all sales representatives and make them marketing representatives. One of the most powerful aspects of Microsoft Access lies in its filtering capabilities. In this chapter, you learn how to filter a table's datasheet so that you can focus on just the data that you need.

Working with Table Data

Tables are the basis of everything that you do in Access. Most of the data for your database resides in tables. So if you create an employee payroll database, your employee data will be stored in a table, your payroll codes might be stored in a table, and your past payroll records could be stored in a table. A table contains data about a specific topic or subject (for example, customers, orders, or employees). Tables are arranged in rows and columns, similar to a spreadsheet. The columns represent the fields, and the rows represent the records (see Figure 3.1).

FIGURE 3.1

A table composed of columns and rows associated with customers.

Opening an Access Table

In working with tables, the first thing to do is open them in Datasheet view and navigate around them. The text that follows covers all the basics of working with tables in Datasheet view.

To open a table in Datasheet view, follow these steps:

1. In the list of objects in the Navigation Pane, select Tables.

2. Select the table you want to open, and click the Open button in the Navigation Pane, or double-click the table you want to open.

Navigating Around a Table

You can move around a table by using the keyboard or mouse. When you edit or add records, your hands are on the keyboard, and you might find it easiest to move around a table by using the keyboard. However, if you look for a specific record, you might find it most convenient to use the mouse.

Table 3.1 shows the keyboard and mouse actions for moving around a table and their resulting effects. As you can see, Microsoft Access provides numerous keyboard and mouse alternatives for moving around a table.

TABLE 3.1 Keyboard and Mouse Actions to Move Around a Table

Keyboard Action	Mouse Action	Effect
Tab or right arrow	Click the right scroll arrow on the bottom scrollbar.	Moves one field to the right of the current field
Shift+Tab or left arrow	Click the left scroll arrow on the bottom scrollbar.	Moves one field to the left of the current field
Down arrow	Click the next record button.	Moves down one record
Up arrow	Click the previous record button.	Moves up one record
Page Down	No equivalent mouse action.	Moves down one screen of records
Page Up	No equivalent mouse action.	Moves up one screen of records
Home	No equivalent mouse action.	Selects the first field of the current record
End	No equivalent mouse action.	Selects the last field of the current record
Ctrl+Home	Click the first record button.	Moves to the first record of the table
Ctrl+End	Click the last record button.	Moves to the last record of the table
F2	Click and drag within a field.	Selects the text in the field

CAUTION   The insertion point does not change locations just because you move your mouse; only the mouse pointer moves when you move your mouse. You need to click *within* a field before you begin typing; otherwise, the changes occur in the original mouse location.

The tab displaying the data includes tools that enable you to scroll through the fields and records, move from record to record, expand and collapse to show and hide related records, and more. Figure 3.2 illustrates these features. Table 3.2 provides a list of these features and provides a description of each.

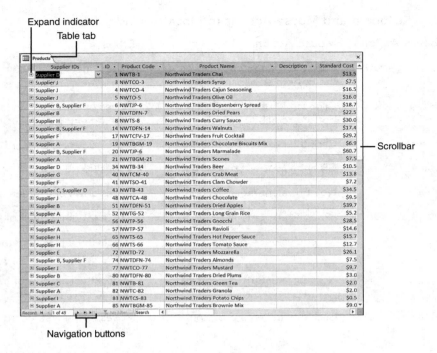

FIGURE 3.2

The Table window.

TABLE 3.2 The Components of the Table Window

Table Component	Description
Table tab	Allows you to easily select the open table.
Scrollbar	You can use the scrollbars to move up, down, right, and left in the table.
Navigation buttons	These icons enable you to select the first record, last record, next record, or previous record in the table.
Expand indicator	The expand indicator enables you to view the data hierarchy by showing you any subdata records that are linked to the main record.

Closing a Table

When you finish working with a table, you need to close it. To close a table, choose File, Close, or click the close button in the upper-right corner of the Table tab.

TIP   Access often prompts you as you close a table, asking if you want to save changes to the layout of the table. You must understand that Access is not asking whether you want to save changes to the data. As you'll learn in a moment, Access saves changes to data the moment you move off a record. When you close a table and Access prompts you, it is asking whether you want to save formatting changes, such as changes to column width, to the look of the datasheet, and so on.

Editing Table Data

You can change the data in a table any time that you are in Datasheet view of a table, the result of a query, or Form view of a form. Access saves changes you make to a record as soon as you move off the record.

Edit Existing Records

One task you might want to perform is to simply modify table data. Here's the process:

1. Select the record you want to change by using any of the techniques listed in Table 3.2.

2. Select the field you want to change by clicking the field or using the arrow keys.

3. Type to make the necessary changes to the data. After you move off the record, Access saves your changes.

NOTE   When entering table data, it is important that you are cognizant of the type of data that you can enter into each field. For example, you can only enter valid numbers into Numeric and Currency fields. You can only enter valid dates into Date fields. If the primary key fields are AutoNumber fields, you cannot enter data into those fields. Finally, if a primary key field allows data entry, you cannot enter duplicate values into those fields.

Undoing Changes

There are different options available when undoing changes to a field or to a record. The options differ depending on whether you are still within a field, have left the field, or have left the record. The following sections explore the various options available to you.

Undoing Changes Made to the Current Field

When you are in the process of making changes to a field, you might realize that you actually didn't want to make changes to that field or to that record. To undo changes to the current field, you can either click the Undo tool on the QuickAccess toolbar or press the Esc key once. For example, if you mean to change the contact's first name from Alison to Alexis but realize that you are accidentally typing Sue in the Customer field, you can press the Esc key once, or click the Undo tool on the QuickAccess toolbar, to undo your change.

Undoing Changes After You Move to Another Field

The process to undo changes after you move to another field is identical to that of the process to undo changes made to the current field. You can either click the Undo tool on the QuickAccess toolbar or press the Esc key once. For example, if you mean to change the contact's first name from Alison to Sue but realize that you accidentally typed Alexis in the Customer field, and then moved to another field, you could click the Undo tool on the QuickAccess toolbar, or press the Esc key once, to undo your change.

Undoing Changes After You Save a Record

When you make changes to a field and then move to another record, Access saves all changes to the modified record. So long as you do not begin making changes to another record, you can still undo the changes you made to the most recently modified record. To do this, you can either click the Undo tool on the QuickAccess toolbar or press the Esc key twice. For example, if you mean to change the contact's first name from Alison to Alexis but realize that you accidentally typed Alexis in the Customer field, and then moved to another record, you either click the Undo tool on the QuickAccess toolbar or press the Esc key twice to undo your change.

Adding Records to a Table

Access adds records to the end of a table, regardless of how you add them to the table.

Add Records to a Table

To add records, follow these steps:

1. Select the table to which you want to add information.

2. Click the New Record Navigation (New (blank) Record) button at the bottom of the Datasheet window.

3. Add the necessary information to the fields within the record. When you move off the record, Access saves the new record.

 TIP   You can use Ctrl + " (quote) to repeat the data in the field directly above the current field.

Access always displays one blank record at the end of a table. When entering data, pressing the Tab key at the end of a record that you just added allows you to continue to add additional records.

Deleting Records

Before you can delete records, you must select them. The following sections cover the process to select records and then the process to delete records.

Selecting One or More Records

To select one record, you just click the gray record selector button to the left of the record within the datasheet.

To select multiple records, you click and drag within the record selector area. Access selects the contiguous range of records in the area over which you click and drag. As an alternative, you can click the gray selector button for the first record you want to select, hold down the Shift key, and then click the gray selector button of the last record that you want to select. When you do this, Access selects the entire range of records between them. Figure 3.3 shows the Customers table with three records selected.

FIGURE 3.3

The Customers table with three records selected.

If you want to select a single record when the cursor is within the record, you can simply choose Select from the Find group on the Home tab, and then choose Select. To select all records, choose Select from the Find group on the Home tab, and then choose Select All.

Deleting Records

When you know how to select records, deleting them is quite simple. You just follow these steps:

1. Select the records you want to delete.

2. Press the Delete key. The dialog box in Figure 3.4 appears, asking whether you're sure you want to delete the records.

3. Click the Yes button. Access deletes the records.

FIGURE 3.4

Access asks if you want to delete the selected records.

NOTE   You will not be able to delete records from many of the tables in the Northwind sample database. This is because relationships and referential integrity have been established between the tables in the database.

Relationships and referential integrity are covered in Chapter 10, "Relating the Information in Your Database," and are explained briefly in the text that follows.

The process of deleting a record is not so simple if you have established referential integrity between the tables in a database and if the row that you are attempting to delete has child rows. Chapter 10 covers relationships and referential integrity. For now, you can think about how customers generally have orders associated with them, and those orders have order detail records associated with them. The relationship between the Customers table and the

Orders table prohibits the user from deleting customers who have orders. Here's how you delete a customer who has orders:

1. Select the records you want to delete.

2. Press the Delete key. The dialog box in Figure 3.5 appears, telling you that the records cannot be deleted because the table includes related records.

FIGURE 3.5

Access notifying you that you cannot delete the selected records.

3. Click OK to close the dialog box.

Access provides a *referential integrity* option with which you can cascade a deletion down to the child table (a table related to a parent table, such as orders related to customers). This means, for example, that if you attempt to delete an order, Access deletes the associated order detail records. If you establish referential integrity with the cascade delete option, the deletion process works like this:

1. Select the records you want to delete.

2. Press the Delete key. The dialog box in Figure 3.6 appears, asking if you're sure you want to delete the records.

3. Click Yes to complete the deletion process.

FIGURE 3.6

Access asking if you want to delete the parent row and the associated child records.

CAUTION   After you have selected records, they appear in black, and you can copy them, delete them, or modify them as a group. Remember that deleting records is a permanent process. **You cannot undo record deletion.**

Finding and Replacing Records

When you work with records in a large data table, you often need a way to locate specific records quickly. By using the Find feature, you can easily move to specific records within a table. After you have found records, you can also replace the text within them.

Find a Record That Meets Specific Criteria

The Find feature enables you to search in a datasheet for records that meet specific criteria. Here's how it works:

1. Select the field containing the criteria for which you are searching.

2. Click the Find button in the Find group on the Home tab of the Ribbon. The Find and Replace dialog box appears (see Figure 3.7).

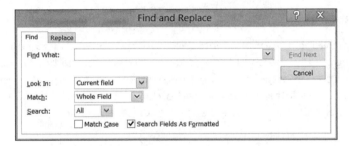

FIGURE 3.7

The Find tab of the Find and Replace dialog box, which you can use to search for values in a datasheet.

3. Type the criteria in the Find What text box.

4. Use the Look In drop-down list box to designate whether you want to search only the current field or all fields in the table.

5. Use the Match drop-down list box to designate whether you want to match any part of the field you are searching, the whole field you are searching, or the start of the field you are searching. For example, if you type **Purchasing** in the Find What text box and you select Whole Field in the Match drop-down list box, you find only entries where Job Title is set to Purchasing. If you select Any Part of Field, you find Purchasing Manager, Purchasing Representative, Purchasing Assistant, Product Purchasing, and so on. If you select Start of Field, you find Purchasing Manager, Purchasing Representative, and Purchasing Assistant, but you do not find Product Purchasing.

6. Use the Search drop-down list box to designate whether you want to search only up from the current cursor position, only down, or in all directions.

7. Use the Match Case check box to indicate whether you want the search to be case-sensitive.

8. Use the Search Fields as Formatted check box to indicate whether you want to find data only based on the display format (for example, 17-Jul-12 for a date).

9. Click the Find Next button to find the next record that meets the designated criteria.

10. To continue searching after you close the dialog box, use the Shift+F4 key-stroke combination.

Replacing Data in a Table

There may be times when you want to update records that meet specific criteria. You can use the Replace feature to automatically insert new information into the specified fields. Here's how:

1. Click within the field that contains the criteria you are searching for.

2. Click the Replace button in the Find group on the Home tab of the Ribbon. The Find and Replace dialog box appears.

3. Select the Replace tab (see Figure 3.8).

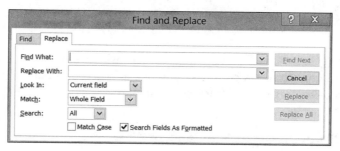

FIGURE 3.8

The Replace tab of the Find and Replace dialog, within which you can replace table data.

4. Type the criteria in the Find What text box.

5. Type the new information (the replacement value) in the Replace with text box.

6. Choose values for the Look In drop-down list box, Match drop-down list box, Search drop-down list box, Match Case check box, and Search Fields as Formatted check box, as described in the "Finding a Record That Meets Specific Criteria" section.

7. Click the Find Next button. Access locates the first record that meets the criteria designated in the Find What text box.

8. Click the Replace button. Access replaces the text for the record and finds the next occurrence of the text in the Find What text box.

9. Repeat step 8 to find all occurrences of the value in the Find What text box and replace them. As an alternative, you can click the Replace All button to replace all occurrences at once.

10. Click Cancel when you finish.

CAUTION You should use Replace All with quite a bit of caution. Remember that the changes you make are *permanent*. Although Replace All is a viable option, when you use it you need to make sure you have a recent backup and that you are quite certain of what you are doing. I usually do a few replaces to make sure that I see what Access is doing before I click Replace All.

NOTE If you search a large table, Access can find a specific value in a field fastest if the field you search on is the primary key or an indexed field. Chapter 5, "Using Forms to Display and Modify Information," covers primary keys and indexes.

When using either Find or Replace, you can use several wildcard characters. A *wildcard* character is a character you use in place of an unknown character. Table 3.3 describes the wildcard characters.

TABLE 3.3 Wildcard Characters You Can Use When Searching

Wildcard Character	Description
*	Acts as a placeholder for multiple characters
?	Acts as a placeholder for a single character
#	Acts as a placeholder for a single number

Filtering Table Data

In a table, you can apply filters to fields to limit what records you view. This is helpful if you want to view just the data associated with a subset of the records. For example, you may want to view just the data associated with sales managers.

Filtering by Selection

The Filter by Selection feature enables you to select text and then filter the data in the table to that selected text. To use the Filter by Selection feature, follow these steps:

1. Open a table in Datasheet view.

2. Select the record and field in the table that contain the value on which you want to filter.

3. Click the Selection drop-down. A menu appears that reflects the data that appears in the current field of the current record. For example, if you select Owner in the Job Title field, the drop-down appears, as shown in Figure 3.9. The choices are Equals Owner, Does Not Equal Owner, Contains Owner, and Does Not Contain Owner. After making your selection, the data is filtered to only the specified rows. For example, in Figure 3.10, the data shows only customers where the Job Title is Owner.

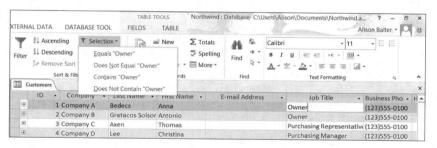

FIGURE 3.9

The choices that appear reflect the data that you selected.

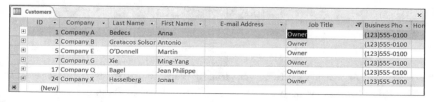

FIGURE 3.10

Data filtered to show customers who are Owners.

Using Right-Click to Filter

Access possesses some intelligent and sophisticated filtering capabilities. Based on where you right-click, the context-sensitive menu that appears reflects the type of data that the current field contains. For example, if you right-click in a Date field, the menu that appears contains filters appropriate for a date. In Figure 3.11, you can right-click within the Order Date field of the Orders table. You can select smart options such as Today, Yesterday, Tomorrow, This Week, Last Week, and much, much more! Microsoft thought of everything! On the other hand, if you right-click a number field, you get options such as Greater Than, Less Than, and Between. For a text field, you get appropriate choices such as Begins With and Ends With. As you can see, the filtering options are both plentiful and practical.

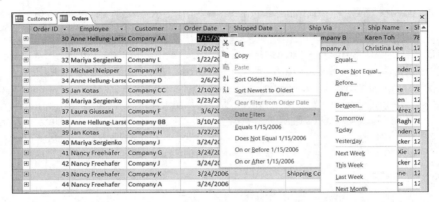

FIGURE 3.11

Filters appropriate for a date field.

NOTE There are some cautions you should be aware of when working with filters. Each time that you perform a filter, you restrict the data that you are viewing. When you close a table, Access will prompt you to save your filters. If you respond affirmatively, Access will remember the filter and next time you open the table, only the filtered data will display. You must explicitly clear the filter to display all of the data.

Removing Filters

After you have applied filters, you might want to remove them so that you can again view all rows or apply a different filter. The process is simple. You just click the Toggle Filter button in the Sort & Filter group on the Home tab of the Ribbon.

THE ABSOLUTE MINIMUM

As you learned in this chapter, tables are a repository for the data that you store in your database. Opening an access table is easy. Your power lies in what you do with the data in the tables that you open.

You must practice navigating around the tables in your database. You can navigate through your table data using the keyboard, your mouse, or any combination of the two. Table 3.1 provides you with everything you want to know about navigating table data.

Remember that when you close a table, you may be prompted to save. This occurs if you have filtered the table data, changed column widths, moved columns around, or have in some way altered the appearance of the datasheet. This prompt has absolutely nothing to do with the process to save changes to the data in your tables. Changes are saved to your table each time you make changes to a record and then move to another record. If you modify a record and then close the table without moving off of the row, Access automatically saves the changes that you made.

Speaking of editing table data, this chapter contained quite a bit of information about the editing process. You learned several techniques that you can use to undo the changes that you make, including how to undo changes when you have already saved changes to a record. You also learned how to add new records, how to select existing records, and how to delete the records that you have selected. Remember that you cannot always delete the data in your table. If you have established referential integrity between tables in your database, and you have not activated the Cascade Delete feature (see Chapter 10), you will be prohibited from deleting records that have related child records. For example, you cannot delete a customer who has associated orders, unless you implement Cascade Delete.

When you have lots of data in a table, two important features are Find and Filter. With the Find feature you can simply find records meeting criteria that you specify, or you can find those records and replace them with alternative data. With the Find feature, all records remain in the datasheet, and you can use Find Next to move from record to record that meets your criteria. With the Filter feature, you apply the wanted filter, and then Access filters the data in the datasheet so that only the wanted records appear. The author generally prefers the Filter feature over the Find feature because it enables you to focus just on the records that you are concerned with.

The techniques that you learned in this chapter are particularly important because they apply not only to table datasheets, but also to query datasheets and to Access forms. They are worth some practice because you will most likely find them invaluable when working with Microsoft Access.

4

USING QUERIES TO RETRIEVE THE DATA YOU NEED

In this chapter, you learn what queries are and why they are important. You learn how to work with queries in both Datasheet view and Design view. You explore the basics of working with queries such as selecting fields, ordering the query result, and using basic criteria. You become comfortable with the process of using **And** and **Or** conditions in the queries that you build. You also learn about comparison operators and wildcards.

What Is a Query and When Should You Use One?

A *Select query* is a stored question about the data stored in a database's tables. Select queries are the foundation of much of what you do in Access. They underlie most forms and reports, and they enable you to view the data you want, when you want. You use a simple Select query to specify the tables and fields whose data you want to view and to specify the criteria that limits the data the query's output displays. A

Select query is a query of a table or tables that just displays data; the query doesn't modify data in any way. An example is a query that enables you to view customers who have placed orders in the last month. You can use more advanced Select queries to summarize data, supply the results of calculations, or cross-tabulate data. You can use Action queries to add, edit, or delete data from tables, based on selected criteria, but this chapter covers Select queries. Chapter 11, "Enhancing the Queries That You Build," shows you how to build queries based on multiple tables. It also covers advanced criteria techniques. Chapter 12, "Advanced Query Techniques," covers other types of queries, including Action queries.

Creating a Simple Query

To create a simple query, you must understand how to add both contiguous and noncontiguous fields to the query grid. You must also know how to complete basic tasks such as how to select fields on the query grid, how to order the query results, and how to add basic criteria to the queries that you build. This section covers all these important topics.

Designing the Query

Creating a basic query is easy because Microsoft provides a user-friendly, drag-and-drop interface. To start a new query, select Query Design from the Queries group of the Create tab on the Ribbon; the Show Table dialog appears (see Figure 4.1). If you prefer, you can select the Query Wizard from the Queries group of the Create tab on the Ribbon. In that case the New Query dialog appears, enabling you to

FIGURE 4.1

The Show Table dialog box.

select from four predefined query wizards (see Figure 4.2). The Simple Query Wizard walks you through the steps to create a basic query. The other wizards help you create three specific types of queries: Crosstab, Find Duplicates, and Find Unmatched queries.

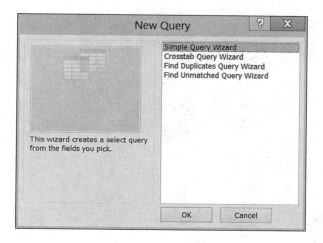

FIGURE 4.2

The New Query dialog box.

Adding Tables to Queries

If you choose to use Design view rather than one of the wizards, the Show Table dialog box appears (refer to Figure 4.1). In this dialog box, you can select the tables or queries that supply data to a query. Access doesn't care whether you select tables or queries as the foundation for the queries that you build. You can select a table or query by double-clicking it, or by single-clicking it and then selecting the Add command button. You can use the Shift key to select a contiguous range of tables or the Ctrl key to select noncontiguous tables. After you have selected the tables or queries you want, you click Add and then click Close. This brings you to the Query Design window, shown in Figure 4.3.

Adding Fields to Queries

After you add tables to a query, you can select the fields you want to include in the query. The query shown in Figure 4.3 is based on the Customers table from the Northwind database that is based on one of the templates available with Microsoft Access. The query window is divided into two sections: The top half of the window shows the tables or queries that underlie the query you're designing, and the bottom

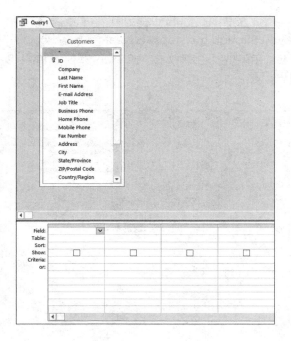

FIGURE 4.3

The Query Design window.

half shows any fields that you include in the query output. You can add a field to the query design grid on the bottom half of the query window in several ways:

- You can double-click the name of the field you want to add.

- You can click and drag a single field from the table in the top half of the query window to the query design grid below.

- You can select multiple fields at the same time by using the Shift key (for a contiguous range of fields) or the Ctrl key (for a noncontiguous range). You can double-click the title bar of the field list to select all fields and then click and drag any one of the selected fields to the query design grid.

Adding a Field to the End of the Query Grid

Sometimes, you want to add a field to the end of the list of existing fields. Fortunately, the process is easy. You just double-click in the field list on the field that you want to add. Access adds the field at the end of the existing field list. This is the technique the author used to add fields to a new query as she built it. She generally double-clicks each field that she wants to add to the query. Access simply adds each field to the query grid in the order that each field was selected.

TIP Shortcut keys are available that allow you to easily toggle between the various query views: Ctrl+>, Ctrl+period, Ctrl+<, and Ctrl+comma. Ctrl+> and Ctrl+period take you to the next view; Ctrl+< and Ctrl+comma take you to the previous view.

Adding a Field Between Other Fields

There are times when you need to insert a field between two existing fields. To do so, just drag the field from the field list to the grid, and drop it where you want it to appear. The fields already included in the query then move to the right. For example, your query already contains City and Zip, and you have decided to add the State field and place it between the City and the Zip fields. You would drag the State field from the field list to add it to the query.

Adding a Group of Contiguous Fields to the Query Grid

It would be tedious if you had to add each field, one field at a time, to add a contiguous group of fields from the field list to the query grid. Fortunately, Access enables you to add the fields as a group. The process is simple: This is a great technique to use when you are lucky because several of the fields you want to include in the query appear together in the field list:

1. Click the first field that you want to add to the query.

2. Scroll through the field list until you can see the last field that you want to add to the query.

3. Hold down the Shift key as you click the last field that you want to add to the query.

4. Drag the fields as a group to the query grid. The fields are placed on the query grid at the position where you dropped them.

Adding a Group of Noncontiguous Fields to the Query Grid

The process to add a noncontiguous group of fields from the field list to the query grid is simpler than to add the fields one at a time. You would add a noncontiguous list of fields when there are several fields that you want to add to the query, but they do not appear together in the field list. Here's what you do:

1. Click the first field that you want to add.

2. Hold down the Ctrl key as you click each additional field that you want to add.

3. Drag the fields to the query grid by clicking any of the selected fields and dragging them to the query grid. Access adds the selected fields to the query grid at the position at which you drop them.

Ordering the Query Result

You might want to modify the sort order designated by the designer of a query. As described in the following sections, you can sort on a single field or you can sort on multiple fields, and you can sort in ascending order or you can sort in descending order. For example, you may want to sort in ascending order by company name in a company table, but in descending order by sales amount in a sales table so that the highest sales amount appears first. An example in which you may want to sort on multiple fields is the employee last name combined with the employee first name.

Sorting on a Single Field

Sorting on a single field is a simple process. It works like this:

1. Open the wanted query in Design view.

2. Click in the Sort row of the field you want to sort by.

3. Click the drop-down arrow button to display the choices for the sort order (see Figure 4.4).

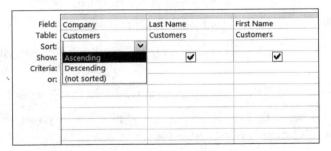

FIGURE 4.4

Selecting the sort order of a query.

4. Select the sort order:

   • **Ascending**—A to Z or 0 to 9

   • **Descending**—Z to A or 9 to 0

   • **Not Sorted**—No sorting

5. Click the Run button on the Design tab. The data appears in the designated sort order.

Sorting on More Than One Field

The process to sort on more than one field is slightly more complicated than the process to sort on one field. It works like this:

1. Return to Design View of the query. Repeat steps 1–4 in the previous section, "Sorting on a Single Field," for the first field that you want to sort by.

2. Click in the Sort row of the second field that you want to sort by.

3. Click the drop-down arrow button to display the choices for sort order.

4. Select the sort order.

5. Click the Run button on the Design tab.

Working with Simple Criteria

You can limit the records that you see in the result of a query by adding criteria to the query. For example, you might want to see only the customers in California, or you may want to view only the orders with sales greater than $500. You can also view sales that occurred within a specific date range. Using criteria, you can easily accomplish any of these tasks, and many, many more!

Using an Exact Match Query

An exact match query locates data only when there is an exact match with the criteria that you enter. Here's how you run an exact match query:

1. Open the wanted query in Design view.

2. Select the cell on the Criteria row below the field for which you want to add the condition.

3. Type the criteria you want to apply for that field. For example, type **Purchasing Manager** in the Job Title field (see Figure 4.5).

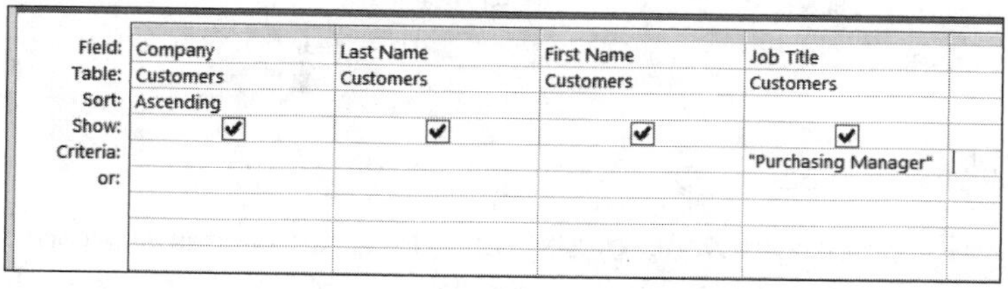

Field:	Company	Last Name	First Name	Job Title	
Table:	Customers	Customers	Customers	Customers	
Sort:	Ascending				
Show:	☑	☑	☑	☑	
Criteria:				"Purchasing Manager"	
or:					

FIGURE 4.5

Entering simple criteria.

4. Click the Run button. Figure 4.6 shows the results of this query.

Query1

Company	Last Name	First Name	Job Title
Company AA	Toh	Karen	Purchasing Manager
Company BB	Raghav	Amritansh	Purchasing Manager
Company CC	Lee	Soo Jung	Purchasing Manager
Company D	Lee	Christina	Purchasing Manager
Company F	Pérez-Olaeta	Francisco	Purchasing Manager
Company I	Mortensen	Sven	Purchasing Manager
Company J	Wacker	Roland	Purchasing Manager
Company K	Krschne	Peter	Purchasing Manager
Company L	Edwards	John	Purchasing Manager
Company O	Kupkova	Helena	Purchasing Manager
Company T	Li	George	Purchasing Manager
Company W	Entin	Michael	Purchasing Manager
Company Y	Rodman	John	Purchasing Manager
*			

FIGURE 4.6

Records with Purchasing Manager in the Job Title field.

Although Access is not case-sensitive, and you therefore can enter criteria in either uppercase or lowercase, the criteria you enter must follow specific rules. These rules vary depending on the type of field the criteria applies to (see Table 4.1).

TABLE 4.1 Rules for Criteria, Based on Type of Field

Type of Field	Description
Text	After you type the text, Access puts quotes around the text entered.
Number/Currency	You type the digits, without commas or dollar signs but with decimals, if applicable.
Date/Time	You enter any date or time format. Access will add # symbols surrounding the date.
Counter	You type the digits.
Yes/No	For yes, you type **yes** or **true**. For no, you type **no** or **false**.

Creating Criteria Based on Multiple Conditions

Sometimes, you might want to create a query that contains two or more conditions. You would do this, for example, if you want only records in the state of California that had sales within a certain date range to appear in the output. The `And` *condition* is used to indicate that *both* of two conditions must be met for the row to be included in the resulting recordset. You can use the `And` condition in the same field or on multiple fields.

Use the And Condition on Multiple Fields

By placing criteria for multiple fields on the *same* line of the query grid, you create an **And** condition. This means that *both* conditions must be true for the records to appear in the result. An example of an **And** condition on two fields is `State Field = 'TX' And Credit limit >=5000`. Here's how you create an **And** condition:

1. Open the wanted query in Design view.

2. Select the cell on the Criteria row below the field that contains the first condition you want to enter.

3. Type the first criterion you want to enter. For example, you can type **Purchasing Manager** as the criterion for Job Title.

4. Select the cell on the Criteria row below the field that contains the second condition you want to apply.

5. Type the second criterion you want to apply. Figure 4.7 shows USA as the criterion for the Country.

Field:	Company	Last Name	First Name	Job Title	Country/Region
Table:	Customers	Customers	Customers	Customers	Customers
Sort:	Ascending				
Show:	✔	✔	✔	✔	✔
Criteria:				"Purchasing Manager"	"USA"
or:					

FIGURE 4.7

The design of a query with criteria for Job Title and Country.

6. Click the Run button to run the query. Only rows that meet both conditions appear in the query result (see Figure 4.8).

Use the And Condition in a Single Field

In only a few situations would you use an **And** condition on the same field. This is because in most situations using the **And** condition on the same field would yield a recordset with no results. For example, the criteria `State = TX and State = CA` would yield no results because the state cannot be equal to both values at the same time. On the other hand, `Shipped Date > 7/1/2006 and Shipped Date < 6/30/2007` would return all orders shipped in that date range. Here's how you would enter this sort of criteria:

1. Open the wanted query in Design view (for example a query based on the Northwind Orders table).

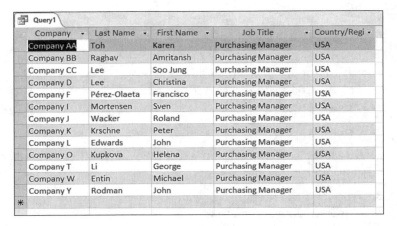

FIGURE 4.8

The Result Includes All Purchasing Managers in the USA.

2. Select the cell on the Criteria row below the field that contains the condition you want to add.

3. Type the first criterion you want to add (for example, **Shipped Date > 7/1/2011**).

4. Type the keyword **And**.

5. Type the second criterion (for example, **Shipped Date < 6/30/2012**).

6. Click the Run button. Access runs the query.

 CAUTION   You need to make sure when you are adding the criteria to each field that you remain on the same row of the query grid.

Use Wildcards in a Query

You can use wildcards to select records that follow a pattern. However, you can use the wildcard characters only in Text or Date/Time fields. You use the * to substitute for multiple characters, and the ? to substitute for single characters. To practice using wildcards in a query, follow these steps:

1. Open the wanted query in Design view. You may wish to use the Northwind Customers table for this example.

2. Select the cell on the Criteria row below the field that contains the condition.

3. Type the criteria, using a wildcard in the wanted expression. In Figure 4.9, the expression `Like Purchasing*` is entered for the Job Title field. This expression returns all rows where the Job Title begins with Purchasing. Note that it is

not necessary to type the keyword "Like." Access will automatically enter it for you when you use the asterisk (*) in your query.

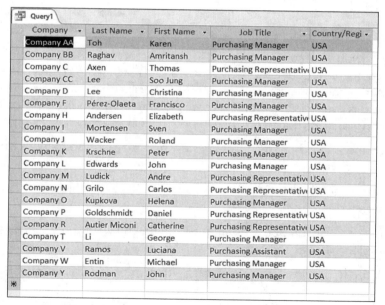

Field:	Company	Last Name	First Name	Job Title	Country/Region
Table:	Customers	Customers	Customers	Customers	Customers
Sort:	Ascending				
Show:	✔	✔	✔	✔	✔
Criteria:				Like "Purchasing*"	
or:					

FIGURE 4.9

Example that contains Purchasing* as the Criteria for the Job Title for the Customers in the USA.

4. Click the Run button. The results of the query are shown in Figure 4.10 and show all the records where the contact title begins with Purchasing.

Company	Last Name	First Name	Job Title	Country/Regi
Company AA	Toh	Karen	Purchasing Manager	USA
Company BB	Raghav	Amritansh	Purchasing Manager	USA
Company C	Axen	Thomas	Purchasing Representative	USA
Company CC	Lee	Soo Jung	Purchasing Manager	USA
Company D	Lee	Christina	Purchasing Manager	USA
Company F	Pérez-Olaeta	Francisco	Purchasing Manager	USA
Company H	Andersen	Elizabeth	Purchasing Representative	USA
Company I	Mortensen	Sven	Purchasing Manager	USA
Company J	Wacker	Roland	Purchasing Manager	USA
Company K	Krschne	Peter	Purchasing Manager	USA
Company L	Edwards	John	Purchasing Manager	USA
Company M	Ludick	Andre	Purchasing Representative	USA
Company N	Grilo	Carlos	Purchasing Representative	USA
Company O	Kupkova	Helena	Purchasing Manager	USA
Company P	Goldschmidt	Daniel	Purchasing Representative	USA
Company R	Autier Miconi	Catherine	Purchasing Representative	USA
Company T	Li	George	Purchasing Manager	USA
Company V	Ramos	Luciana	Purchasing Assistant	USA
Company W	Entin	Michael	Purchasing Manager	USA
Company Y	Rodman	John	Purchasing Manager	USA

FIGURE 4.10

The result of running a query with criteria that contains the wildcard*.

Table 4.2 provides examples of how to use wildcards.

TABLE 4.2 Examples of Using Wildcards

Expression	Results
Sm?th	Finds Smith or Smyth
L*ng	Finds any record that starts with *L* and ends in *ng*
*th	Finds any record that ends in *th* (for example, 158th or Garth)
on	Finds any record that has *on* anywhere in the field
*/2012	Finds all dates in 2000
6/*/2012	Finds all dates in June 2000

 NOTE Access displays the word Like in the criteria cell before a wildcard criteria. It is not necessary to type the word Like in the criteria cell before the criteria.

Use Comparison Operators in a Query

Sometimes, you want to select records in a table that fall within a range of values. You can use comparison operators (=, <, >, <=, and >=) to create criteria based on the comparison of the value contained in a field to a value that you specify in your criteria. Each record is evaluated, and only records that meet the condition are included in the recordset. To practice using comparison operators in your queries, follow these steps:

1. Open the wanted query in Design view. You may wish to follow along with the Nothwind Orders table.

2. Select the cell on the Criteria row below the field for which you want to apply the condition.

3. Type a comparison operator and the criteria you want the query to apply (for example, > 100 as the criteria for the Shipping Fee).

4. Click the Run button. The result of the query appears in Datasheet view.

Table 4.3 gives an example of comparison operators used for a field called Sales. It shows the operators, provides an example of each, and discusses the records that Access would include in the output.

TABLE 4.3 Comparison Operators Used to Compare Against a Field Called Sales

Operator	Indicates	Example	Includes Records Where
>	Greater than	>7500	Sales are greater than 7500.
>=	Greater than or equal to	>=7500	Sales are 7500 or more.
<	Less than	<7500	Sales are less than 7500.
<=	Less than or equal to	<=7500	Sales are 7500 or less.
<>	Does not equal	<>7500	Sales are not 7500.
Between	Range of values	Between 5000 and 7500	Sales are between 5000 and 7500.

Use the Or Condition on a Single Field

The Or condition states that *either* condition of two conditions should be met for the record to appear in the result set. You can use the Or condition on a single field or on more than one field. To practice using an Or condition on a single field, follow these steps:

1. Open the wanted query in Design view.

2. Select the cell on the Criteria row below the field that contains the condition.

3. Type the first criterion you want the query to apply. For example, you could type **Purchasing Manager** as criterion for the Job Title field.

4. Select the cell below the current cell. (This is the Or row.)

5. Type the second criterion you want the query to apply. For example, you could type **Purchasing Assistant** as criterion for the Job Title field (see Figure 4.11).

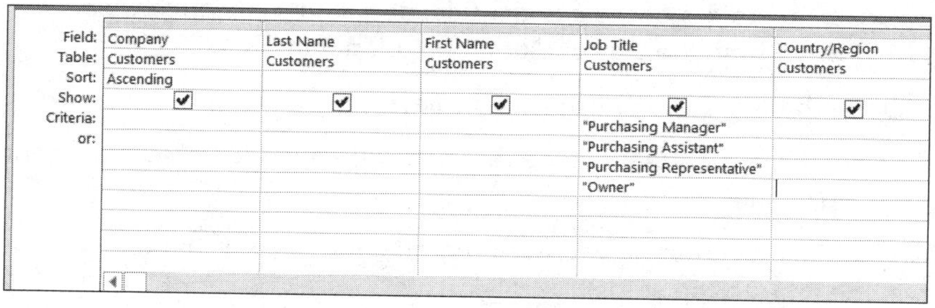

Field:	Company	Last Name	First Name	Job Title	Country/Region
Table:	Customers	Customers	Customers	Customers	Customers
Sort:	Ascending				
Show:	✔	✔	✔	✔	✔
Criteria:				"Purchasing Manager"	
or:				"Purchasing Assistant"	
				"Purchasing Representative"	
				"Owner"	

FIGURE 4.11

Using an Or condition on the Job Title field.

6. Click the Run button. The result of this query is shown in Figure 4.12. The result contains all the purchasing managers, purchasing assistants, purchasing representatives, and owners.

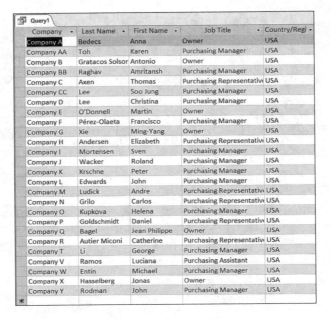

Company	Last Name	First Name	Job Title	Country/Regi
Company A	Bedecs	Anna	Owner	USA
Company AA	Toh	Karen	Purchasing Manager	USA
Company B	Gratacos Solsor	Antonio	Owner	USA
Company BB	Raghav	Amritansh	Purchasing Manager	USA
Company C	Axen	Thomas	Purchasing Representative	USA
Company CC	Lee	Soo Jung	Purchasing Manager	USA
Company D	Lee	Christina	Purchasing Manager	USA
Company E	O'Donnell	Martin	Owner	USA
Company F	Pérez-Olaeta	Francisco	Purchasing Manager	USA
Company G	Xie	Ming-Yang	Owner	USA
Company H	Andersen	Elizabeth	Purchasing Representative	USA
Company I	Mortensen	Sven	Purchasing Manager	USA
Company J	Wacker	Roland	Purchasing Manager	USA
Company K	Krschne	Peter	Purchasing Manager	USA
Company L	Edwards	John	Purchasing Manager	USA
Company M	Ludick	Andre	Purchasing Representative	USA
Company N	Grilo	Carlos	Purchasing Representative	USA
Company O	Kupkova	Helena	Purchasing Manager	USA
Company P	Goldschmidt	Daniel	Purchasing Representative	USA
Company Q	Bagel	Jean Philippe	Owner	USA
Company R	Autier Miconi	Catherine	Purchasing Representative	USA
Company T	Li	George	Purchasing Manager	USA
Company V	Ramos	Luciana	Purchasing Assistant	USA
Company W	Entin	Michael	Purchasing Manager	USA
Company X	Hasselberg	Jonas	Owner	USA
Company Y	Rodman	John	Purchasing Manager	USA

FIGURE 4.12

The result contains all the records that meet the specified criteria for the Job Title field.

Use the Or Condition on Multiple Fields

An alternative to using the Or condition on a single field is to use the Or condition to create criteria on multiple fields. An example is `City equals Las Vegas or Contact Title equals Owner`. These criteria would return all companies in Las Vegas, regardless of the contact title, and all owners, regardless of the city. Here's how you use the Or condition on multiple fields:

1. Open the wanted query in Design view.

2. Select the cell on the Criteria row below the field for which you want to apply the first condition.

3. Type the first criterion you want the query to apply (from the criteria mentioned in the intro to the steps).

4. Select the cell in the Or row below the second field for which you want to apply the criterion.

5. Type the second criterion you want the query to apply (see Figure 4.13).

Field:	Company	Last Name	First Name	Job Title	City	Country/Region
Table:	Customers	Customers	Customers	Customers	Customers	Customers
Sort:	Ascending					
Show:	✔	✔	✔	✔	✔	✔
Criteria:				"owner"		
or:					"Las Vegas"	

FIGURE 4.13

Using the Or condition on multiple fields.

6. Click the Run button. The result of this query is shown in Figure 4.14. The output contains all rows where the city is Las Vegas or the contact title is Purchasing Manager.

Company	Last Name	First Name	Job Title	City	Country/Regi
Company A	Bedecs	Anna	Owner	Seattle	USA
Company AA	Toh	Karen	Purchasing Manager	Las Vegas	USA
Company B	Gratacos Solsor	Antonio	Owner	Boston	USA
Company E	O'Donnell	Martin	Owner	Minneapolis	USA
Company G	Xie	Ming-Yang	Owner	Boise	USA
Company L	Edwards	John	Purchasing Manager	Las Vegas	USA
Company Q	Bagel	Jean Philippe	Owner	Seattle	USA
Company X	Hasselberg	Jonas	Owner	Salt Lake City	USA

FIGURE 4.14

The result contains the rows where the city is Las Vegas or the job title is owner.

NOTE When you use two fields in an Or condition, you need to make sure the criteria are listed on two separate lines. If not, they will combine as an And condition.

You need to use the Or condition to find dates or numbers that fall outside a range (for example, before 6/1/2010 or after 1/1/2012).

You can use the word In and list the multiple criteria, separated by commas, in parentheses (for example, In ("USA", "France", "Canada")).

Saving a Query

To save a query, click the Save button on the toolbar. The Save As dialog box appears (see Figure 4.15). After you provide a name and click OK, Access saves the Structured Query Language (SQL) statement underlying the query. It does not save the result of the query.

FIGURE 4.15

The Save As dialog box.

 TIP   The industry standard for naming queries is to prefix the name with qry.

Closing a Query

You close a query using the close button (the X) in the upper-right corner of the Query Design tab. How Access responds depends on the following three conditions:

- Whether you previously named and saved the query
- Whether you made design changes to the query
- Whether you made changes to the layout of the query while you were in Datasheet view

If you did not previously name and save the query, Access prompts you with the Save As dialog box when you attempt to close the query. If you previously named and saved the query, but did not make any design or layout changes Access provides no prompts. If you made design changes or design and layout changes, Access asks whether you want to save those design changes. If you made *only* layout changes, Access asks if you want to save the layout changes.

THE ABSOLUTE MINIMUM

Access Select queries are stored questions about data. You can create an Access query using one of four wizards or by designing the query from scratch. This chapter focused on designing queries from scratch.

To design an Access query, you must first select the tables that you want to include in your query. After you add one or more tables to your query, you are ready to add fields to the query. There are several techniques that you can use to accomplish this task. You can add one field at a time to the query grid; you can add contiguous fields to the grid; or you can add multiple noncontiguous fields to the grid.

You probably want to sort the data in your query output. You can sort on one or more fields using the Sort row on the query grid.

The real power of queries lies in your ability to designate criteria for the query output. You can create exact match queries. In doing so, you can base criteria on a single condition or on multiple conditions. You can also introduce wildcards into the queries that you build. Using wildcards, you can select records that follow a pattern. Comparison operators enable you to return records that fall within a range of values. For example, you can return records where the sales are greater than a designated value.

When you are happy with your query, you should save it. You can then close it and open it again at a later time. When you run an Access query, it always runs based on the current data in the table. Therefore, any criteria contained in the query is properly reflected in the output.

IN THIS CHAPTER

- How do I open an existing form?
- How can I use a form to insert, delete, and modify table data?
- How can I filter form data?
- How do I close a form?

5

USING FORMS TO DISPLAY AND MODIFY INFORMATION

In this chapter, you learn what forms are and why they are important. You learn how to work with forms in Form view. You explore the basics of working with forms such as opening an existing form, working with data, finding, sorting, and filtering. Finally, you learn how to close a form when you finish working with it.

Moving from Record to Record in a Form

The Navigation Bar appears at the bottom of the Form tab (see Figure 5.1). It enables you to move from record to record. The first button on the Navigation Bar moves you to the first record in the form, and the second button moves you to the record that precedes the record you're currently viewing. Between the second and third navigation button is a record indicator. By typing a record number in the record indicator box, you can quickly move to a wanted record. To the right of the record indicator are the next record button, the last record button, and the new record button.

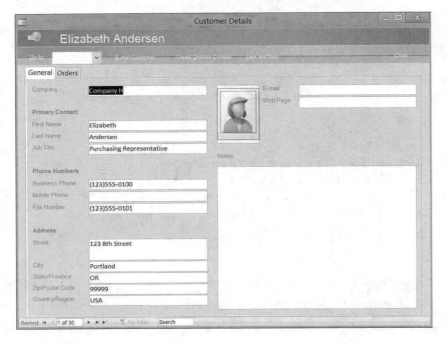

FIGURE 5.1

The Navigation Bar.

You can also you use keystrokes to move from record to record. Pressing Page Down moves you forward through the records, one record at a time. Pressing Page Up moves you backward through the records, one record at a time. Pressing Ctrl+End moves you to the last record, and pressing Ctrl+Home moves you to the first record. Finally, Ctrl++ (plus sign) moves you to a new record.

Edit the Data Underlying a Form

You can modify the table data from within a form. For example, you may want to change a customer's company name or address. Here's how:

1. Select the record you want to change by using any of the techniques covered in the previous section, "Moving from Record to Record in a Form."

2. Select the field you want to change by clicking the field or using the directional keys.

3. Type to make the necessary changes to the data.

Delete Field Contents Within a Form

Now that you know how to modify the contents of a field, consider how to delete the contents of a field. In following along with this section, make sure that you understand that you are not deleting records; you are simply deleting the contents of an individual field *within* a record. You would do this, for example, if you enter a region for a company and then realize that it was located in a country that did not have regions. The process is simple:

1. Select the field contents you want to delete.

2. Press the Delete key.

NOTE If you press the Esc key twice, Access cancels all changes you made to that record. You must recognize that Access saves the record you are working with as soon as you move off of it onto another record.

Undoing Changes Made Within a Form

There are many times when you need to undo changes that you made to a control or to a record. An example is when you start making changes to the incorrect control, or even to the incorrect record. Undo comes to the rescue! You have several different options for how to do this, depending on whether you are still within a field, have left the field, or have left the record. You can use the Undo feature only to undo the last change made to a control or changes made to the most recently modified record.

Undoing Changes Made to the Current Control

When you are in the process of making changes to a field, you might realize that you don't want to make changes to that field or to that record. To undo changes to the current control, you can either click the Undo tool on the QuickAccess toolbar, select Edit, Undo Typing, or press the Esc key once.

Undoing Changes After You Move to Another Control

The process of undoing changes after you move to another control is the same as the process of undoing changes made to the current control. You can either click the Undo tool on the QuickAccess toolbar or press the Esc key once.

 NOTE After you make changes to more than one control in a record, you can undo those changes only by undoing the changes to the entire record. This requires selecting Undo twice on the QuickAccess toolbar.

Undoing Changes After You Save the Record

When you make changes to a field and then move to another record, Access saves all changes to the modified record. If you do not begin making changes to another record, you can still undo the changes you made to the most recently modified record. To do this, you can either click the Undo tool on the toolbar or press the Esc key twice.

 NOTE If Access is unable to undo a change, the Undo tool appears dimmed.

Use a Form to Add New Records to a Table

Access adds records to the end of a table, regardless of how you add them to the table. To use a form to add new records to a table, follow these steps:

1. On the Navigation Bar at the bottom of the form, click the New Record tool.

2. Type the data for the new record (see Figure 5.2).

3. Press Tab to go to the next control.

4. Repeat steps 2 and 3 to enter all the data for the record.

5. Click the New Record tool to move to another new record. Access saves the record you were working on.

 NOTE Access always displays one blank record at the end of a table. This blank record is ready to act as the new record. By default, you can press the Tab key to add a record when you are on the last field of the last record in the table. You can change this behavior by changing a property of the form called the Cycle property. By default Access sets this property to All Records. In the Customer Details form, shown in this example, Microsoft has set this property to Current record. The Tab key therefore cycles you through the fields in the current record and does not bring you to a new record.

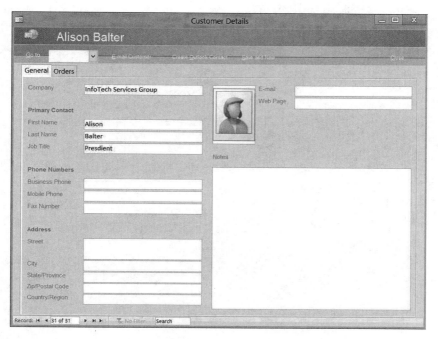

FIGURE 5.2

Adding a new record.

Using a Form to Delete Records from a Table

Before you can delete records, you must first select them. Therefore the process of selecting records is covered before the process of deleting records. The Northwind Customer List form illustrates the process.

To select a record, you just click the gray record selector button to the left of a record within a form (see Figure 5.3). Access selects the record.

To select multiple records (when the form is in Continuous Forms view or Datasheet view), click and drag within the record selector area. Continuous Forms view enables you to view multiple rows of data in a form at a time. Access selects the contiguous range of records in the area over which you click and drag. As an alternative, you can click the selector button for the first record you want to select, hold down the Shift key, and then click the selector button of the last record that you want to select. Access selects the entire range of records between the two selector buttons. Figure 5.4 shows the Customer List form with three records selected.

If you want to select a single record when the cursor is within the record, you can simply choose Select from the Find group on the Home tab of the Ribbon. Then choose Select from the drop-down menu.

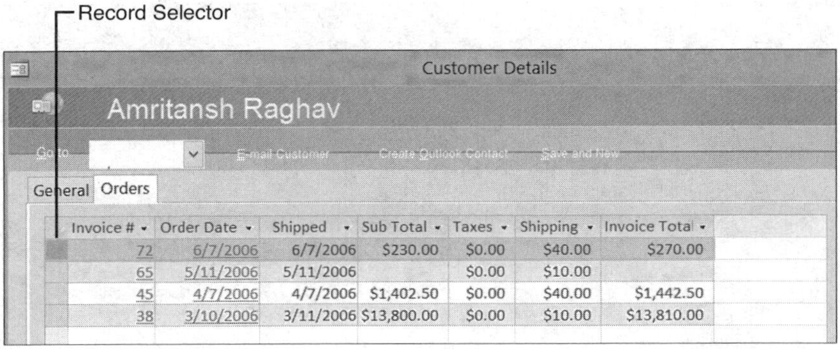

Record Selector

FIGURE 5.3

The gray selector button.

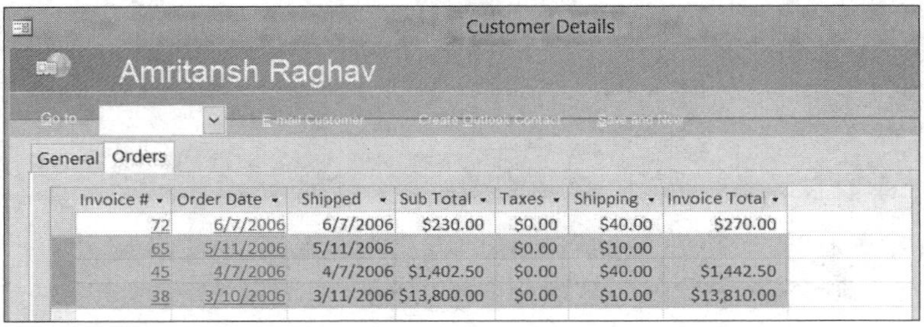

FIGURE 5.4

The Orders table, with three records selected.

Delete a Record

When you know how to select records, deleting them is simple. The process is almost identical to that of deleting records in a datasheet:

1. Select the record you want to delete.

2. Press the Delete key. A dialog box appears, asking whether you're sure you want to delete the records (see Figure 5.5).

3. Click the Yes button.

Delete Records from Tables with Referential Integrity

The process of deleting a record is not simple if you have established referential integrity between the tables in a database and the row that you want to delete has child rows. Chapter 10, "Relating the Information in Your Database," covers relationships and referential integrity. For now, consider that customers generally

FIGURE 5.5

A dialog box that asks if you want to delete the selected records.

have orders associated with them, and those orders have order detail records associated with them. The relationship between the Customers table and the Orders table prohibits the user from deleting customers who have orders. Here's how you delete a customer who has orders:

1. Select the records you want to delete.

2. Press the Delete key. A dialog box appears, saying that the record cannot be deleted or changed because the table includes related records (see Figure 5.6).

FIGURE 5.6

Access notifies you that you cannot delete the selected records.

3. Click OK to close the dialog box.

Access provides a referential integrity option with which you can cascade a deletion down to the child table. This means, for example, that if you attempt to delete an order, Access deletes the associated order detail records. If you establish referential integrity with the cascade delete option, the deletion process works like this:

1. Select the records you want to delete.

2. Press the Delete key. A dialog box appears, asking whether you are sure you want to delete the records (see Figure 5.7).

3. Click Yes to complete the deletion process.

> **Microsoft Access** ⚠
>
> Relationships that specify cascading deletes are about to cause 1 record(s) in this table, along with related records in related tables, to be deleted.
>
> Are you sure you want to delete these records?
>
> [Yes] [No] [Help]
>
> Was this information helpful?

FIGURE 5.7

Access asks whether you want to delete the parent row and the associated child records.

Copying Records Within a Form

At times, you want to copy an entire record. This generally occurs because you are creating a new record and the new record is similar to an existing record. For example, you might have two contacts at the same company who share similar information. You can copy the existing record and then make the necessary changes to the new record. Here's the process:

1. Select the record you want to copy. You can select the record by clicking the gray record selector or by choosing Select from the Find group on the Home tab of the Ribbon and then choosing Select from the drop-down menu.

2. On the Home tab of the Ribbon, select Copy in the Clipboard group.

3. On the Home tab of the Ribbon, select Paste in the Clipboard group, and then from the drop-down, choose Paste Append. Access copies the original record and places you in the new record (the copy).

Copying a record often results in an *entity integrity error*. This occurs, for example, when copying a record would cause a duplicate primary key (that is, unique record identifier). In such a situation, you see an error message, as shown in Figure 5.8. You can either change the data in the field or fields that constitute the duplicate key or you can press the Escape key to cancel the process of appending the new row. For example, you can modify the company name (refer to Figure 5.8).

> **Microsoft Access** ⚠
>
> The changes you requested to the table were not successful because they would create duplicate values in the index, primary key, or relationship. Change the data in the field or fields that contain duplicate data, remove the index, or redefine the index to permit duplicate entries and try again.
>
> [OK] [Help]
>
> Was this information helpful?

FIGURE 5.8

The error that appears when copying a record results in an entity integrity error.

Finding a Record That Meets Specific Criteria

If you edit records in a form, you need to find specific records quickly. The same procedure used in Datasheet view helps you to quickly locate data in a form:

1. Select the field that contains the criteria for which you are searching (in this case, Salesperson in the Order List form).

2. On the Home tab of the Ribbon, click the Find button in the Find group. The Find and Replace dialog box appears (see Figure 5.9).

FIGURE 5.9

The Find tab of the Find and Replace dialog box, where you search for values in the data underlying a form.

3. Type the criteria in the Find What text box. For this example, type **Nancy Freehafer**.

4. Use the Look In drop-down list box to designate whether to search only the current field or all fields in the table. For this example, designate that you want to search only the current field.

5. Use the Match drop-down list box to designate whether to match any part of the field you are searching, the whole field you are searching, or the start of the field you are searching. For example, if you type the word **Federal** in the Find What text box and you select Whole Field in the Match drop-down list box, you find only entries where Ship Via is set to Federal. If you select Any Part of Field, you find Federal Shipping, Federal Express, United Federal Shipping, and so on. If you select Start of Field, you find Federal Shipping and Federal Express, but you do not find United Federal Shipping. For this example, designate that you want to match the whole field.

6. Use the Search drop-down list box to designate whether to search only up from the current cursor position, only down, or in all directions. For this example, designate that you want to search in all directions.

7. Use the Match Case check box to indicate whether you want the search to be case-sensitive.

8. Use the Search Fields as Formatted check box to indicate whether you want to find data based only on the display format (for example, 04-Jul-96 for a date).

9. Click the Find Next button to find the next record that meets the designated criteria.

10. To continue searching after you close the dialog box, use the Shift+F4 keystroke combination or select Find again from the Ribbon.

Replace Data in the Table Underlying a Form

Sometimes you might want to update records that meet specific criteria. You might want to do this, for example, if a company changes its name or you realize that you have improperly entered an employee's Social Security number. The Replace feature automatically inserts new information into the specified fields. Here's the process:

1. Click within the field that contains the criteria you are searching for (Job Title in the Customer List form for this example).

2. Click the Replace button in the Find group on the Home tab of the Ribbon. The Find and Replace dialog box appears.

3. Select the Replace tab (see Figure 5.10).

FIGURE 5.10

The Replace tab of the Find and Replace dialog box, where you can replace table data.

4. Type the criteria in the Find What text box. Type **Owner** for this example.

5. Type the new information (the replacement value) in the Replace With text box. Type **CEO** for this example.

6. Choose values for the Look In drop-down list box, Match drop-down list box, Search drop-down list box, Match Case check box, and Search Fields as

Formatted check box, as described in section, "Finding a Record That Meets Specific Criteria," of this chapter.

7. Click the Find Next button. Access locates the first record that meets the criteria designated in the Find What text box.

8. Click the Replace button.

9. Repeat steps 7 and 8 to find all occurrences of the value in the Find What text box and replace them. As an alternative, you can click the Replace All button to replace all occurrences simultaneously.

 CAUTION You should use Replace All with quite a bit of caution. Remember that the changes you make are *permanent*. Although Replace All is a viable option, when you use it, you need to make sure you have a recent backup and that you are quite certain of what you are doing. You might do a few replaces to make sure that you see what Access is doing before clicking Replace All.

10. Click Cancel when you finish.

 NOTE If you search a large table, Access can find a specific value in a field fastest if the field you search on is the primary key or an indexed field. Chapter 9, "Creating Your Own Tables," covers primary keys and indexes.

When using either Find or Replace, you can use several wildcard characters. A *wildcard character* is a character you use in place of an unknown character. Table 5.1 describes the wildcard characters.

TABLE 5.1   Wildcard Characters You Can Use When Searching

Wildcard Character	Description
*	Acts as a placeholder for multiple characters
?	Acts as a placeholder for a single character
#	Acts as a placeholder for a single number

Sorting Records

You can change the order of records by using sort buttons. You use this feature when you want to view your records in a particular order. For example, you may want to first view the records in order by company name, and later view them in order by most recent order date. The wonderful thing is that with this easy-to-use feature, changing the sort order involves a simple mouse click.

Sort Records on a Single Field

To sort on a field, follow these steps:

1. Click anywhere within the field.

2. Click the Ascending button or click the Descending button. These buttons are found in the Sort & Filter group on the Home tab of the Ribbon. Access reorders the form data by the designated column.

 NOTE Another way to do this is to right-click a field and then choose Sort A to Z or Sort Z to A. (Options differ for numeric and date fields.)

Filtering the Data Underlying a Form

From the Form view, you can apply a filter to view a select group of records. You do this when you want to focus on a select group of records. For example, you may just want to work with the records in the Customers table where the contact title is the owner. You can use the filter by form feature to accomplish this task. When you learn how to use the filter by form feature, you need to know how to remove filters, and how to work with multiple filter criteria.

Use the Filter by Form Feature

The Filter by Form feature is a wonderful feature built in to Access 2013. It enables you to easily implement filtering while viewing data within a form. Here's how you use it:

1. Open the form whose data you want to filter. For this example, I use the Orders form.

2. Choose the Advanced drop-down from the Sort & Filter group on the Home tab of the Ribbon. Select Filter by Form from the drop-down. The Filter by Form feature appears.

3. Click in the field whose data you want to use as the filter criteria.

4. Select the field data to filter on from the drop-down list (see Figure 5.11).

5. From the Sort & Filter group on the Home tab of the Ribbon, choose the Advanced drop-down. Select Apply Filter/Sort from the drop-down. Access filters the data to just the designated rows.

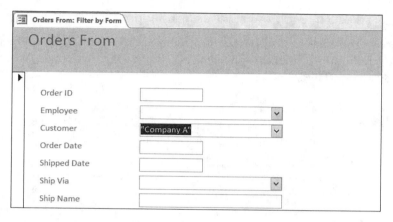

FIGURE 5.11

The Filter by Form feature.

Removing a Filter

To remove a filter, in the Sort & Filter group on the Home tab of the Ribbon, select the Toggle Filter button. Access then displays all the records in the record source underlying the form.

Use Multiple Filter Criteria

So far in this chapter you have learned how to apply a single filter criterion for a single field. The following steps describe how to apply multiple filter criteria for multiple fields or multiple filter criteria for a single field. The process is similar to applying a single filter criterion for a single field:

1. Open the form whose data you want to filter.

2. From the Sort & Filter group on the Home tab of the Ribbon, choose the Advanced drop-down. Select Filter by Form from the drop-down. The Filter by Form feature appears.

3. Click in the first field you want to filter by.

4. Select the field data to filter on from the drop-down list that automatically appears when you click the Filter by Form tool, and then click in a text box.

5. Select the Or tab.

6. Click in the next field you want to filter by. A drop-down list appears for that field.

7. Select the field data to filter on from the drop-down list.

8. Repeat steps 5 through 7 to apply as many additional filter options as wanted.

9. Choose the Advanced drop-down from the Sort & Filter group on the Home tab of the Ribbon. Select Apply Filter/Sort from the drop-down. Access applies the designated filter.

NOTE You can filter by right-clicking a field and selecting from one of the available filter options. Figure 5.12 shows the filtering options available for a text field. Appropriate options are available for numeric and date fields.

If you create multiple filters by using the Or tab, the records that meet either condition appear in the output.

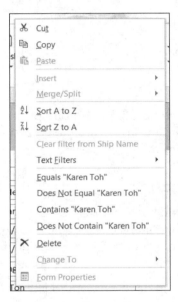

FIGURE 5.12

Filtering options available when you right-click a text field.

CAUTION It is important to understand that the filters that you apply remain with the form. Even after toggling the filter, if you activate the Filter By Form feature you will see that the filters still exist. You must select Clear All Filters from the Advanced dropdown in the Sort & Filter group to permanently remove the filters you apply.

Closing a Form

To close a form, click the close button (the X) in the upper-right corner of the form. If you try to close a form without having made any *design changes*—that is, changes that you make to the design of the form—Access does not prompt you to save. This is because Access saves all data changes as you move from row to row. If you close a form and save design changes, those changes are permanent for all users of the form.

THE ABSOLUTE MINIMUM

Access forms enable you to view, edit, insert, and delete table data in a user-friendly fashion. This chapter focused on the process of manipulating table data via forms.

When you open an existing form, you must become familiar with the process of moving from record to record. You can navigate from record to record using either the Navigation Bar or your mouse, or by using the keyboard. After you locate the record you want to modify, you can easily edit the data within the record.

This chapter showed you several techniques that you can use to undo the changes that you have made. If you read Chapter 3, "Tables: The Repository for Your Data," you should already be somewhat familiar with these techniques. Fortunately, Microsoft made the process of editing and undoing changes to data consistent whether you are in a table datasheet, query datasheet, or a form.

The process of inserting and deleting rows should also be familiar from Chapter 3. When deleting records, you must understand whether referential integrity has been established between the tables in your database. If it has been established, you cannot delete parent records that have associated children, unless you have activated the Cascade Delete functionality. Beware that if you have activated Cascade Delete, all child rows are removed when you delete the parent record. For example, all orders associated with a customer are deleted when you delete the customer.

In this chapter, you saw how you can copy table data from within a form. As you learned in the chapter, you may get an error when copying a record. This error is generally due to a primary key violation. This means that you are duplicating data in the primary or unique key of the duplicated record. You can rectify this problem by modifying the primary key of the duplicate before you save the record.

You will probably agree that Find and Replace in a form are similar to that in a datasheet. An added feature available in a form is the powerful Filter by Form feature. Using Filter by Form you get a nice interface to filtering the data underlying the form. And, of course, you can always right-click within a field and get filtering options appropriate to the type of data in the current field (just like in a datasheet).

Finally, remember that any changes made to table data are automatically saved as you move from record to record. If you are prompted to save when you close a form, it means that you have changed something relating to the design of the form. If, for example, you filter form data, close the form, and opt to save, Access will reapply the filter the next time you open the form.

IN THIS CHAPTER

- How do I use AutoForm to create my own form?
- How do I use a Form Wizard to build a form?
- What is a Split form and how do I build one?
- How do I create a form with multiple items?

CREATING YOUR OWN FORMS

What is a Navigation form and how can I build one? In this chapter, you learn how to create your own forms. You start with the simplest but least flexible method to create a form: the AutoForm feature. You then explore the Form Wizard that provides you with a flexible and powerful method to create forms. After exploring the Form Wizard, you look at three types of forms available to you: Split forms, forms with multiple items, and Navigation forms.

The AutoForm Feature

You can quickly build forms by using the AutoForm feature. The AutoForm feature gives you absolutely no control over how a form appears but provides you with an instantaneous means of data entry.

Create a Form by Using the AutoForm Feature

Creating a form by using the AutoForm feature is amazingly easy. Here's how it works:

1. Select the table or query on which you want to base the new form. Select the Customers table for this example.

2. On the Create tab of the Ribbon, select Form in the Forms group. Access creates a form based on the selected table or query (see Figure 6.1). Notice that the form includes data from the Orders table. The AutoForm feature included this data because there is a relationship established between the Customers and Orders tables. Chapter 10, "Relating the Information in Your Database," covers the process of establishing relationships between the tables in your database.

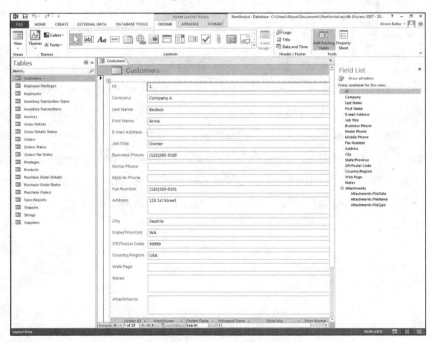

FIGURE 6.1

Access creating a form based on the selected table or query.

Saving a Form

Although Access automatically saves all the data changes that you make to a form, it is up to you to save all the design changes that you make to the form. As you work with the design of a form, you should periodically click the Save tool on the QuickAccess toolbar to save changes. When you close the form, Access prompts you to again save your changes. Here's the process:

1. Click the close button (the X). A dialog box appears, asking whether you want to save your changes.

2. Click the Yes button.

3. If you have not yet named the form, Access prompts you with the Save As dialog box, asking you to provide a name for the form.

4. Enter a form name and click OK.

Form Guidelines

Naming standards suggest that you use the `frm` prefix to name every form.

The name of a form can be up to 64 characters and can contain text, numbers, and spaces.

Subdatasheets are available within forms, just as they are in datasheets.

Using the Form Wizard to Build a Form

Using the Form Wizard gives you more flexibility than using the AutoForm feature to create forms. It also requires more knowledge on your part. Here's how to use it:

1. In the Forms group on the Create tab of the Ribbon, select Form Wizard. The Form Wizard appears.

2. Select the table or query on which you want to base the form.

3. Select the fields you want to include on the form (see Figure 6.2).

4. Click Next. Select a layout for the form .

5. Click Next. Provide a title for the form.

6. Click Finish. The completed form appears with all the options that you selected.

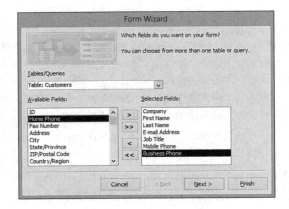

FIGURE 6.2

Select the fields.

Creating Split Forms

Using the Split Form feature, you can create a form that includes a datasheet in one section of the form, and a data entry form in another section of the form, as shown in Figure 6.3. The data entry form appears on the top section of the form

FIGURE 6.3

A Split Form with the data entry form on the top and the datasheet on the bottom.

and the datasheet appears at the bottom of the form. You can use a property of the form to determine whether the datasheet appears at the bottom, top, left, or right side of the form. You use the Format tab of the form's property sheet to create a split form. Chapter 13, "Building Powerful Forms," covers the process to work with and modify form properties. It is the Split Form Orientation property that affects the position of the data entry form and datasheet.

The process to create a Split Form is simple:

1. Use the Navigation Pane to select the table or query on which you want to base the split form.

2. In the Forms group on the Create tab, use the More Forms drop-down to view the types of forms you can create.

3. Select Split Form. Access instantly creates the form. As you select different records in the datasheet, the data from the corresponding record appears in the data entry form.

To view the design of the form that you just created, from the View drop-down on the Design tab of the Ribbon, select Design View. The design appears, as shown in Figure 6.4. Notice that the datasheet does not appear when in Design view.

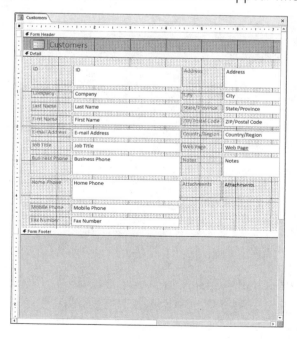

FIGURE 6.4

The design of a Split Form shows only the data entry form.

Creating Multiple Item Forms

Multiple Item forms are also referred to as Continuous forms. Multiple Item forms show multiple records at once (see Figure 6.5). To create a Multiple Item form:

1. Use the Navigation Pane to select the table or query on which you want to base the split form.

2. Use the More Forms drop-down in the Forms group on the Create tab to view the types of forms you can create.

3. Select Multiple Items. Access instantly creates the form. The form displays multiple records. You can move from record to record, making data changes as necessary.

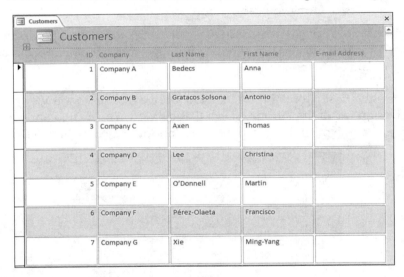

FIGURE 6.5

A form that displays multiple records simultaneously.

NOTE A multiple item form is one in which the Default View property is set to Continuous Forms. With Continuous Forms, the detail section of the form repeats for each record underlying the form.

To view the design of the form that you just created, from the View drop-down on the Design tab of the Ribbon, select Design View. The design appears, as shown in Figure 6.6.

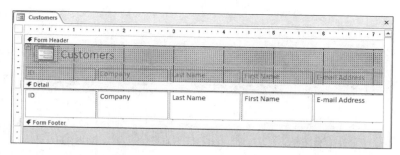

FIGURE 6.6

The design of a Multiple Item form.

Creating Navigation Forms

Navigation forms are powerful and elegant. They enable you to provide an easy-to-use interface to the forms within your application. To create a Navigation form, follow these steps:

1. In the Forms group on the Create tab of the Ribbon, open up the Navigation drop-down.

2. Select the style of Navigation form you want to create. Access creates the form and places you in Layout View (see Figure 6.7).

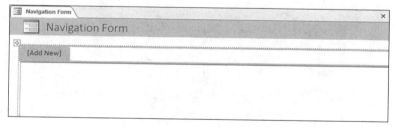

FIGURE 6.7

Layout View of a Navigation form with Horizontal tabs.

3. Drag and drop a form or report onto the Add New tab, as shown in Figure 6.8.

4. Click within the tab, if wanted, and supply the text for the tab. You can click and drag the edge of the tab to make the tab wider or taller if the text for the tab does not fit.

5. Repeat steps 3 and 4 to add as many forms and reports to your Navigation form as wanted. Figure 6.9 shows a completed example.

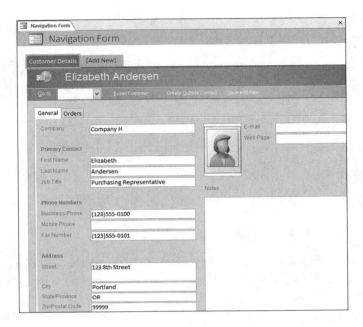

FIGURE 6.8

Layout View of a Navigation form after adding a form.

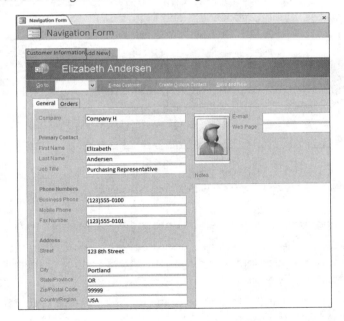

FIGURE 6.9

A completed Navigation form.

Customizing a Navigation Form

After you create a Navigation form, you can customize its look and feel. Follow these steps:

1. You must first switch to Layout view. To do this, from the Views drop-down on the Home or Design tab of the Ribbon, select Layout View.

2. Click to select the Format tab on the Ribbon.

3. Click to select one of the tabs you want to customize.

4. Hold down your Ctrl key, and select the other tabs you want to customize.

5. Open the Quick Styles drop-down in the Control Formatting group on the Format tab (see Figure 6.10).

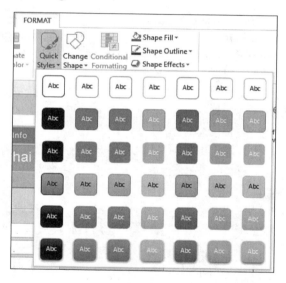

FIGURE 6.10

The Quick Styles drop-down enables you to select a style for the selected buttons.

6. Select the wanted style for the selected buttons.

7. Click the Change Shape drop-down in the Control Formatting group on the Format tab (see Figure 6.11).

8. Select the wanted shape for the selected buttons.

9. Click the Shape Fill drop-down in the Control Formatting group on the Format tab. Either select a solid fill, or click Gradient and select the wanted gradient.

10. In the Control Formatting group on the Format tab, click the Shape Outline drop-down. Here you can designate the line color, type, and thickness.

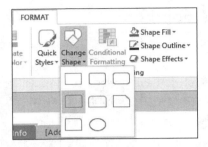

FIGURE 6.11

The Change Shape drop-down enables you to select a shape for the selected buttons.

11. In the Control Formatting group on the Format tab, click the Shape Effects drop-down. Here you can select Shadow, Glow, Soft Edges, or Bevel. For example, Figure 6.12 shows the options available to you if you select Glow. A completed example appears in Figure 6.13.

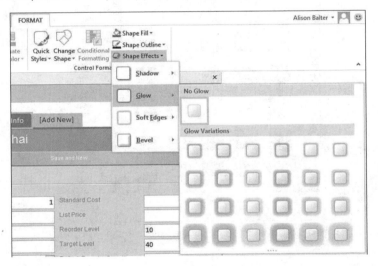

FIGURE 6.12

One of the options under Shape Effects enables you to apply a glow to the selected buttons.

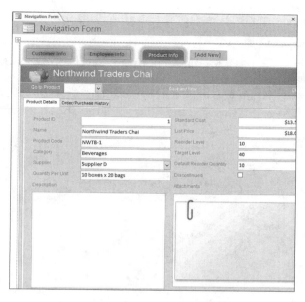

FIGURE 6.13

A Navigation form after applying several formatting options.

Creating a Navigation Form with Horizontal and Vertical Tabs

The process to creating a Navigation form with both Horizontal and Vertical tabs is a little different. It looks like this:

1. In the Forms group on the Create tab of the Ribbon, open the Navigation drop-down.

2. Select Horizontal Tabs and Vertical Tabs Left. Access creates the form and places you in Layout View (see Figure 6.14). The vertical tabs appear on the left with the horizontal tabs going across the top.

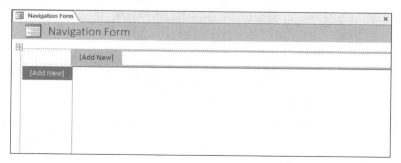

FIGURE 6.14

A Navigation form with horizontal and vertical tabs.

3. Drag and drop a form or report onto the horizontal Add New tab.

4. Drag and drop forms and reports onto the vertical Add New tab.

5. Repeat steps 3 and 4 for all the horizontal and corresponding vertical tabs.

When you finish, when you click a horizontal tab, you see all the associated vertical tabs (see Figure 6.15). Clicking the horizontal tab shows all of the associated vertical tabs.

FIGURE 6.15

Viewing all associated vertical tabs.

THE ABSOLUTE MINIMUM

There are many types of forms available to you in Microsoft Access, and there are many ways to create those forms. They range from the simplest to create, but least flexible, to the more complex to create, but extremely flexible.

The author rarely uses the AutoForm feature because it takes more work to modify the forms that it creates than to build the same form using a wizard or from scratch. However, the author does use the Form Wizard, which makes it easy to quickly build a form containing just the fields that you need.

After exploring AutoForm and the Form Wizard, you experimented with three additional types of forms: Split, Multiple Item, and Navigation. Split forms provide you with a quick-and-easy way to navigate a datasheet, viewing each record in a data entry form. Multiple Item forms enable you to view the contents of multiple records simultaneously. Multiple Item forms are "datasheets on steroids" because they offer the features of a datasheet (you can view multiple records), but they give you much more control than a datasheet. Finally, you learned about Navigation forms. Using Navigation forms, you can provide a rich user interface with all the forms and reports contained in your databases.

There is more to learn about creating and working with forms. Chapter 13, "Building Powerful Forms," and Chapter 14, "Advanced Form Techniques," cover the more advanced aspects of creating forms. In those chapters, you learn how to further customize the forms that you learned how to create in this chapter.

- How do I work with an existing report?

- How do I preview what a report will look like when it prints?

- How do I perform basic tasks such as moving from page to page and zooming in and out?

- What is the difference between Report view, Layout view, and Print Preview?

USING REPORTS TO PRINT INFORMATION

In this chapter, you learn how to work with existing reports. You begin by opening and viewing an existing report. You explore the process to move from page to page, and zoom in and out so that you can see just the data you need to see. You learn the differences between Print Preview, Layout view, and Report view and will know when each view is appropriate. Finally, you see how easy it is to print the data displayed on the report.

Opening and Viewing a Report

Microsoft Access provides an excellent means to work with existing reports. You can either send a report directly to the printer, or you can first preview a report that you want to work with.

Preview a Report

Begin by looking at the process to preview a report:

1. Click the Reports list of objects in the Navigation Pane (see Figure 7.1).

2. Right-click the report you want to open. Then from the context-sensitive menu, select Print Preview. The report appears in Preview mode.

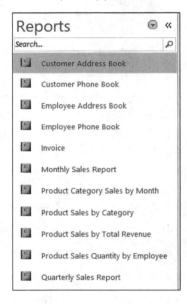

FIGURE 7.1

The Reports list of objects.

Moving from Page to Page

A report is a way to present the data from a table or query in a formatted document. Although you can print datasheets, reports control how you present and summarize the data. When you open a report, you can use the navigation buttons to easily move from page to page. You accomplish this by using the page navigation buttons at the bottom of the report window (see Figure 7.2). By using these buttons, you can easily navigate to the first page of the report, the previous page, the next page, or the last page of the report. By typing a number into the text box on the navigation bar, you can easily navigate to any page in the report.

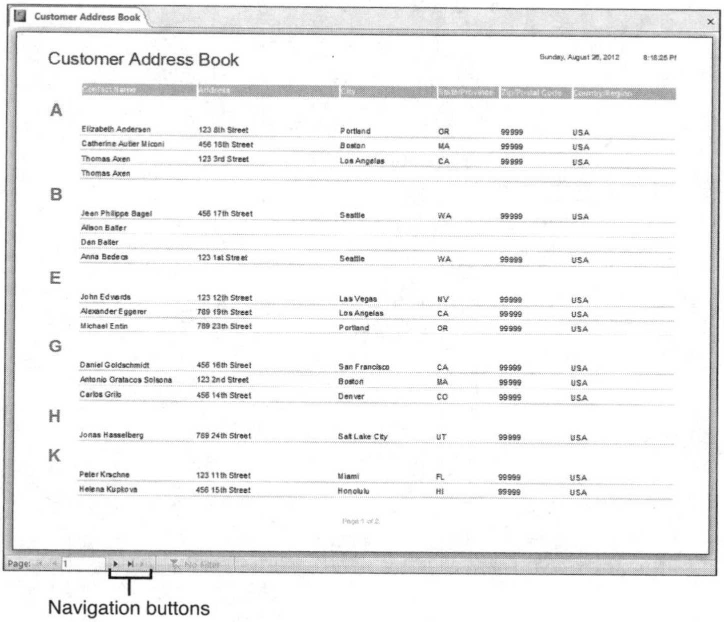

Navigation buttons

FIGURE 7.2

Report navigation buttons.

Zooming In and Out

When previewing reports, you can change the amount of text (and the size of the text) that you see onscreen in a report. You do this by zooming in and out of the report page. There are three different techniques that you can use to set the zoom level. Here's the first technique:

1. Place the mouse pointer over the report so that it appears as a magnifying glass.

2. Click the mouse. The page zooms in.

3. Click the mouse again. The page zooms out.

Here's the second technique:

1. Click the Zoom drop-down list box in the Zoom group on the Print Preview tab on the Ribbon (see Figure 7.3).

2. Select a size. The report zooms to the designated level.

NOTE The third technique involves the use of the Zoom control found in the lower right-hand corner of the Preview window. Using the Zoom control you can click and drag to select the desired zoom level.

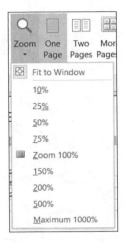

FIGURE 7.3

The Zoom drop-down list box, which enables you to select a zoom level.

 NOTE You may wonder what the Fit option is within the Zoom drop-down. The Fit option fits the report within the available screen real estate of the report window.

Viewing Multiple Pages

While you're previewing an Access report, you can preview more than one page at a time. To view two pages, click the Two Pages button in the Zoom group on the Print Preview tab of the Ribbon. To view multiple pages, click the Multiple Pages button, and select how many pages you want to view (see Figure 7.4).

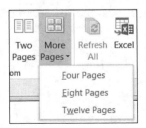

FIGURE 7.4

Selecting how many pages you want to view.

Working in Layout View

You just learned how to preview a report. The preview option enables you to view what the report will look like when it is printed, but you cannot make structural changes to a report while in Print Preview. Layout view enables you to modify many of the design aspects of a report while viewing what it will look like when it is printed. It is an excellent way for you to size a control on a report while instantly determining whether the actual table data will fit within the new column size. Figure 7.5 shows the Employee Address Book report in Layout view with the Employee Name column selected. You can size the Employee Name column and instantly see whether the existing employee names fit in the columns. You can also do things such as bold and italicize report data, all with instant results.

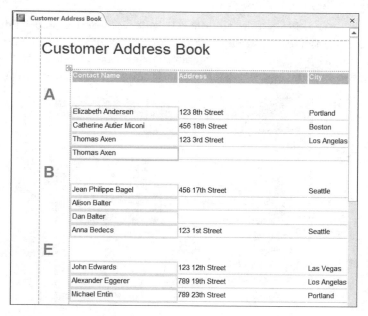

FIGURE 7.5

The Employee Address Book report in Layout view.

Working in Report View

Report view differs both from Print Preview and from Layout View. Whereas Print Preview displays the data just as it will display when it is printed, Report view differs significantly. The goal of Report view is to quickly display data to the screen. Not only does this not reflect what the report will look like when printed, but also no programming code is executed in Report view. This means that if you, or a programmer, place programming code in a form event, the code is not executed. Even page breaks don't appear in Report view. Although this view can be useful to take a quick look at a report on the screen, beware that what you see may not be what you get when you print your report!

Printing a Report

Before you print your report, you can change the report margins, orientation, paper size, and several other important options. You accomplish this using the Page Setup feature.

Use Page Setup

Here's how Page Setup works:

1. While previewing the report, in the Page Layout group on the Print Preview tab of the Ribbon, click the Page Setup button. The Page Setup dialog box appears (see Figure 7.6). Note that as an alternative, you can select the Page Setup tab while in Layout view of the report, and then click the Page Setup button.

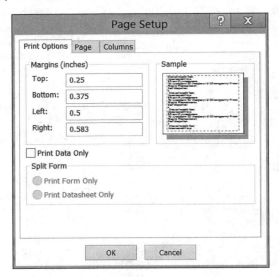

FIGURE 7.6

The Page Setup dialog box where you select report settings.

2. The Print Options tab enables you to modify the margins. The Page tab enables you to customize important settings such as the orientation, paper size and source, and the printer you want to use. The Columns tab enables you

to designate column size and other information applicable for multicolumn reports. Select the wanted options.

3. Click OK to accept your changes.

 TIP If you prefer, you can use the appropriate Ribbon buttons to designate the settings available in the Page Setup dialog box. For example, you can easily switch from portrait to landscape using the Landscape tool available in the Page Layout group of the Print Preview tab of the Ribbon.

Sending Reports to the Printer

You can print the reports you create by using the context-sensitive menu. You can just right-click the report that you want to print, and then select Print. You can also print from Print Preview mode. Just click the Print button in the Print group on the Print Preview tab on the Ribbon. To print a report by using the context-sensitive menu, follow these steps:

1. In the list of objects in the Navigation Pane, click Reports.

2. Right-click the report you want to print.

3. Choose Print.

4. Complete the dialog box, entering information such as the number of copies that you want to print, the printer you want to print to, and so on.

5. Click OK to complete the process.

The process to print a report by using the Print button while previewing the report works like this:

1. In the list of objects in the Database window, click Reports.

2. Right-click the report you want to print, and then select Preview.

3. Click the Print tool in the Print group on the Print Preview tab on the Ribbon. Again the Print dialog appears, prompting you for additional information.

Closing a Report

To close an Access report, click the close button (X) on the upper-right corner of the report tab (see Figure 7.7). If you have made changes to a report in Layout view, or in Design view (covered in Chapter 8, "Building Your Own Reports"), Access prompts you and asks you if you want to save your changes to the report (see Figure 7.8). If you click Yes, the changes you made to your report will be permanent. If you click No, Access discards the changes you made to you report.

Click to close

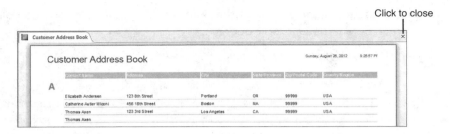

FIGURE 7.7

To close an Access report, click the close button.

FIGURE 7.8

Access prompts you and asks you if you want to save your changes.

THE ABSOLUTE MINIMUM

Before you can learn how to build your own reports, it is helpful for you to learn how to work with existing reports. Using the Print Preview feature in Access, you can view a report exactly how it will appear when printed. While in Print Preview, you can zoom in and out, move from page to page, and view a specified number of pages simultaneously.

Whereas you use Print Preview to get a look at how your report will print, you use Layout View to dynamically modify the design of a report. Using Layout view, you can change the width of controls, change the properties of control (for example, bold, italicize, and change the font), and more. The beauty of Layout view is that you can see the effect of your design changes immediately. For example, if you increase the size of the font associated with a control, the data may no longer fit within the control.

Yet another view for a report is called Report view, which is optimized for viewing data on the screen. There are no page breaks. Furthermore, Access does not execute any programming code placed in events, such as the Format event of the Detail section of the report. If all you want to do is to view data on the screen, this view is for you, but remember to beware that what you see is not always what you will get when you print.

When printing a report, you can use the Page Setup features to refine how Access prints the report. For example, you can use Page Setup to modify report margins.

Remember that you can use two different techniques to print a report. You can right-click a report in the navigation pane and select print. You can also select Print from the ribbon while in Print Preview mode. With either method, Access sends the report to the printer.

Finally, don't be surprised when closing a report if Access prompts you to save. This means that you made a change to the design of the report, probably in Layout view. Remember that if you select Yes, all your changes will be permanent.

BUILDING YOUR OWN REPORTS

In this chapter, you learn how to create your own reports. You learn how to use both the AutoReport and Report Wizard features, and how to view the design of a report so that you can modify the reports that you build. You explore the types of reports available in Access 2013. Finally, you learn how to create custom mailing labels from your table data.

Using the AutoReport Feature

Using the AutoReport feature is the quickest and easiest way to create a report. Access creates a report via the AutoReport feature without asking you any questions. Although you can create this type of report effortlessly, as you will see, it is not flexible because it does not prompt you with any options.

Create a Report with AutoReport

Here's how AutoReport works:

1. Select Tables or Queries in the list of objects in the Navigation Pane.

2. Select the table or query on which you want to base the report.

3. Click the Create tab (see Figure 8.1).

4. Select Report. Access creates a report based on the selected table or query.

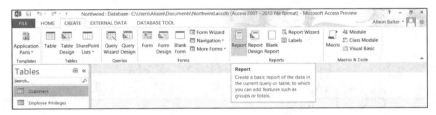

FIGURE 8.1

The Create tab enables you to quickly and easily create a report based on a table or query.

Create a Report by Using the Report Wizard

Although the AutoReport feature is great at producing a quick report, it does not offer much in terms of flexibility. The Report Wizard asks a series of questions and then better customizes the report to your needs. Now take a look at how it works:

1. Select the Create tab.

2. Click the Report Wizard tool in the Reports group.

3. In the first step of the wizard, you select the tables or queries on which you want to base the report. For this example, I use the Customers table.

4. Select the fields you want to include in the report (see Figure 8.2). You can add any type of field to a report. You can also add as many fields or as few fields as you like. You can even use the Tables/Queries dropdown to include fields from more than one table! You simply select the first table (for example Customers) from the Tables/Queries dropdown, select the desired fields from that table,

and then select the next table (for example Orders) from the Tables/Queries dropdown, and then select the fields you want to include from that table. Chapter 15, "Building Powerful Reports," covers the process of building reports based on multiple tables in more detail. To follow along with this example select only the Customers table. Click Next to continue.

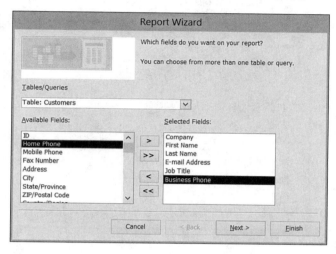

FIGURE 8.2

Step 1: Selecting the fields you want to include in a report.

5. In the second step the wizard prompts you to select any fields that you want to group by (see Figure 8.3). To add a grouping, click the field you want to group by and then click the right arrow. The field will appear as a grouping in

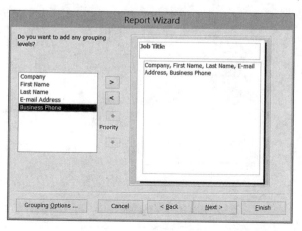

FIGURE 8.3

Step 2: Selecting the fields that you want to group by.

the image on the right. If you make a mistake and want to remove a grouping, click the left arrow. Click Next.

6. In the third step of the wizard, you select the wanted sort order (see Figure 8.4). You can select either ascending or descending. Ascending is selected (refer to Figure 8.4). Click Next.

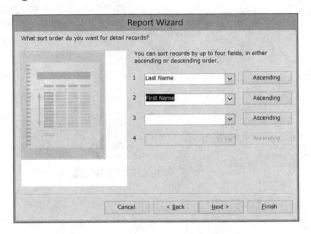

FIGURE 8.4

Step 3: Selecting a sort order for a report.

7. In the fourth step of the wizard, you select the wanted layout for the report (see Figure 8.5). The layout you select is a matter of personal preference and that works best with the data you selected for the report. Click Next.

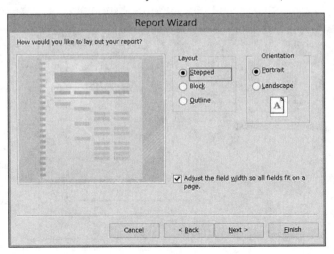

FIGURE 8.5

Step 4: Selecting a layout for a report.

8. The fifth step of the wizard prompts you to type the report title.

9. Click the Finish button. Access creates the report and places you in Preview mode.

As you can see, the Report Wizard offers more flexibility than the AutoReport feature. Using the Report Wizard, you can designate the fields you want to include on the report, the data groupings you want to add to the report, the sort order for the report, the layout for the report, and a style for the report. The Report Wizard can generally do most of the work for you. It's then up to you to add those finishing touches.

Viewing the Design of a Report

AutoReports are limiting because they create such generic reports. But after you create such a rather-dull, generic report the easy way using the AutoReport feature, you then can begin to make modifications using the Design view. Access does the basics, and then you add bells and whistles to make the report individual and better suited to your specific application. Furthermore, although the Report Wizard gives you many choices, you still may want to customize many of the options that it set.

After you create a report by using the AutoReport feature or the Report Wizard, you probably want to customize the report. You must switch to Design view of the report to accomplish this task. While previewing the report, you must first right-click the report and then select Design View from the context-sensitive menu. Or, while in Report view, just click the View tool in the Views group on the Home tab on the Ribbon (see Figure 8.6) to switch to Design view. The report is shown in

FIGURE 8.6

The View tool switches you to Design view.

Design view in Figure 8.7. You can easily toggle between Design view and Preview mode to view the report and then modify its design.

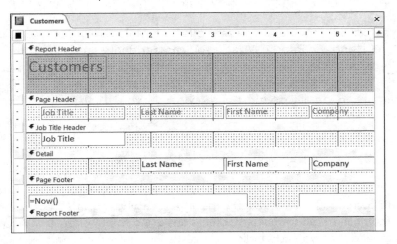

FIGURE 8.7

The report in Design view.

Types of Reports Available

The reporting engine of Microsoft Access is powerful, with a wealth of features. Many types of reports are available in Access 2007:

- Detail reports
- Summary reports
- Reports containing graphics
- Reports containing forms
- Reports containing labels
- Reports including any combination of the preceding

Detail Reports

A Detail report supplies an entry for each record included in the report. As you can see in Figure 8.8, there's an entry for each customer in the Customers table. The report's detail is grouped by the first character of the customer's last name.

Customer Address Book

Contact Name	Address	City	State/Province	Zip/Postal Co
A				
Elizabeth Andersen	123 8th Street	Portland	OR	99999
Catherine Autier Miconi	456 18th Street	Boston	MA	99999
Thomas Axen	123 3rd Street	Los Angelas	CA	99999
Thomas Axen				
B				
Jean Philippe Bagel	456 17th Street	Seattle	WA	99999
Alison Balter				
Dan Balter				
Anna Bedecs	123 1st Street	Seattle	WA	99999
E				
John Edwards	123 12th Street	Las Vegas	NV	99999
Alexander Eggerer	789 19th Street	Los Angelas	CA	99999

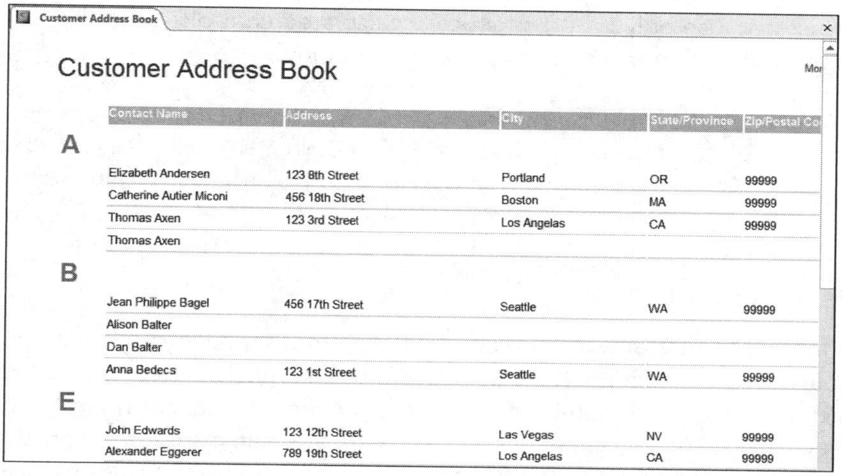

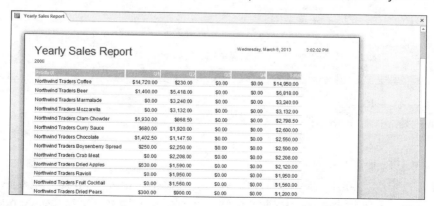

FIGURE 8.8

An example of a Detail report.

Summary Reports

A Summary report gives you summary data for all the records included in the report. In Figure 8.9, only total sales by product for each quarter display in the report. The underlying detail records that compose the summary data don't display in the report. The report contains only programmatically calculated controls in its Detail section. The remainder of the controls are placed in report Group Headers and Footers that are grouped on the month and year of the

Yearly Sales Report
2006
Wednesday, March 6, 2013 3:02:02 PM

Product	Q1	Q2	Q3	Q4	Total
Northwind Traders Coffee	$14,720.00	$230.00	$0.00	$0.00	$14,950.00
Northwind Traders Beer	$1,400.00	$5,418.00	$0.00	$0.00	$6,818.00
Northwind Traders Marmalade	$0.00	$3,240.00	$0.00	$0.00	$3,240.00
Northwind Traders Mozzarella	$0.00	$3,132.00	$0.00	$0.00	$3,132.00
Northwind Traders Clam Chowder	$1,930.00	$868.50	$0.00	$0.00	$2,798.50
Northwind Traders Curry Sauce	$680.00	$1,920.00	$0.00	$0.00	$2,600.00
Northwind Traders Chocolate	$1,402.50	$1,147.50	$0.00	$0.00	$2,550.00
Northwind Traders Boysenberry Spread	$250.00	$2,250.00	$0.00	$0.00	$2,500.00
Northwind Traders Crab Meat	$0.00	$2,208.00	$0.00	$0.00	$2,208.00
Northwind Traders Dried Apples	$530.00	$1,590.00	$0.00	$0.00	$2,120.00
Northwind Traders Ravioli	$0.00	$1,950.00	$0.00	$0.00	$1,950.00
Northwind Traders Fruit Cocktail	$0.00	$1,560.00	$0.00	$0.00	$1,560.00
Northwind Traders Dried Pears	$300.00	$900.00	$0.00	$0.00	$1,200.00

FIGURE 8.9

An example of a Summary report.

order. Because only programmatically calculated controls are in the report's Detail section, Access prints summary information only.

 NOTE To run the sample summary report, first open the Northwind form Sales Report Dialog. Select the Sales by Product report for the Yearly Sales period. Select 2006 as the year and then click Preview.

Reports with Graphics

Although the statement "A picture paints a thousand words" is a cliché, it's also quite true; research proves that you retain data much better when it's displayed as pictures rather than numbers. Fortunately, Access makes including graphics in your reports easy. As you can see in Figure 8.10, you can design a report that contains one or more graphics. The report in Figure 8.10 shows the sales by product for the each day. The main report is grouped by order date and product category. The report includes a company logo in its header. This report is not included in the Northwind database.

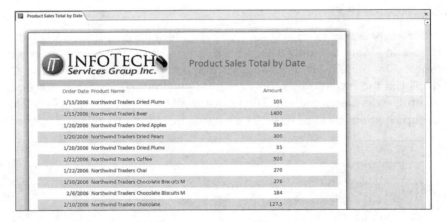

FIGURE 8.10

An example of a report with a graphic.

Reports with Forms

Users often need a report that looks like a printed form. The Access Report Builder, with its many graphical tools, enables you to quickly produce reports that emulate the most elegant data entry form. The report shown in Figure 8.11 produces an invoice for a customer. The report is based on a query that draws information from the `Customers`, `Orders`, `Order_Details`, `Products`, `Employees_Extended`, and `Shippers` tables. The report's `Filter` property is filled in, limiting the data that appears on the report to a particular order in the `Orders` table. Using graphics, color, fonts, shading, and other special effects gives the form a professional look. You run the Invoice report from the Northwind Order List form. Open the form and then click the View Invoice command button.

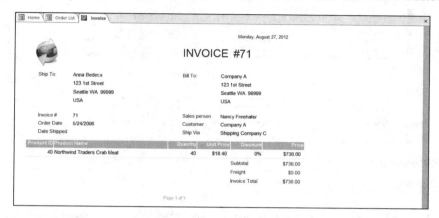

FIGURE 8.11

An example of a report containing a form.

Reports with Labels

Creating mailing labels in Access 2013 is easy using the Label Wizard. Mailing labels are simply a special type of report with a page setup indicating the number of labels across the page and the size of each label. An example of a mailing label report created by using the Label Wizard is shown in Figure 8.12. This report is based on the `Customers` table but could have just as easily been based on a query that limits the mailing labels produced.

Creating Mailing Labels

As you saw in the previous section, one of the types of reports that you can create is a report that generates mailing labels. Mailing labels are fun and easy to create:

1. In the list of objects in the Navigation Pane, select Tables or Queries.

2. Click to select the table or query on which you want to base the mailing labels.

3. Click to select the Create tab.

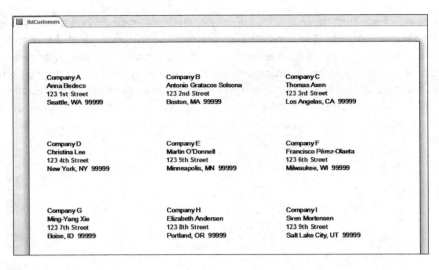

FIGURE 8.12

An example of a Mailing Labels.

4. Click Labels in the Reports group. The Label Wizard appears (see Figure 8.13). The Labels button is not available if you forget to select a table or query in step 2.

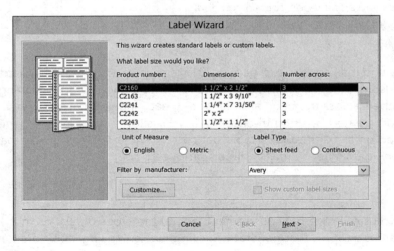

FIGURE 8.13

The Label Wizard facilitates the process of creating labels.

5. Select the size of label you want to create. You can filter by manufacturer, if you want. You can skip to step 10 if you find the label size that you need.

6. If you do not find the label size that you need, click Customize. The New Label Size dialog appears (see Figure 8.14). The New Label Size dialog enables you to create a label with any dimensions.

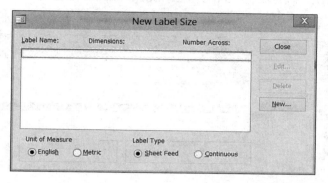

FIGURE 8.14

Use the New Label Size dialog to create a label with any dimensions.

7. Click New. The New Label dialog appears (see Figure 8.15). Here you can designate all the specifics of a custom label. Note that you cannot leave the spacing options at zero.

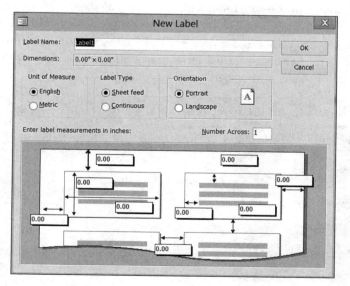

FIGURE 8.15

Use the New Label dialog to designate the specifics of the custom label.

8. Click OK to close the New Label dialog and return to the New Label Size dialog.

9. Click Close to close the New Label Size dialog and return to the wizard. The new label appears, and the Show Custom Label Sizes check box is selected (see Figure 8.16).

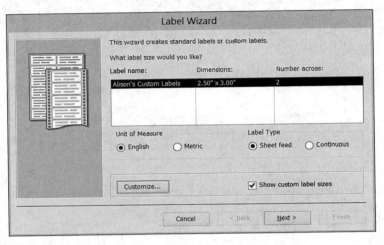

FIGURE 8.16

If you click the Show Custom Label Sizes check box, all the custom labels appear.

10. Click Next to move to the next step of the wizard. Access prompts you to select a font and size for the label text. You can also designate the font weight, text color, italic, and underline (see Figure 8.17).

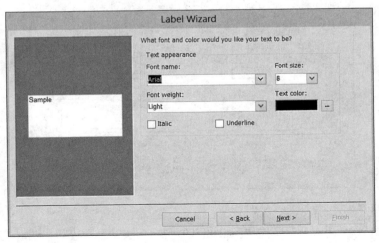

FIGURE 8.17

The Label wizard enables you to control the appearance of the labels.

11. Click Next. It is now time for you to lay out the fields on the label.

12. Double-click to add the first field to the first line of the label.

13. Press the Enter key to move to the second line of the label. Double-click to add the second field to the label. If you want, you can add more than one field to a line on the label. For example, you may want to add the first name, a space, and the last name to the same line of the label (see Figure 8.18). You can even add characters such as commas to your labels, and your labels can include graphics such as your company logo.

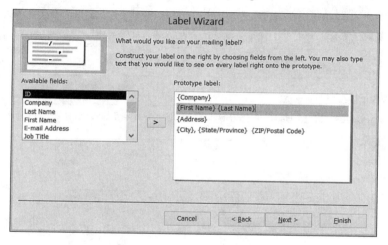

FIGURE 8.18

You can add multiple fields to each line of the label.

14. Click Next after you add all wanted fields to the label. The wizard prompts you for the fields you want to sort by. Figure 8.19 shows the fields sorted by Company Name, Last Name, and First Name.

15. Click Next. Access prompts you to name the labels. You have the option of previewing the labels or viewing them in Design view. If you select Modify the Label Design and click Finish, the completed labels appear, as shown in Figure 8.20. Your labels appear in the list of objects under Reports.

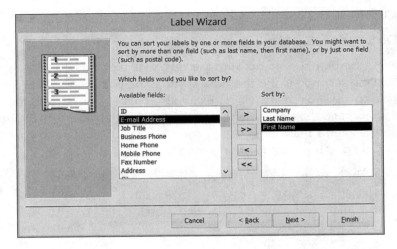

FIGURE 8.19

Access enables you to designate the sort order for the labels that you create.

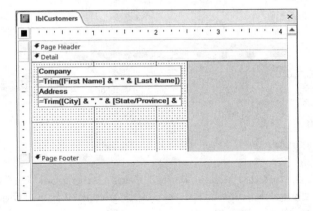

FIGURE 8.20

Labels in Design view.

THE ABSOLUTE MINIMUM

This chapter began by providing you with an introduction to the AutoReport feature. You'll probably agree that although easy to use, this method of creating a report is not usually particularly helpful. This is because the AutoReport feature creates a report based on the selected table or query, without asking you any questions.

Unlike its cousin, the AutoReport, the Report Wizard is an extremely powerful tool. It walks you through a series of steps, after which it generates a report that is most likely close to what you are looking for. The best news is that whether you use the AutoReport feature or the Report Wizard, you can switch to Design view (covered briefly in this chapter) and customize the report to your liking. Chapter 15 covers the details of working with a report in Design view.

To be considered a powerful Access user, you must understand the types of reports you can build in Access. This chapter took you on an extensive tour of report examples. You saw everything from simple detail reports to mailing labels, and everything in between.

Speaking of mailing labels, the Mailing Label Wizard is one of the more elegant tools in Microsoft Access. After answering a series of questions, you can not only select from a list of standard labels, but you can also design your own. Mailing labels are simple to create, but the end product is extremely powerful.

IN THIS CHAPTER

- How do you build your tables?

- What are field types and why do you care?

- How can you benefit from indexes?

- What field properties are available, and how can you take advantage of them?

9

CREATING YOUR OWN TABLES

It is useful to think of the process of table design as being similar to the process of building a foundation for a house. Just as a house with a faulty foundation will fall over, an application with a poor table design will be difficult to build, maintain, and use. This chapter covers all the ins and outs of table design in Access 2013. After reading this chapter, you will be ready to build the other components of an application, knowing that the tables you design provide the application with a strong foundation.

Building a New Table

You can add a new table to an Access 2013 database in several ways: You can design the table from scratch, build the table from a *datasheet* (a spreadsheet-like format), import the table from another source, or link to an external table. This chapter discusses the processes of building a table from a datasheet and designing a table from scratch. Chapter 19, "Sharing Data with Other Applications," covers the processes of importing and linking.

Regardless of which method you choose, you should start building a new table by selecting the Create tab. The icons that appear enable you to create a table in Design view or to create a table by entering data (see Figure 9.1).

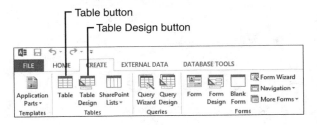

FIGURE 9.1

Creating a new table.

Building a Table from a Datasheet

Building a table from a datasheet was limited in earlier versions of Access. With Access 2013, you can do quite a bit while in Datasheet view. To use the datasheet method, follow these steps:

1. On the Ribbon select the Create tab.

2. From the Tables group click the Table button. A new datasheet appears, ready for you to design your table.

3. Click to add a column. A drop-down appears with a list of the available field types (see Figure 9.2). Select the appropriate field type from the list.

4. Enter a name for the field. Press Enter. The focus appears on the next field. At any time, you can refine the properties associated with a field. You accomplish the task with the buttons on the Fields tab on the Ribbon. For example, you can designate a field as Required or Unique. The user must populate a required field with data. If you designate a field as unique, no two records in the table can contain the same value in that field.

5. After you add all the columns and data you want, click the Save button on the QuickAccess toolbar. Access prompts you for a table name. Enter a table name, and click OK.

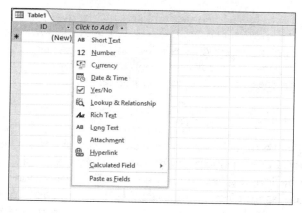

FIGURE 9.2

Selecting the appropriate field type.

6. After the save operation is complete, click the View button on the Home tab of the Ribbon to look at the design of the resulting table.

7. You can add a description to each field to help make the table self-documenting. Your table design should look something like Figure 9.3.

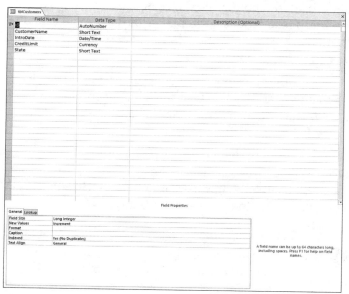

FIGURE 9.3

The table design results from building a table with the datasheet method.

NOTE Adding descriptions to table, query, form, report, macro, and module objects goes a long way toward making an application self-documenting. Such documentation helps you, or anyone who modifies an application, perform any required maintenance on the application's objects.

Designing a Table from Scratch

Many people believe that designing tables from scratch offers flexibility and encourages good design principles. Although it requires some knowledge of database and table design, it gives you more control and precision than designing a table from the Datasheet view. It enables you to select each field name and field type, and to define field properties. To design a table from scratch, you select Tables from the list of objects and double-click the Create Table in Design View icon. The Table Design view window appears.

When the Table Design view window appears, follow these steps to design a table:

1. Define each field in the table by typing its name in the Field Name column.

2. Tab to the Data Type column. Select the default field type, which is Text, or use the drop-down combo box to select another field type. You can find details on which field type is appropriate for data in the section "Selecting the Appropriate Field Type for Data." If you use the Field Builder, it sets a data type value for you that you can modify.

3. Tab to the Description column, and enter a description for the data. What you type in this column appears on the status bar when the user is entering data into the field. This column is also great for documenting what data is actually stored in the field.

4. Continue entering fields. If you need to insert a field between two existing fields, click the Insert Rows button in the Tools group of the Design tab on the Ribbon. Access inserts the new field above the field you were on. To delete a field, select it and click the Delete Rows button.

 NOTE If you forget a field and need to insert it later, you can right-click the column heading to the right of where you want to insert the new column and then select Insert Field from the context menu. Access inserts a column that you can rename by double-clicking the column heading. You can then use the Fields tab on the Ribbon to set properties of the field.

5. To save your work, click the Save tool on the QuickAccess toolbar. The Save As dialog box appears. Enter a table name and click OK. A dialog box appears,

recommending that you establish a primary key. Every table should have a primary key. Primary keys are discussed in the section "The All-Important Primary Key." Because the process of creating a primary key is covered later, this table does not contain a primary key.

Field names can be up to 64 characters. For practical reasons, you should try to limit them to 10 to 20 characters, which is enough to describe the field without making the name difficult to type.

 NOTE Access supplies default names for the tables that you create (for example, Table1 and Table2). You can supply a more descriptive name. The author generally follows the industrywide naming convention of prefixing all the table names with *tbl.*

Field names can include any combination of letters, numbers, spaces, and other characters, excluding periods, exclamation points, accents, and brackets. The author recommends that you use letters. Spaces in field names can be inconvenient when you build queries, modules, and other database objects. You shouldn't be concerned that users can see the field names without the spaces. The `Caption` property of a field enables you to designate the text that Access displays for users.

A field name cannot begin with leading spaces. As mentioned previously, field names shouldn't contain any spaces, so the rule to not begin a field name with spaces shouldn't be a problem. Field names also cannot include ASCII control characters (ASCII values 0 to 31).

You should try not to duplicate property names, keywords, function names, or the names of other Access objects when naming fields (for example, naming a field Date). Although the code might work in some circumstances, you might get unpredictable results in others.

To make a potential move to the client/server platform as painless as possible, you should be aware that not all field types are supported by every back-end database. Furthermore, most back-end databases impose stricter limits than Access does on the length of field names and the characters that are valid in field names. To reduce the number of problems you'll encounter if you migrate tables to a back-end database server, you should consider these issues when you name the fields in Access tables.

Selecting the Appropriate Field Type for Data

The data type you select for each field can greatly affect the performance and functionality of an application. Several factors can influence your choice of data type for each field in a table:

- The type of data that's stored in the field
- Whether the field's contents need to be included in calculations
- Whether you need to sort the data in the field
- The way you want to sort the data in the field
- How important storage space is to you

The type of data you need to store in a field has the biggest influence on which data type you select. For example, if you need to store numbers that begin with leading zeros, you can't select a Number field because leading zeros entered into a Number field are ignored. This rule affects data such as ZIP codes (some of which begin with leading zeros) and department codes.

If the contents of a field need to be included in calculations, you must select a Number or Currency data type. You can't perform calculations on the contents of fields defined with the other data types. The only exception to this rule is Date data type fields, which you can include in date/time calculations.

 NOTE If it is unimportant that leading zeros be stored in a field and you just need them to appear on forms and reports, you can accomplish this by using the Format property of the field.

You must also consider whether you will sort or index the data in a field. You can't sort the data in OLE Object and Hyperlink fields, so you shouldn't select these field types if you must sort or index the data in the field. Furthermore, you must think about the *way* you want to sort the data. For example, in a Text field, a set of numbers would be sorted in the order of the numbers' leftmost character, then the second character from the left, and so on (that is, 1, 10, 100, 2, 20, and 200) because data in the Text field is sorted as characters rather than numbers. On the other hand, in a Number or Currency field, the numbers would be sorted in ascending value order (that is, 1, 2, 10, 20, 100, and 200). You might think you would never want data sorted in a character sequence, but sometimes it makes sense to sort certain information, such as department codes, in this fashion. Access 2003 introduced the ability to sort or group based on a Memo field, but Access performs the sorting or grouping based only on the first 255 characters. Finally, you should consider how important disk space is to you. Each field type takes up a different amount of storage space on a hard disk, and this could be a factor when you select a data type for a field.

Nine field types are available in Access: Text, Memo, Number, Date/Time, Currency, AutoNumber, Yes/No, OLE Object, and Hyperlink. Table 9.1 briefly describes the appropriate uses for each field type and the amount of storage space each type needs.

TABLE 9.1 Appropriate Uses and Storage Space for Access Field Types

Field Type	Appropriate Use	Storage Space
Short Text	Data containing text, a combination of text and numbers, or numbers that don't need to be included in calculations. Examples are names, addresses, department codes, and phone numbers.	Based on what's actually stored in the field; ranges from 0 to 255 bytes
Long Text	Long text and numeric strings. Examples are notes and descriptions.	Ranges from 0 to 65,536 bytes
Number	Data included in calculations (excluding money). Examples are ages, codes (such as employee IDs), and payment methods.	1, 2, 4, or 8 bytes, depending on the field size selected (or 16 bytes for replication ID)
Date/Time	Dates and times. Examples are date ordered and birth date.	8 bytes
Currency	Currency values. Examples are amount due and price.	8 bytes
AutoNumber	Unique sequential or random numbers. Examples are invoice numbers and project numbers.	4 bytes (16 bytes for replication ID)
Yes/No	Fields that contain one of two values (for example, yes/no or true/false). Sample uses are indicating bills paid and tenure status.	1 bit
OLE Object	Objects such as Word documents or Excel spreadsheets. Examples are employee reviews and budgets.	0 bytes to 1GB, depending on what's stored within the field
Hyperlink	Text or a combination of text and numbers, stored as text and used as a hyperlink for a web address (uniform resource locator [URL]) or a universal naming convention (UNC) path.	0 to 2,048 bytes for text for each of the three parts that compose the address (up to 64,000 characters total)
Attachment	Examples are web pages and network files.	
Calculated	Stores attachments to other file types.	

The most difficult part of selecting a field type is knowing which type is best in each situation. The following detailed descriptions of each field type and when you should use them should help you with this process.

 NOTE   Although Microsoft loosely considers the Lookup Wizard a field type, it is actually not its own field type. You use it to create a field that enables the user to select a value from another table or from a list of values via a combo box that the wizard helps define for you. As far as storage, it requires that same storage size as the primary key for the lookup field.

Short Text Fields: The Most Common Field Type

Most fields are Short Text fields. Many developers don't realize that it's best to use Text fields for any numbers that are not used in calculations. Examples of such numbers are phone numbers, part numbers, and ZIP codes. Although the default size for a Text field is 50 characters, you can store up to 255 characters in a Text field. Because Access allocates disk space dynamically, a large field size doesn't use hard disk space, but you can improve performance if you allocate the smallest field size possible. You can control the maximum number of characters allowed in a `Text` field by using the `FieldSize` property.

Long Text Fields: For Long Notes and Comments

A Long Text field (previously referred to as a Memo field) can store up to 65,536 characters of text, meaning that it can hold up to 16 pages of text for each record. `Long Text` fields are excellent for any types of notes you want to store with table data. Remember that in Access 2013 you can sort by a Memo field.

Number Fields: For When You Need to Calculate

You use Number fields to store data that you must include in calculations. If currency amounts are included in calculations or if calculations require the highest degree of accuracy, you should use a Currency field rather than a Number field.

The Number field is actually several types of fields in one because Access 2013 offers seven sizes of numeric fields. Byte can store integers from 0 to 255, Integer can hold whole numbers from –32768 to 32767, and Long Integer can hold whole numbers ranging from less than –2 billion to just more than 2 billion. Although all three of these sizes offer excellent performance, each type requires an increasingly large amount of storage space. Two of the other numeric field sizes, Single and Double, offer floating decimal points and, therefore, much slower performance than integer and long integer. Single can hold fractional numbers to 7 significant digits; Double extends the precision to 14 significant digits. Decimal, a specialized numeric data type, enables storage of large numbers and provides decimal precision up to 28 digits!

Date/Time Fields: For Tracking When Things Happened

You use the Date/Time field type to store valid dates and times. Date/Time fields enable you to perform date calculations and make sure dates and times are always sorted properly. Access actually stores the date or time internally as an 8-byte floating-point number. Access represents time as a fraction of a day.

Currency Fields: For Storing Money

The Currency field is a number field used when currency values are stored in a table. A Currency field prevents the computer from rounding off data during calculations. It holds 15 digits of whole dollars, plus accuracy to one-hundredth of a cent. Although accurate, this type of field is quite slow to process.

 NOTE Any date and time settings you establish in the Windows Control Panel are reflected in your data. For example, if you modify Short Date Style in Regional Settings within the Control Panel, your forms, reports, and datasheets immediately reflect those changes.

AutoNumber Fields: For Unique Record Identifiers

The AutoNumber field in Access 2013 automatically generates AutoNumber field values when the user adds a record. The AutoNumber field type in Access 2013 can be either sequential or random. The random assignment is useful when several users are adding records offline because it's unlikely that Access will assign the same random value to two records.

 NOTE Any changes to the currency format made in the Windows Control Panel are reflected in your data. Of course, Access doesn't automatically perform any actual conversion of currency amounts. As with dates, if you modify the currency symbol in Regional Settings within the Control Panel, your forms, reports, and datasheets immediately reflect those changes.

You should note a few important points about sequential AutoNumber fields. If a user deletes a record from a table, its unique number is lost forever. Likewise, if a user adds a record but cancels the action, the unique counter value for that record is lost forever. If this behavior is unacceptable, you can generate your own counter values.

Yes/No Fields: For When One of Two Answers Is Correct

You should use Yes/No fields to store a logical true or false. What Access actually stores in the field is −1 for yes, 0 for no, or Null for no specific choice. The display format for the field determines what the user actually sees (normally Yes/No, True/False, On/Off, or a third option [Null] if you set the `TripleState` property of the associated control on a form to True). Yes/No fields work efficiently for any data that can have only a true (yes) or false (no) value. Not only do they limit the user to valid choices, but they also take up only 1 bit of storage space.

OLE Object Fields: For Storing Just About Anything

OLE Object fields are designed to hold data from any OLE server application registered in Windows, including spreadsheets, word processing documents, sound, and video. There are many business uses for OLE Object fields, such as storing resumes, employee reviews, budgets, or videos. However, in many cases, it is more efficient to use a Hyperlink field to store a link to the document rather than store the document in an OLE Object field.

Hyperlink Fields: For Linking to the Internet

Hyperlink fields are used to store uniform resource locator addresses, which are links to web pages on the Internet or on an intranet, or UNC paths, which are links to a file location path. The Hyperlink field type is broken into three parts:

- What the user sees
- The URL or UNC
- Subaddress such as a range name or bookmark

After the user places an entry in a Hyperlink field, the entry serves as a direct link to the file or page it refers to.

 TIP Although you can enter the full path to the URL (http://www.google.com), it is sufficient to enter just the domain name (google.com).

Attachment Fields: For Storing File Attachments Associated with a Record

With Attachment fields you can associate and manage multiple attachments with each record in your database. When a field is an attachment field, it appears as in Figure 9.4. When you double-click the paperclip, the Attachments dialog appears (see Figure 9.5). This is where you manage attachments associated with a record.

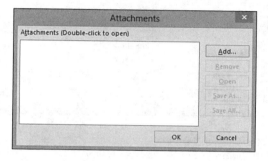

FIGURE 9.4

Attachment fields appear as paperclips in a table datasheet.

FIGURE 9.5

The Attachment dialog enables you to manage the attachments associated with a record.

 CAUTION Attachment fields are not supported in SQL Server. Therefore, if you plan to upsize your database to SQL Server, you probably won't want to use Attachment fields.

Calculated Fields: For Storing Your Database Calculations

Calculated fields, as their name implies, enable you to store dynamic calculations in your tables. These fields automatically recalculate as users enter data in the tables contained within the database. A perfect example is the ability to add extended quantity to the Northwind Order Details table. Extended quantity is price times the quantity. When you select Calculated as the data type, the Expression Builder appears. Here you enter the desired calculation (see Figure 9.6). After you click OK and return to Datasheet view, the result of the calculation appears (see Figure 9.7).

Using Indexes to Improve Performance

Indexes improve performance when you're searching, sorting, or grouping on a field or fields. Primary key indexes are used to maintain unique values for records. For example, you can create a single-field index that does not allow a duplicate order number or a multiple-field index that does not allow records with the same first and last names.

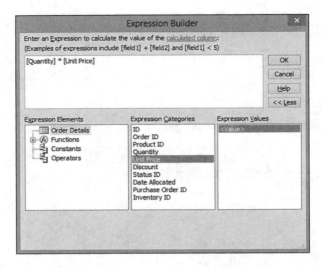

FIGURE 9.6

You enter the calculation in the Expression Builder.

Order Details

ID	Order ID	Product	Quantity	Unit Price	ExtendedPrice	Discount	Status ID	Date Allocat	Purchase Or
27	30	Northwind Tra	100	$14.00	1400	0.00%	Invoiced		9
28	30	Northwind Tra	30	$3.50	105	0.00%	Invoiced		
29	31	Northwind Tra	10	$30.00	300	0.00%	Invoiced		
30	31	Northwind Tra	10	$53.00	530	0.00%	Invoiced		
31	31	Northwind Tra	10	$3.50	35	0.00%	Invoiced		
32	32	Northwind Tra	15	$18.00	270	0.00%	Invoiced		
33	32	Northwind Tra	20	$46.00	920	0.00%	Invoiced		
34	33	Northwind Tra	30	$9.20	276	0.00%	Invoiced		9
35	34	Northwind Tra	20	$9.20	184	0.00%	Invoiced		
36	35	Northwind Tra	10	$12.75	127.5	0.00%	Invoiced		
37	36	Northwind Tra	200	$9.65	1930	0.00%	Invoiced		9
38	37	Northwind Tra	17	$40.00	680	0.00%	Invoiced		
39	38	Northwind Tra	300	$46.00	13800	0.00%	Invoiced		9
40	39	Northwind Tra	100	$12.75	1275	0.00%	Invoiced		10

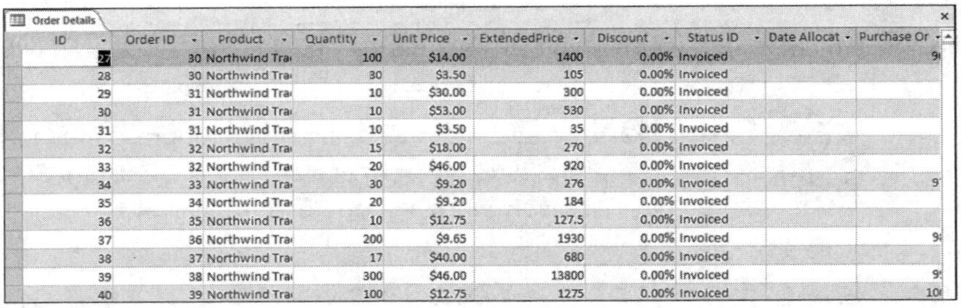

FIGURE 9.7

The result of the calculation automatically appears in Datasheet view.

Create an Index Based on a Single Field

To create an index based on a single field (from Design view), follow these steps:

1. Select the field to be indexed.

2. Click the Indexed row of the Field Properties pane.

3. Select the desired index type: No, Yes (Duplicates OK), or Yes (No Duplicates). The Yes (Duplicates OK) option means that you are creating an index and that you will allow duplicates within that field. The Yes (No Duplicates) option means that you are creating an index and you will *not* allow duplicate values within the index. If the index is based on company name and you select Yes (Duplicates OK), you can enter two companies with the same name. If you select Yes (No Duplicates), you cannot enter two companies with the same name.

Create an Index Based on Multiple Fields

To create an index based on multiple fields (from Design view), follow these steps:

1. Select Indexes from the Show/Hide group on the Design tab on the Ribbon. The Indexes window appears (see Figure 9.8).

2. Type the index name in the Index Name column.

3. From the Field Name column, select the desired fields to include in the index.

4. Select the desired index properties.

5. Close the Indexes window if desired.

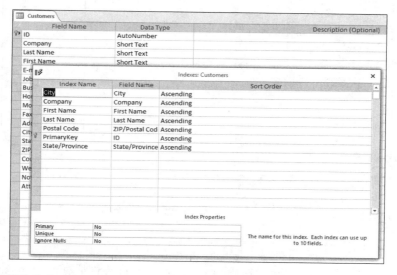

FIGURE 9.8

Use the Indexes window to add and remove indexes.

The All-Important Primary Key

A primary key is a field or a combination of fields in a table that uniquely identifies each row in the table (for example, the Order ID). The most important index in a table is called the *Primary Key index*; it ensures uniqueness of the fields that make up the index and also gives the table a default order. You must set a primary key for the fields on the one side of a one-to-many relationship. To create a Primary Key index, you select the fields you want to establish as the primary key and then click the Primary Key button in the Tools group of the Design tab on the Ribbon.

Figure 9.9 shows the Northwind Orders table with a Primary Key index based on the Order ID field. Notice that the index name of the field designated as the primary key of the table is called PrimaryKey. The `Primary` and `Unique` properties for this index are both set to Yes (true).

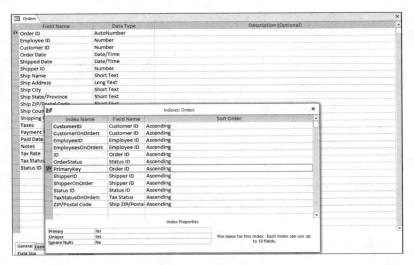

FIGURE 9.9

A Primary Key index based on the Order ID field.

 CAUTION It is important to understand some rules about primary keys. You cannot have non-unique data in a field or fields, and then create a primary key or unique index based on those fields. No fields that make up the primary key can contain null values. Tables cannot contain more than one autonumber field. Finally, it is best to create autonumber primary keys for each table in your database. This both improves performance and helps to ensure data integrity.

Working with Field Properties

After you add fields to a table, you need to customize their properties. Field properties let you control how Access stores data and what data the user can enter into a field. The available properties differ depending on which field type you select. You can find a comprehensive list of properties under the Text data type (see Figure 9.10). The following sections describe the various field properties. Notice that the lower portion of the Design view window in Figure 9.10 is the Field Properties pane. This is where you can set properties for the fields in a table.

Field Properties pane

Field Properties

General	Lookup
Field Size	50
Format	
Input Mask	
Caption	
Default Value	
Validation Rule	
Validation Text	
Required	No
Allow Zero Length	No
Indexed	Yes (Duplicates OK)
Unicode Compression	Yes
IME Mode	No Control
IME Sentence Mode	Phrase Predict
Text Align	General

A field name can be up to 64 characters long, including spaces. Press F1 for help on field names.

NUM LOCK

FIGURE 9.10

Using the Field Properties pane of the Design view window to set the properties of a field.

The Field Size Property: Limiting What the User Enters into a Field

The `Field Size` property is available for Text and Number fields only. It's best to set the `Field Size` property to the smallest value possible. For Number fields, a small size means lower storage requirements and faster performance. The same is true for Text fields. To modify the `Field Size` property, follow these steps:

1. Select the desired field name from the top pane of the Design view window.

2. Click the `Field Size` property text box in the Field Properties pane.

3. Type the desired field size.

The Format Property: Determining How Access Displays Data

The `Format` property enables you to customize the way Access displays and prints numbers, dates, times, and text. You can select a predefined format or create a custom format.

 NOTE   Here's a tip to save you a lot of time: You can move between the two panes of the Design view window by pressing F6.

To select a predefined display format (from Design view), follow these steps:

1. Select the desired field.

2. Click the `Format` property text box in the Field Properties pane.

3. Click the drop-down arrow that appears after you click in the `Format` property.

4. Select the desired format based on the type of field you are formatting.

You create a custom format by using a combination of the special characters, called *placeholders*, listed in Table 9.2.

TABLE 9.2   Placeholders That Enable You to Build a Custom Format

Placeholder	Function
0	Displays a digit if one exists in the position; otherwise, displays a zero. You can use the 0 placeholder to display leading zeros for whole numbers and trailing zeros for decimals.
#	Displays a digit if one exists in the position; otherwise, displays a blank space.
$	Displays a dollar sign in the position.
. % ,	Displays a decimal point, percent sign, or comma at the indicated position.
/	Separates the day, month, and year to format date values.
M	Used as a month placeholder: m displays 1, mm displays 01, mmm displays Jan, and mmmm displays January.
D	Used as a day placeholder: d displays 1, dd displays 01, ddd displays Mon, and dddd displays Monday.
Y	Used as a year placeholder: yy displays 95, and yyyy displays 1995.
:	Separates hours and minutes.
h, n, s	Used as time placeholders for h hours, n minutes, and s seconds.
AM/PM	Displays time in 12-hour format, with AM or PM appended.
@	Indicates that a character is required in the position in a text or memo field.
&	Indicates that a character is optional.
>	Changes all the text characters to uppercase.
<	Changes all the text characters to lowercase.

Create a Custom Display Format

To create a custom display format, follow these steps while in Design view of a form:

1. Select the desired field.

2. Click the Format text box in the Field Properties pane.

3. Type the desired format, using the placeholders listed in Table 9.2.

Figure 9.11 provides an example of a custom display format. The example shows the custom format for the Shipping Fee field in the Orders table. The format causes Access to display both positive and negative values with two decimal points. Positive values appear in green type. Negative values appear in parentheses with red type. Zero values display as the word Zero, and null values display with the word Null.

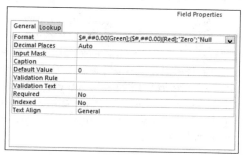

FIGURE 9.11

Using the Custom Format property to determine how numeric data displays.

The Caption Property: Providing Alternatives to the Field Name

The text you place in the `Caption` property becomes the caption for fields in Datasheet view. Access also uses the contents of the `Caption` property as the caption for the attached label it adds to data-bound controls when you add them to forms and reports. The `Caption` property becomes important whenever you name fields without spaces. Whatever is in the `Caption` property overrides the field name for use in Datasheet view, on forms, and on reports.

 NOTE Field names, as a general rule, should be short and should not contain spaces. You can, however, assign to the field a `Caption` property that is descriptive of the field's contents. Access displays the `Caption` property as the field label on forms and reports. For example, you can assign "Fax Number" to the `Caption` property for a field named FaxNum.

Set the `Caption` Property from Design View

To set the `Caption` property (from Design view), follow these steps:

1. Select the desired field name from the top pane of the Design view window.

2. Click the Caption text box in the Field Properties pane.

3. Type the desired caption.

NOTE A *data-bound control* is a control that is bound to a field in a table or query. The term *attached label* refers to the label that is attached to a data-bound control.

The Default Value Property: Saving Data-Entry Time

Assigning a `Default Value` property to a field causes a specified value to be filled in for the field in new records. Setting a commonly used value as the `Default Value` property facilitates the data entry process. When adding data, you can accept the default entry or replace it with another value. For example, if most of your customers are in California, you can assign a default value of "CA". When doing data entry, if the customer is in California, you do not need to change the value for the state. If the customer is in another state, you just replace the "CA" with the appropriate state value.

Set the Default Value Property from Design View

To set a `Default Value` property (from Design view), follow these steps:

1. Select the desired field from the top pane of the Design view window.

2. Click the Default Value property text box in the Field Properties pane.

3. Type the desired value.

The data users enter in tables must be accurate if the database is to be valuable to you or your organization. You can use the `Validation Rule` property to add data entry rules to the fields in tables.

NOTE A `Default Value` property can be constant, such as CA for California, or a function that returns a value, such as `Date()`, which displays the current date, or `Now()` which displays the current date and time.

The Validation Rule and Validation Text Properties: Controlling What the User Enters in a Field

The `Default Value` property suggests a value to the user, but the `Validation Rule` property actually limits what the user can place in the field. Validation rules cannot be violated; the database engine strictly enforces them. As with the `Default Value` property, this property can contain either text or a valid Access expression, but you cannot include user-defined functions in the `Validation Rule` property. You also cannot include references to forms, queries, or tables in the `Validation Rule` property.

NOTE Date() is a built-in Visual Basic for Applications (VBA) function that returns the current date. When it is used as a default value for a field, Access enters the current date into the field when the user adds a new row to the table. Now() is a similar function which returns the current date and time.

You can use operators to compare two values; the less than (<) and greater than (>) symbols are examples of comparison operators. And, Or, Is, Not, Between, and Like are called *logical operators*. Table 9.3 provides a few examples of validation rules.

Whereas the validation rule limits what the user can enter into the table, the validation text provides the error message that appears when the user violates the validation rule.

TABLE 9.3 Examples of Validation Rules

Validation Rule	Validation Text Example
>0	Enter a valid Employee ID number.
"H", "S", or "Q"	Only H, S, or Q codes will be accepted.
Between Date() 365 and Date()+365	Date cannot be later than 1 year ago today or more than 1 year from today.
>0 or is Null	Enter a valid ID number or leave blank if not approved.
Between 0 and 9 or is Null	Rating range is 0 through 9 or is blank.
>Date()	Date must be after today.

 NOTE If you set the Validation Rule property but do not set the Validation Text property, Access automatically displays a standard error message whenever the user violates the validation rule. To display a custom message, you must enter message text in the Validation Text property.

Set the Validation Rule Property from Design View

To establish a field-level validation rule (from Design view), follow these steps:

1. Select the desired field name from the top pane of the Design view window.

2. Click the Validation Rule text box in the Field Properties pane.

3. Type the desired validation rule (for example, **Between 0 and 120**).

Set the `Validation Text` Property from Design View

To add validation text, follow these steps:

1. Click the Validation Text text box in the Field Properties pane.

2. Type the desired text (for example, **Age Must Be Between 0 and 120**).

You can require users of a database to enter a valid value in selected fields when editing or adding records. For example, you can require a user to enter a date for each record in an Invoice table.

The Required Property: Making the User Enter a Value

The `Required` property is important: It determines whether you require a user to enter a value in a field. This property is useful for foreign key fields, when you want to make sure the user enters data into the field. It's also useful for any field containing information that's needed for business reasons (company name, for example).

 NOTE A *foreign key field* is a field that is looked up in another table. For example, for a Customers table and an Orders table, both might contain a CustomerID field. In the Customers table, the CustomerID field is the primary key field. In the Orders table, the CustomerID field is the foreign key field because its value is looked up in the Customers table.

Set the Required Property from Design View

To designate a field as required (from Design view), follow these steps:

1. Select the desired field.

2. Click the Required text box in the Field Properties pane.

3. Type **Yes**.

The `Allow Zero Length` Property: Accommodating for Situations with Nonexistent Data

You can use the `Allow Zero Length` property to allow a string of no characters. You enter a zero-length string by typing a pair of quotation marks with no space between them (""). You use the `Allow Zero Length` property to indicate that you know there is no value for a field.

Set the `Allow Zero Length` Property from Design View

To allow a zero-length field (from Design view), follow these steps:

1. Select the desired field.

2. Click the Allow Zero Length text box in the Field Properties pane.

3. Select Yes from the drop-down list box.

The Input Mask Property: Determining What Data Goes into a Field

An input mask controls data the user enters into a field. For instance, a short date input mask appears as --/--/---- when the field is active. You can then simply type **07042005** to display or print 7/4/2013. Based on the input mask, you can ensure that the user enters only valid characters into the field.

Table 9.4 lists some of the placeholders that you can use in character strings for input masks in fields of the Text data type.

TABLE 9.4 Placeholders That Can Be Included in an Input Mask

Placeholder	Description
0	A number (0–9) is required.
9	A number (0–9) is optional.
#	A number (0–9), a space, or a plus or minus sign is optional; a space is used if no number is entered.
L	A letter (A–Z) is required.
?	A letter (A–Z) is not required; a space is used if no letter is entered.
A	A letter (A–Z) or number (0–9) is required.
A	A letter (A–Z) or number (0–9) is optional.
&	Any character or space is required.
C	Any character or space is optional.
>	Any characters to the right are converted to uppercase.
<	All the text characters to the right are changed to lowercase.

Set the Input Mask Property from Design View

To create an input mask (from Design view), follow these steps:

1. Select the desired field.

2. Click the Input Mask text box.

3. Type the desired format, using the placeholders listed in Table 9.4.

Access includes an Input Mask Wizard that appears when you place the cursor in the Input Mask text box and click the build button to the right of the text box. The wizard, as shown in Figure 9.12, provides common input mask formats from which to choose. To start the Input Mask Wizard, click the button to the right of the `Input Mask` property.

FIGURE 9.12

Entering an input mask with the Input Mask Wizard.

For example, the input mask `000-00-0000;;_` (converted to `000\-00\-0000;;_` as soon as you tab away from the property) forces the entry of a valid Social Security number. Everything that precedes the first semicolon designates the actual mask. The zeros force the entry of the digits 0 through 9. The dashes are literals that appear within the control as the user enters data. The character you enter between the first and second semicolon determines whether literal characters (the dashes, in this case) are stored in the field. If you enter a 0 in this position, literal characters are stored in the field; if you enter 1 or leave this position blank, the literal characters aren't stored. The final position (after the second semicolon) indicates what character is displayed to denote the space where the user types the next character (in this case, the underscore).

Here's a more detailed example: In the mask `\(999") "000\-0000;;_`, the first backslash causes the character that follows it (the open parenthesis) to be displayed as a literal. The three nines enable the user to enter optional numbers or spaces. Access displays the close parenthesis and space within the quotation marks as literals. The first three zeros require values 0 through 9. The dash that follows the next backslash is displayed as a literal. Four additional numbers are then required. The two semicolons have nothing between them, so the literal characters aren't stored in the field. The second semicolon is followed by an underscore, so an underscore is displayed to indicate the space where the user types the next character. This sounds complicated, but here's how it works. The user types **8054857632**. What appears is (805)485-7632. What is actually stored is 8054857632. Because the input mask contains three nines for the area code, the area code is not required. The remaining characters are all required numbers.

 NOTE The Input Mask Wizard is available only if you selected the Additional Wizards component during Access setup. If you did not select this component and then you try to open the Input Mask Wizard, Access prompts you to install the option on-the-fly the first time you use it.

The Lookup Wizard

You can select the Lookup Wizard as a field's data type. The Lookup Wizard guides you through the steps to create a list of values from which you can choose. You can select the values from a table or a query, or you can create a list of your own values.

Use the Lookup Wizard

To use the Lookup Wizard (from Design view), follow these steps:

1. Select the desired field.

2. Choose the Lookup Wizard as the data type.

3. Select the desired source of the values, and then click Next.

4. Select the table or query to provide the values, and then click Next.

5. Double-click the fields that contain the desired values, and then click Next.

6. Drag the Lookup column to the desired width, and then click Next.

7. Type a name for the Lookup column, and then click Finish. Figure 9.13 illustrates the result of running the Lookup Wizard to look up the Customer from the Orders table.

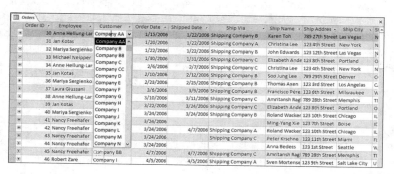

FIGURE 9.13

While in the Customer field in the Orders table, a dropdown appears displaying valid customers.

NOTE   When working with the Lookup Wizard, you should be aware of a few things. When you create a form based on a table with a Lookup field, the form automatically displays a combo box (or another designated control) for that field. As you add records to the table that is the source for the lookup values, the new information appears in the list.

THE ABSOLUTE MINIMUM

Building the tables that you want to include in your database is like building the foundation of a house. Without a strong foundation, the house will fall over. Without a sound table design, you cannot easily build the queries, forms, reports, macros, and modules you need to successfully retrieve the data in your database.

This chapter covered the process of creating your own tables. Two methods were presented that you can use to create new tables: from a datasheet and in Design view. The author prefers Design view. Although a bit more difficult at first, it is less clumsy. Furthermore, not all options (such as certain field properties) are available to you in Datasheet view.

We spent quite a bit of time talking about field types. You learned the type of data you can store in each field type and when each field type is appropriate. If you select the incorrect field type, you will have trouble both storing and retrieving data. For example, if you need to perform date/time calculations, you will need to store your data in a Date field.

The use of indexes can make or break your database. Using indexes properly, you can dramatically improve the performance of your database. The following story illustrates the importance of indexes. I once had a very large database with lots of data (hundreds of thousands of rows in each table). A particular report was taking 15 minutes to run. My client was quite disappointed when they saw how the report behaved. It occurred to me that I hadn't indexed a date field that was used for the report criteria, and for sorting and grouping within the report. I added the missing index. Voila! The report appeared in 1–2 seconds.

The use of an appropriate primary key is also very important. If you don't select an appropriate primary key, it will be difficult, if not impossible to use queries to retrieve your data. The primary key is the unique identifier for a table. It should be short, stable, and simple. The most common type of primary key is an

AutoNumber. An AutoNumber field provides you with a unique identifier for the record that is short (long integer), stable (cannot change), and fairly simple.

Finally, you learned how to work with field properties. Using field properties you can totally control how each field in each table behaves. For example, you can use a Validation Rule to control what data a user can enter in a field. The Validation Text is a related property that you use to specify the error message a user receives when they violate the Validation Rule. Working with field properties can take a little bit of practice, but I believe that you'll find it well worth the effort!

IN THIS CHAPTER

- What is relational database design?

- What are the goals and rules of relational database design?

- What is normalization, and why should I care?

- What types of relationships are available in Microsoft Access?

- How do I establish relationships in Microsoft Access?

- What are referential integrity, cascade update, and cascade delete?

10

RELATING THE INFORMATION IN YOUR DATABASE

A *relationship* exists between two tables when one or more key fields from one table are matched to one or more key fields in another table. The fields in both tables usually have the same name, data type, and size. This chapter first introduces you to relational database design. You then learn the types of relationships available in Access and how to establish those relationships. Finally, you learn how to establish referential integrity between the tables in your database.

Introduction to Relational Database Design

Many people believe Access is such a simple product to use that database design is something they don't need to worry about. The author couldn't disagree more! Just as a poorly planned vacation is generally not fun, a database with poorly designed tables and relationships fails to meet the needs of its users.

The History of Relational Database Design

Dr. E. F. Codd first introduced formal relational database design in 1969 while he was at IBM. *Relational theory*, which is based on set theory and predicate logic, applies to both databases and database applications. Codd developed 12 rules that determine how well an application and its data adhere to the relational model. Since Codd first conceived these 12 rules, the number of rules has expanded into the hundreds.

You should be happy to learn that, although Microsoft Access is not a perfect application development environment, it measures up quite well as a relational database system.

Goals of Relational Database Design

The number one goal of relational database design is to, as closely as possible, develop a database that models some real-world system. This involves breaking the real-world system into tables and fields and determining how the tables relate to each other. Although on the surface this might appear to be a trivial task, it can be an extremely cumbersome process to translate a real-world system into tables and fields.

A properly designed database has many benefits. The processes of adding, editing, deleting, and retrieving table data are greatly facilitated in a properly designed database. In addition, reports are easy to build. Most important, the database is easy to modify and maintain.

Rules of Relational Database Design

To adhere to the relational model, you must follow certain rules. These rules determine what you store in a table and how you relate the tables. The rules are as follows:

- The rules of tables
- The rules of uniqueness and keys
- The rules of foreign keys and domains

The Rules of Tables

Each table in a system must store data about a single entity. An *entity* usually represents a real-life object or event. Examples of objects are customers, employees, and inventory items. Examples of events include orders, appointments, and doctor visits.

The Rules of Uniqueness and Keys

Tables are composed of rows and columns. To adhere to the relational model, each table must contain a unique identifier. Without a unique identifier, it is programmatically impossible to uniquely address a row. You guarantee uniqueness in a table by designating a *primary key*, which is a single column or a set of columns that uniquely identifies a row in a table.

Each column or set of columns in a table that contains unique values is considered a *candidate key*. One candidate key becomes the *primary key*. The remaining candidate keys become *alternate keys*. A primary key made up of one column is considered a *simple key*. A primary key composed of multiple columns is considered a *composite key*.

It is generally a good idea to choose a primary key that is

- Minimal (has as few columns as possible)

- Stable (rarely changes)

- Simple (is familiar to the user)

Following these rules greatly improves the performance and maintainability of a database application, particularly if it deals with large volumes of data.

Consider the example of an employee table. An employee table is generally composed of employee-related fields such as the Social Security number, first name, last name, hire date, salary, and so on. The combination of the first name and the last name fields could be considered a primary key. This might work until the company hires two employees who have the same name. Although the first and last names could be combined with additional fields (for example, hire date) to constitute uniqueness, that would violate the rule of keeping the primary key minimal. Furthermore, an employee might get married, and her last name might change. This violates the rule of keeping a primary key stable. Therefore, using a name as the primary key violates the principle of stability. The Social Security number might be a valid choice for primary key, but a foreign employee might not have a Social Security number. This is a case in which a derived, rather than a natural, primary key is appropriate. A *derived key* is an artificial key that you create. A *natural key* is one that is already part of the database.

In examples such as this, consider adding EmployeeID as an AutoNumber field. Although the field would violate the rule of simplicity (because an employee number is meaningless to the user), it is both small and stable. Because it is numeric, it is also efficient to process. You can use `AutoNumber` fields as primary keys for most of the tables that you build.

The Rules of Foreign Keys and Domains

A *foreign key* in one table is the field that relates to the primary key in a second table. For example, the CustomerID field may be the primary key in a Customers table and the foreign key in an Orders table.

A domain is a pool of values from which columns are drawn. A simple example of a domain is the specific data range of employee hire dates. In the case of the Orders table, the domain of the CustomerID column is the range of values for the CustomerID in the Customers table.

Normalization and Normal Forms

Some of the most difficult decisions that you face as a developer are what tables to create and what fields to place in each table and how to relate the tables that you create. *Normalization* is the process of applying a series of rules to ensure that a database achieves optimal structure. *Normal forms* are a progression of these rules. Each successive normal form achieves a better database design than the previous form. Although there are several levels of normal forms, it is generally sufficient to apply only the first three levels of normal forms. The following sections describe the first three levels of normal forms.

First Normal Form

To achieve first normal form, all columns in a table must be *atomic*. This means, for example, that you cannot store the first name and last name in the same field. The reason for this rule is that data becomes difficult to manipulate and retrieve if you store multiple values in a single field. Use the full name as an example. It would be impossible to sort by first name or last name independently if you stored both values in the same field. Furthermore, you or the user would need to perform extra work to extract just the first name or just the last name from the field.

Another requirement for the first normal form is that the table must not contain repeating values. An example of repeating values is a scenario in which Item1, Quantity1, Item2, Quantity2, Item3, and Quantity3 fields are all found within the Orders table (see Figure 10.1). This design introduces several problems.

tblNotNormalized

Order#	CustInfo	OrderTotal	OrderDate	Item1Name	Item1Supplier	Item1Quantity	Item1Price
1	12 Any Street Anywhere, CA	$350.00	5/1/2001	Widget	Good Supplier	5	$1.50
2	12 Any Street Anywhere, CA	$0.00		Gadget	Bad Supplier	2	$2.25
3	12 Any Street Anywhere, CA	$0.00		Nut	Okay Supplier	7	$7.70
4	12 Any Street Anywhere, CA	$0.00		Bolt	Another Supplier	9	$3.00
5	45 Any Street Somewhere,	$0.00		Pencil	Good Supplier	2	$1.50
6	45 Any Street Somewhere,	$0.00		Eraser	Someone	4	$2.20
* (New)		$0.00				0	$0.00

FIGURE 10.1

A table that contains repeating groups.

What if the user wants to add a fourth item to the order? Furthermore, finding the total ordered for a product requires searching several columns. All numeric and statistical calculations on the table are extremely cumbersome. Repeating groups make it difficult to summarize and manipulate table data. The alternative, as shown in Figure 10.2, achieves the first normal form. Notice that each item ordered is located in a separate row. All fields are atomic, and the table contains no repeating groups.

tblOrderDetails2NF | tblOrders2NF | tblNotIn2NF

OrderID	CustID	CustInfo	OrderDate	Item
1	1	InfoTech Services Group, Inc.	12/14/2011	Mother Board
1	1	InfoTech Services Group, Inc.	12/14/2011	Computer
1	1	InfoTech Services Group, Inc.	12/14/2011	Monitor
2	2	Balter Realty	12/1/2011	RAM
2	2	Balter Realty	12/1/2011	Computer
3	1	InfoTech Services Group, Inc.	9/15/2012	Printer
3	1	InfoTech Services Group, Inc.	9/15/2012	SIM Card
3	1	InfoTech Services Group, Inc.	9/15/2012	USB Cable
4	3	Achieve Your Dreamz Coaching Center	9/19/2012	Computer
4	3	Achieve Your Dreamz Coaching Center	9/19/2012	Printer
4	3	Achieve Your Dreamz Coaching Center	9/19/2012	Monitor
4	3	Achieve Your Dreamz Coaching Center	9/19/2012	Scanner
* 0	0			

FIGURE 10.2

A table achieves the first normal form.

Second Normal Form

For a table to achieve a second normal form, all nonkey columns must be fully dependent on all the fields that make up the primary key. This rule applies only to tables that have a composite key: a key made up of two or more fields. For example, the table shown in Figure 10.2 has a primary key made up of the

OrderID and CustomerID. The combination of those two keys ensures that the primary key is unique for every row in the table, which is the purpose of the primary key.

However, this table is not in the second normal form because some of the information in the table depends only on part of the primary key. For instance, the CustInfo field depends only on the CustomerId field: If you were to change the CustomerId field, you'd also need to change the CustInfo field. In real life, of course, there is every possibility that the CustomerId field would be changed and the CustInfo would not, leading to problems in the application.

To achieve the second normal form, you must break this data into two tables: an order table and a customer table. The customer table would contain the CustomerId field from the primary key and the fields that depend on it (the CustInfo field, in this case); the order table would consist of the OrderId field and the fields that depend upon it. The order table would still have the CustomerId field (so you'd know which customer to ship the order to) but wouldn't have any other customer information. (All other customer information would be in the customer table.) If you assign the order to another customer, you'd have to change only the CustomerId field.

The process to break the data into two tables is called *decomposition*, which is considered to be a *nonloss* decomposition because no data is lost during the decomposition process. After you separate the data into two tables, you can easily bring the data back together by joining the two tables via a query. Figure 10.3 shows the data separated into two tables. These two tables achieve the second normal form for two reasons. First, neither table has a composite key—their primary keys

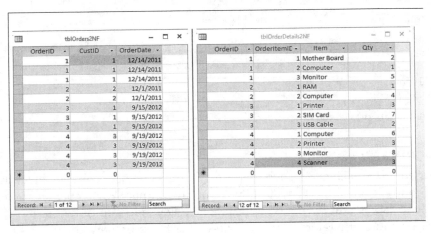

FIGURE 10.3

Tables that achieve the second normal form.

now have only a single field. (The second normal form applies only to tables with a composite primary key.) Second, the fields in each table depend on the whole of the primary key rather than on just part of the key.

Third Normal Form

To attain the third normal form, a table must meet all the requirements for the first and second normal forms, and all nonkey columns dependent only on the primary key field and not dependent on each other—all the fields are independent of each other. This means that you must eliminate any calculations, and you must break out the data into lookup tables. Lookup tables include tables such as Inventory tables, Course tables, State tables, and any other table where you look up a set of values from which you select the entry that you store in the foreign key field. For example, from your Customer table, you look up within the set of states in the state table to select the state associated with the customer.

An example of a calculation stored in a table is the product of price multiplied by quantity; the extended price is dependent on two other fields in the table: the price and the quantity. If either of those fields is changed, the extended price would also need to be changed. As with the example in the second normal form, there is every possibility of changing one or two of these fields without changing the third one, leading to problems in the application. Instead of storing the result of this calculation in the table, you would generate the calculation in a query or in the control source of a control on a form or a report.

The example in Figure 10.3 does not achieve the third normal form because the description of the inventory items is stored in the Order Details table. If the description changes, all rows with that inventory item need to be modified. The Order Details table, as shown in Figure 10.4, shows the item

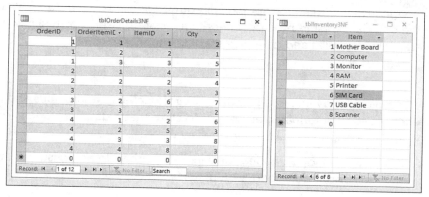

FIGURE 10.4

A table (on the right) that achieves the third normal form.

descriptions broken into an Inventory table. This design achieves the third normal form. You have moved the description of the inventory items to an Inventory table, and ItemID is stored in the Order Details table. All fields are mutually independent. You can modify the description of an inventory item in one place.

Denormalization: Purposely Violating the Rules

Although a developer's goal is normalization, sometimes it makes sense to deviate from normal forms. This process is called *denormalization*. The primary reason for applying denormalization is to enhance performance.

An example of when denormalization might be the preferred tact could involve an open invoices table and a summarized accounting table. It might be impractical to calculate summarized accounting information for a customer when you need it. Instead, you can maintain the summary calculations in a summarized accounting table so that you can easily retrieve them as needed. Although the upside of this scenario is improved performance, the downside is that you must update the summary table whenever you make changes to the open invoices. This imposes a definite trade-off between performance and maintainability. You must decide whether the trade-off is worth it.

If you decide to denormalize, you should document your decision. You should make sure that you make the necessary application adjustments to ensure that you properly maintain the denormalized fields. Finally, you need to test to ensure that the denormalization process actually improves performance.

Integrity Rules

Although integrity rules are not part of normal forms, they are definitely part of the database design process. Integrity rules are broken into two categories: overall integrity rules and database-specific integrity rules.

Overall Integrity Rules

The two types of overall integrity rules are referential integrity rules and entity integrity rules. *Referential integrity rules* dictate that a database does not contain any orphan foreign key values. This means that

- Child rows cannot be added for parent rows that do not exist. In other words, an order cannot be added for a nonexistent customer.

- A primary key value cannot be modified if the value is used as a foreign key in a child table. This means that a CustomerID in the customers table cannot be changed if the Orders table contains rows with that CustomerID.

- A parent row cannot be deleted if child rows have that foreign key value. For example, a customer cannot be deleted if the customer has orders in the Orders table.

Entity integrity dictates that the primary key value cannot be `Null`. This rule applies not only to single-column primary keys, but also to multicolumn primary keys. In a multicolumn primary key, no field in the primary key can be `Null`. This makes sense because if any part of the primary key can be `Null`, the primary key can no longer act as a unique identifier for the row. Fortunately, the Microsoft Database Engine does not allow a field in a primary key to be `Null`.

Database-Specific Integrity Rules

Database-specific integrity rules are not applicable to all databases, but are, instead, dictated by business rules that apply to a specific application. Database-specific rules are as important as overall integrity rules. They ensure that the user enters only valid data into a database. An example of a database-specific integrity rule is requiring the delivery date for an order to fall after the order date.

The Types of Relationships

Three types of relationships can exist between tables in a database: one to many, one to one, and many to many. Setting up the proper type of relationship between two tables in a database is imperative. The right type of relationship between two tables ensures

- Data integrity
- Optimal performance
- Ease of use in designing system objects

The reasons behind these benefits are covered throughout this chapter. Before you can understand the benefits of relationships, though, you must understand the types of relationships available.

One-to-Many Relationships

A one-to-many relationship is by far the most common type of relationship. In a *one-to-many relationship*, a record in one table can have many related records in another table. A common example is a relationship set up between a Customers table and an Orders table. For each customer in the Customers table, you want to have more than one order in the Orders table. On the other hand, each order in the Orders table can belong to only one customer. The Customers table is on the "one" side of the relationship, and the Orders table is on the "many" side. For you to implement this relationship, the field joining the two tables on the one side of the relationship must be unique.

In the Customers and Orders tables example, the CustomerID field that joins the two tables must be unique within the Customers table. If more than one customer in the Customers table has the same customer ID, it is not clear which customer belongs to an order in the Orders table. For this reason, the field that joins the two tables on the one side of the one-to-many relationship must be a primary key or have a unique index. In almost all cases, the field relating the two tables is the primary key of the table on the one side of the relationship. The field relating the two tables on the many side of the relationship is the foreign key.

One-to-One Relationships

In a one-to-one relationship, each record in the table on the one side of the relationship can have only one matching record in the table on the many side of the relationship. This relationship is not common and is used only in special circumstances. Usually, if you have set up a one-to-one relationship, you should have combined the fields from both tables into one table. The following are the most common reasons to create a one-to-one relationship:

- The number of fields required for a table exceeds the number of fields allowed in an Access table.

- Several fields in a table are required for only a subset of records in the table.

The maximum number of fields allowed in an Access table is 255. There are few reasons a table should ever have more than 255 fields. Before you even get close to 255 fields, you should take a close look at the design of the system. On the rare occasion when having more than 255 fields is appropriate, you can simulate a single table by moving some of the fields to a second table and creating a one-to-one relationship between the two tables.

The second situation in which you would want to define one-to-one relationships is when you use certain fields in a table for only a relatively small subset of records. An example is an Employees table and a Vesting table. Certain fields are required only for employees who are vested. If only a small percentage of a company's employees are vested, it is not efficient, in terms of performance or disk space, to place all the fields containing information about vesting in the Employees table. This is especially true if the vesting information requires a large number of fields. By breaking the information into two tables and creating a one-to-one relationship between the tables, you can reduce disk-space requirements and improve performance. This improvement is particularly pronounced if the Employees table is large.

Many-to-Many Relationships

In a *many-to-many relationship*, records in two tables have matching records. You cannot directly define a many-to-many relationship in Access; you must develop this type of relationship by adding a table called a *junction table*. You relate the junction table to each of the two tables in one-to-many relationships. For example, with an Orders table and a Products table, each order probably contains multiple products, and each product is likely to be found on many different orders. The solution is to create a third table, called OrderDetails. You relate the OrderDetails table to the Orders table in a one-to-many relationship based on the OrderID field. You relate it to the Products table in a one-to-many relationship based on the ProductID field.

Establishing Relationships in Access

You use the Relationships window to establish relationships between Access tables, as shown in Figure 10.5. To open the Relationships window, you must select Relationships from the Relationships group on the Database Tools tab on the Ribbon. If you have not established any relationships, the Show Table dialog box appears. The Show Table dialog box enables you to add tables to the Relationships window.

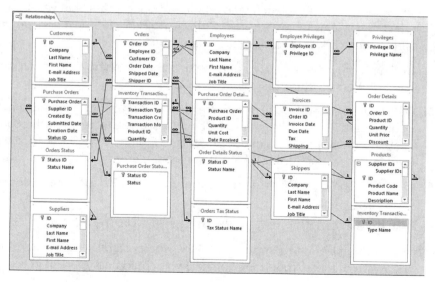

FIGURE 10.5

The Relationships window, which enables you to view, add, modify, and remove relationships between tables.

By looking at the Relationships window, you can see the types of relationships for each table. All the one-to-many and one-to-one relationships defined in a database are represented with join lines. If you enforce referential integrity between the tables involved in a one-to-many relationship, the join line between the tables appears with the number 1 on the one side of the relationship and with an infinity symbol on the many side of the relationship. A one-to-one relationship appears with a 1 on each end of the join line.

Establish a Relationship Between Two Tables

To establish a relationship between two tables, follow these steps:

1. Open the Relationships window.

2. If this is the first time that you've opened the Relationships window of a particular database, the Show Table dialog box appears. Select each table you want to relate, and click Add.

3. If you have already established relationships in the current database, the Relationships window appears. If the tables you want to include in the relationship do not appear, click the Show Table button in the Relationships group of the Design tab on the Ribbon. To add the wanted tables to the Relationships window, select a table and then click Add. Repeat this process for each table you want to add. To select multiple tables at once, press Shift while clicking to select contiguous tables, or press Ctrl while clicking to select noncontiguous tables; then click Add. Click Close when you finish.

4. Click and drag the field from one table to the matching field in the other table. The Edit Relationships dialog box appears.

5. Determine whether you want to establish referential integrity and whether you want to cascade update related fields or cascade delete related records by enabling the appropriate check boxes (see Figure 10.6). These topics are covered in the section "Establishing Referential Integrity."

6. Click OK. The dialog closes and you return to the Relationships window.

Following Guidelines for Establishing Relationships

You must remember a few important things when establishing relationships. If you are not aware of these important gotchas, you could find yourself in some hairy situations:

- You must understand the correlation between the Relationships window and the actual relationships established within a database. The Relationships window enables you to view and modify the existing relationships. When you establish relationships, Access creates the relationship the moment you click

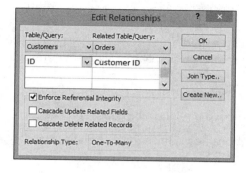

FIGURE 10.6

The Edit Relationships dialog box, which enables you to view and modify the relationships between the tables in a database.

OK. You can delete the tables from the Relationships window (by selecting them and pressing Delete), but the relationships still exist. (The "Modifying an Existing Relationship" section covers the process of permanently removing relationships.) The Relationships window provides a visual blueprint of the relationships that are established. If you modify the layout of the window by moving around tables, adding tables to the window, or removing tables from the window, Access prompts you to save the layout after you close the Relationships window. Access is not asking whether you want to save the relationships you have established; it is simply asking whether you want to save the visual layout of the window.

- When you add tables to the Relationships window by using the Show Tables dialog box, it is easy to accidentally add a table to the window many times. This is because the tables you add can hide behind the Show Tables dialog box, or they can appear below the portion of the Relationships window that you view. If this occurs, you see multiple occurrences of the same table when you close the Show Tables dialog box. Access gives each occurrence of the table a different alias, and you must remove the extra occurrences.

- You can add queries to the Relationships window by using the Show Tables dialog box. Although this method is rarely used, it might be useful if you regularly include the same queries within other queries and want to permanently establish relationships between them.

- If you remove tables from the Relationships window (remember that this does not delete the relationships) and you want to again show all relationships that exist in the database, you can click All Relationships in the Relationships group on the Design tab on the Ribbon. All existing relationships are then shown.

- To delete a relationship, click the join line and press Delete.

Modifying an Existing Relationship

Modifying an existing relationship is easy. Access gives you the capability to delete an existing relationship or to simply modify the nature of the relationship.

Delete a Relationship Between Tables

To permanently remove a relationship between two tables, follow these steps:

1. Click the Relationships button in the Relationships group on the Database Tools tab on the Ribbon.

2. Click the line joining the two tables whose relationship you want to delete.

3. Press Delete. Access prompts you to verify your actions. Click Yes.

Modify a Relationship Between Tables

You often need to modify the nature of a relationship rather than remove it. To modify a relationship, follow these steps:

1. Click the Relationships button in the Relationships group on the Database Tools tab on the Ribbon.

2. Double-click the line joining the two tables whose relationship you want to modify.

3. Make the required changes.

4. Click OK. All the normal rules regarding the establishment of relationships apply.

Establishing Referential Integrity

As you can see, establishing a relationship is easy. Establishing the right kind of relationship is a little more difficult. When you attempt to establish a relationship between two tables, Access makes some decisions based on a few predefined factors:

- Access establishes a one-to-many relationship if one of the related fields is a primary key or has a unique index.

- Access establishes a one-to-one relationship if both of the related fields are primary keys or have unique indexes.

- Access creates an indeterminate relationship if neither of the related fields is a primary key and neither has a unique index. You cannot establish referential integrity in this case.

As discussed earlier, *referential integrity* consists of a series of rules that Access applies to ensure that it properly maintains the relationships between tables. At the most basic level, referential integrity rules prevent the creation of orphan records in the table on the many side of the one-to-many relationship. After you establish a relationship between a Customers table and an Orders table, for example, all orders in the Orders table must be related to a particular customer in the Customers table. Before you can establish referential integrity between two tables, the following conditions must be met:

- The matching field on the one side of the relationship must be a primary key field or must have a unique index.

- The matching fields must have the same data types. (For linking purposes, AutoNumber fields match Long Integer fields.) With the exception of Text fields, the matching fields also must have the same size. Number fields on both sides of the relationship must have the same size (for example, Long Integer).

- Both tables must be part of the same Access database.

- Both tables must be stored in one of the proprietary Access file (MDB or ACCDB) formats. (They cannot be external tables from other sources.)

- The database that contains the two tables must be open.

- Existing data within the two tables cannot violate any referential integrity rules. All orders in the Orders table must relate to existing customers in the Customers table, for example.

 NOTE   Although Text fields involved in a relationship do not have to be the same size, it is prudent to make them the same size. Otherwise, you degrade performance and risk the chance of unpredictable results when you create queries based on the two tables.

After you establish referential integrity between two tables, Access applies the following rules:

- You cannot enter in the foreign key of the related table a value that does not exist in the primary key of the primary table. For example, you cannot enter in the CustomerID field of the Orders table a value that does not exist in the CustomerID field of the Customers table.

- You cannot delete a record from the primary table if corresponding records exist in the related table. For example, you cannot delete a customer from the Customers table if related records (for example, records with the same value in the CustomerID field) exist in the Orders table.

- You cannot change the value of a primary key on the one side of a relationship if corresponding records exist in the related table. For example, you cannot change the value in the CustomerID field of the Customers table if corresponding orders exist in the Orders table.

If you attempt to violate any of these three rules and you have enforced referential integrity between the tables, Access displays an appropriate error message, as shown in Figure 10.7.

FIGURE 10.7

An error message that appears when you attempt to delete a customer who has orders.

When you establish referential integrity in Access, its default behavior is to prohibit the deletion of parent records that have associated child records and to prohibit the change of a primary key value of a parent record when that parent has associated child records. You can override these restrictions by using the Cascade Update Related Fields and Cascade Delete Related Records check boxes that are available in the Relationships dialog box when you establish or modify a relationship.

The Cascade Update Related Fields Option

The Cascade Update Related Fields option is available only if you have established referential integrity between tables. When this option is selected, the user can change the primary key value of the record on the one side of the relationship. When the user attempts to modify the field joining the two tables on the one side of the relationship, Access cascades the change down to the foreign key field on the many side of the relationship. This is useful if the primary key field is modifiable. For example, a purchase number on a purchase order master record might be updateable. If the user modifies the purchase order number of the parent record, you would want to cascade the change to the associated detail records in the purchase order detail table.

It is easy to accidentally introduce a loophole into a system. If you create a one-to-many relationship between two tables but forget to set the `Required` property of the foreign key field to `Yes`, you allow the addition of orphan records. Figure 10.8 illustrates this point. This example shows an added order to tblOrders without entering a Customer ID. This record is an orphan record

⊞	76	Anne Hellung-Lar	Company Y	6/5/2006
⊞	77	Anne Hellung-Lar	Company Z	6/5/2006
⊞	78	Nancy Freehafer	Company CC	6/5/2006
⊞	79	Andrew Cencini	Company F	6/23/2006
⊞	80	Andrew Cencini	Company D	4/25/2006
⊞	81	Andrew Cencini	Company C	4/25/2006
⊞	82	Michael Neipper		9/19/2012

Record: I◄ ◄ 49 of 49 ► ►I ► No Filter Search ◄

FIGURE 10.8

An orphan record with Null in the foreign key field.

because no records in `tblCustomers` have `CustomerID` set to `Null`. To eliminate the problem, you set the `Required` property of the foreign key field to `Yes`.

 TIP There is no need to select the Cascade Update Related Fields option when the related field on the one side of the relationship is an AutoNumber field. You can never modify an AutoNumber field. The Cascade Update Related Fields option has no effect on AutoNumber fields.

The Cascade Delete Related Records Option

The Cascade Delete Related Records option is available only if you have established referential integrity between tables. When this option is selected, the user can delete a record on the one side of a one-to-many relationship, even if related records exist in the table on the many side of the relationship. A user can delete a customer even if the customer has existing orders, for example. The Jet Engine maintains referential integrity between the tables because it automatically deletes all related records in the child table.

If you attempt to delete a record from the table on the one side of a one-to-many relationship and no related records exist in the table on the many side of the relationship, you get the usual warning message, as shown in Figure 10.9.

FIGURE 10.9

A message that appears after the user attempts to delete a parent record that does not have related child records.

On the other hand, if you attempt to delete a record from the table on the one side of a one-to-many relationship and related records exist in the child table, Access warns you that you are about to delete the record from the parent table and any related records in the child table (see Figure 10.10).

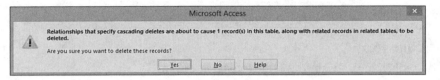

FIGURE 10.10

A message that appears after the user attempts to delete a parent record that has related child records.

THE ABSOLUTE MINIMUM

Although one of the more difficult and dryer subjects to learn about, understanding relationships is imperative when designing the databases that you will build. Without understanding database design and relationships is like building a house without understanding the importance of the foundation.

In this chapter you learned the importance of selecting a primary key: the unique identifier for each table. It is important that the primary key is minimal (short), stable (doesn't change), and simple (familiar to the user of the database). Most tables benefit from the use of an AutoNumber field as the primary key; although, a meaningless number, AutoNumber fields are minimal and stable.

Although theoretical, gaining a basic understanding of normalization and normal forms is important to your success in working with Microsoft Access. You must remember that you don't want your tables to contain repeating groups (Item1, Qty1, Item2, Qty2, and so on), and that all fields in a table should relate to the primary key. This means that the customer table should not contain the order date, and the order detail table should not contain the description of the item being ordered. Following the rules of normalization ensures that queries, forms, and reports will be easy to design and build.

As their name implies, integrity rules ensure the integrity of the data in your databases. For example, with integrity rules in place, you cannot add an order for a customer that doesn't exist. You cannot delete a customer who has orders, unless you opt to cascade the delete so that Access deletes related orders from the Orders table.

Most tables participate in one-to-many relationships. An example of a one-to-many relationship is that between the Customers and Orders tables. Generally, one customer has multiple orders. Many-to-many relationships are also common. An example of a many-to-many relationship is between the Orders table and the Products table. Each order contains multiple products, and each product is contained on multiple orders. Because Access cannot represent a many-to-many relationship, use a junction table to create two one-to-many relationships. In this case you can create an OrderDetails table that relates to the Orders table in a one-to-many relationship and to the Products table in a one-to-many relationship. One order has multiple detail items, and one product is contained in multiple detail items.

Although a little difficult to digest, when you are comfortable with relational databases and relational design principles, you can create databases that accomplish just about anything and your learning efforts are rewarding!

IN THIS CHAPTER

- What other query basics should I know?
- How do I build a query based on multiple tables?
- How do I modify the datasheet view of a query?
- How do I print my query results?
- Are my query results updateable?
- How do I further refine my queries with criteria?

11

ENHANCING THE QUERIES THAT YOU BUILD

Chapter 4, "Using Queries to Retrieve the Data You Need," taught you the basics of working with queries. This chapter takes your knowledge of designing and working with queries to a whole new level. You begin by covering some essential query basics. We'll then talk about the update-ability of query results. You then learn how to work with queries based on data in more than one table. After you learn how to add multiple tables to a query, you see the pitfalls of multitable queries. Although multitable queries are extremely powerful and useful, you should be aware of these potential pitfalls. After discussing multitable queries, you move to the pro-cess of customizing the datasheet view of a query and printing your query results. Finally, you expand your knowledge of working with criteria in your discussion of some more advanced criteria techniques, including working with dates and criteria.

Everything You Ever Needed to Know About Query Basics

You should be aware of some basics when working with queries not yet covered. These include removing a field from the query Design grid, inserting a field after a query is built, and moving fields to different locations on the query grid. The following text covers these topics.

Removing a Field from the Query Design Grid

To remove a field from the query design grid, follow these steps:

1. Find the field you want to remove.

2. Click the column selector (that is, the small, horizontal gray button) immediately above the name of the field. The entire column of the query design grid should become black (see Figure 11.1).

3. Press the Delete key, or select Delete Columns from the Query Setup group on the Design tab of the ribbon. Access removes the field from the query.

FIGURE 11.1

Removing a field from the query design grid.

Inserting a Field After a Query Is Built

The process for inserting a field after you have built a query depends on where you want to insert the new field. If you want to insert it after the existing fields, it's easiest to double-click the name of the field you want to add. If you prefer to insert the new field between two existing fields, it's best to click and drag the field you want to add and drop it onto the field you want to appear to the right of the inserted field.

Moving a Field to a Different Location on the Query Grid

Although the user can move a column while in a query's Datasheet view, sometimes you want to permanently alter the position of a field in the query output. You can do this as a convenience to the user or, more important, to use the query as a foundation for forms and reports. The order of the fields in the query becomes the default order of the fields on any forms and reports you build by using any of the wizards. You can save quite a bit of time by ordering queries effectively.

To move a single column, follow these steps:

1. Select a column while in the query's Design view by clicking its column selector.

2. Click the selected column a second time, and then drag it to a new location on the query design grid.

Move More Than One Column

Follow these steps to move more than one column at a time:

1. Drag across the column selectors of the columns you want to move.

2. Click any of the selected columns a second time, and then drag them to a new location on the query design grid.

 NOTE Moving a column in Datasheet view doesn't modify the query's underlying design. If you move a column in Datasheet view, subsequent reordering in Design view isn't reflected in Datasheet view. In other words, Design view and Datasheet view are no longer synchronized, and you must reorder both manually. This actually serves as an advantage in most cases. For example, if you want to sort by the Country field and then by the CompanyName field, the Country field must appear to the left of the CompanyName field in the design of the query. If you want the CompanyName field to appear to the left of the Country field in the query's result, you must make that change in Datasheet view. Because Access maintains the order of the columns separately in both views enables you to easily accomplish both objectives.

Updating Query Results

The results of most queries are updateable. This means that if you modify the data in the query output, Access permanently modifies the data in the tables underlying the query.

Update Results of a Query

To see how this works, follow these steps:

1. Build a query based on the Customers table.

2. Add the ID, Company, Address, City, and State/Province fields to the query design grid and then run the query.

3. Change the address of a particular customer and make a note of the ID of the customer whose address you changed. Make sure you move off the record so that Access writes the change to disk.

4. Close the query, open the actual table in Datasheet view, and find the record whose address you modified. The change you made was written to the original table; this is because a query result is a dynamic set of records that maintains a link to the original data. This happens whether you're on a standalone machine or on a network.

 NOTE It's essential that you understand how Access updates query results; otherwise, you might mistakenly update table data without realizing you've done so. Updating multitable queries is covered in the section "Pitfalls of Multitable Queries."

Building Queries Based on Multiple Tables

If you have properly normalized your table data, you probably want to bring the data from your tables back together by using queries. An example is where you have separated the data into Customers, Orders, and Order Detail tables. You now want to see all the items that a customer ordered. Fortunately, you can do this quite easily by using Access queries.

The query in Figure 11.2 joins the Customers, Orders, and Order Details tables, pulling fields from each. Notice in the figure that the ID and Company fields are selected from the Customers table, the Order ID, and Order Date fields from the Orders table, and the Unit Price and Quantity fields from the Order Details table. You can add tables to the Design grid of the query using the Show Table button in the Query Setup group on the Design tab of the ribbon. After you run this query, you should see the results shown in Figure 11.3. Notice that you get a record in the query's result for every record in the Order Details table. In other words, there are 67 records in the Order Details table, and that's how many records appear in the query output. By creating a multitable query, you can look at data from related tables, along with the data from the Order Details table.

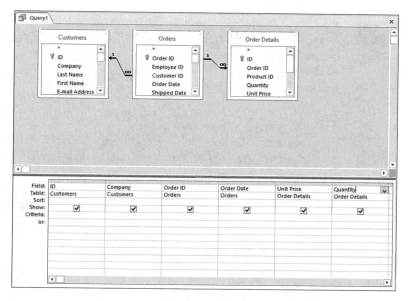

FIGURE 11.2

A query joining the Customers, Orders, and Order Details tables.

ID	Company	Order ID	Order Date	Unit Price	Quantity
27	Company AA	30	1/15/2006	$14.00	100
27	Company AA	30	1/15/2006	$3.50	30
4	Company D	31	1/20/2006	$30.00	10
4	Company D	31	1/20/2006	$53.00	10
4	Company D	31	1/20/2006	$3.50	10
12	Company L	32	1/22/2006	$18.00	15
12	Company L	32	1/22/2006	$46.00	20
8	Company H	33	1/30/2006	$9.20	30
4	Company D	34	2/6/2006	$9.20	20
29	Company CC	35	2/10/2006	$12.75	10
3	Company C	36	2/23/2006	$9.65	200
6	Company F	37	3/6/2006	$40.00	17
28	Company BB	38	3/10/2006	$46.00	300
8	Company H	39	3/22/2006	$12.75	100
10	Company J	40	3/24/2006	$2.99	200
7	Company G	41	3/24/2006	$46.00	300
10	Company J	42	3/24/2006	$25.00	10
10	Company J	42	3/24/2006	$22.00	10
10	Company J	42	3/24/2006	$9.20	10
11	Company K	43	3/24/2006	$3.50	20
11	Company K	43	3/24/2006	$2.99	50
1	Company A	44	3/24/2006	$18.00	25
1	Company A	44	3/24/2006	$46.00	25
1	Company A	44	3/24/2006	$2.99	25
28	Company BB	45	4/7/2006	$9.65	50
28	Company BB	45	4/7/2006	$18.40	50
9	Company I	46	4/5/2006	$19.50	100
9	Company I	46	4/5/2006	$34.80	50
6	Company F	47	4/8/2006	$14.00	300
8	Company H	48	4/5/2006	$40.00	25
8	Company H	48	4/5/2006	$9.20	25
25	Company Y	50	4/5/2006	$10.00	20
26	Company Z	51	4/5/2006	$21.35	25
26	Company Z	51	4/5/2006	$9.65	30
26	Company Z	51	4/5/2006	$18.40	30
29	Company CC	55	4/5/2006	$14.00	87
6	Company F	56	4/3/2006	$12.75	10
27	Company AA	57	4/22/2006		
4	Company D	58	4/22/2006	$81.00	40
4	Company D	58	4/22/2006	$7.00	40

Record: I ◄ 1 of 67 ► ► ► No Filter   Search

FIGURE 11.3

The results of querying multiple tables.

NOTE Chapter 10, "Relating the Information in Your Database," discusses how setting up the right type of relationship ensures ease of use in designing system objects. By setting up relationships between tables in a database, Access knows how to properly join them in the queries that you build.

TIP To remove a table from a query, you click anywhere on the table in the top half of the query design grid and then press the Delete key. You can add tables to the query at any time by clicking the Show Table button on the Ribbon. If you prefer, you can select the Navigation Pane and then click and drag tables directly from the Navigation Pane to the top half of the query design grid.

Pitfalls of Multitable Queries

You should be aware of some pitfalls of multitable queries: They involve updating and which records you see in the query output.

You cannot update certain fields in a multitable query. You cannot update the join fields on the "one" side of a one-to-many relationship (unless you've activated the Cascade Update Referential Integrity feature). You also can't update the join field on the "many" side of a relationship after you've updated data on the "one" side. More important, which fields you *can* update, and the consequences of updating them, might surprise you. If you update the fields on the "one" side of a one-to-many relationship, you must be aware of that change's impact. You're actually updating that record in the original table on the "one" side of the relationship, and several records on the "many" side of the relationship may be affected.

For example, Figure 11.4 shows the result of a query based on the Customers, Orders, and Order Details tables. I have changed Company D to InfoTech Services Group on a specific record of the query output. You might expect this change to affect only that specific order detail item. However, pressing the down arrow key to move off the record shows that all records associated with Company D are changed (see Figure 11.5). This happens because all the orders for Company D were actually getting their information from one record in the Customers table—the record for ID 12—and that is the record I modified while viewing the query result.

The second pitfall of multitable queries has to do with figuring out which records result from a multitable query. So far, you have learned how to build only inner joins. You need to understand that the query output contains only customers who have orders and orders that have order details. This means that not all the

ID	Company	Order ID	Order Date	Unit Price	Quantity
27	Company AA	30	1/15/2006	$14.00	100
27	Company AA	30	1/15/2006	$3.50	30
4	InfoTech Services Group	31	1/20/2006	$30.00	10
4	Company D	31	1/20/2006	$53.00	10
4	Company D	31	1/20/2006	$3.50	10
12	Company L	32	1/22/2006	$18.00	15
12	Company L	32	1/22/2006	$46.00	20
8	Company H	33	1/30/2006	$9.20	30
4	Company D	34	2/6/2006	$9.20	20
29	Company CC	35	2/10/2006	$12.75	10
3	Company C	36	2/23/2006	$9.65	200
6	Company F	37	3/6/2006	$40.00	17
28	Company BB	38	3/10/2006	$46.00	300

FIGURE 11.4

Changing a record on the "one" side of a one-to-many relationship.

ID	Company	Order ID	Order Date	Unit Price	Quantity
27	Company AA	30	1/15/2006	$14.00	100
27	Company AA	30	1/15/2006	$3.50	30
4	InfoTech Services Group	31	1/20/2006	$30.00	10
4	InfoTech Services Group	31	1/20/2006	$53.00	10
4	InfoTech Services Group	31	1/20/2006	$3.50	10
12	Company L	32	1/22/2006	$18.00	15
12	Company L	32	1/22/2006	$46.00	20
8	Company H	33	1/30/2006	$9.20	30
4	InfoTech Services Group	34	2/6/2006	$9.20	20
29	Company CC	35	2/10/2006	$12.75	10
3	Company C	36	2/23/2006	$9.65	200
6	Company F	37	3/6/2006	$40.00	17
28	Company BB	38	3/10/2006	$46.00	300

FIGURE 11.5

The result of changing a record on the "one" side of a one-to-many relationship.

customers or orders might be listed. In the next chapter, Chapter 12, "Advanced Query Techniques" you learn how to build queries in which you can list all customers, regardless of whether they have orders. You'll also learn how to list only the customers that do not have orders.

AutoLookup in Multitable Queries

The AutoLookup feature is automatically available in Access. As you fill in key values on the "many" side of a one-to-many relationship in a multitable query, Access automatically looks up the nonkey values in the parent table. Most database developers refer to this as *enforced referential integrity*. A foreign key must first exist on the "one" side of the query to be entered successfully on the "many" side. As you can imagine, you don't want to add to a database an order for a nonexistent customer.

For example, the author based the query in Figure 11.6 on the `Customers` and `Orders` tables. The fields included in the query are `CustomerID` from the `Orders` table; `Company`, `Address`, and `City` from the `Customers` table; and `Order ID` and `Order Date` from the `Orders` table. If you change the `CustomerID` field associated with an order, Access looks up the `Company`, `Address`, and `City` fields from the `Customers` table and immediately displays them in the query result.

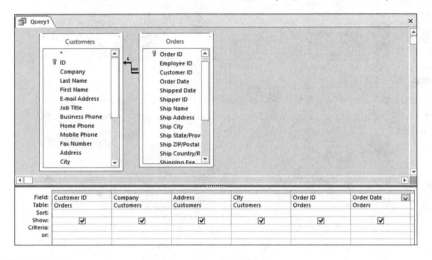

FIGURE 11.6

Using AutoLookup in a query with multiple tables.

Notice in Figure 11.7 how the information for `Company F` is displayed in the query result. Figure 11.8 shows that the `Company` and `Address` fields change automatically when the `Customer` field is changed to `Company C.` Don't be confused by the combo box used to select the customer ID. The presence of the combo box within the query is a result of Access's Lookup feature. The customer ID associated with a particular order is actually being modified in the query. If you add a new record to the query, Access fills in the customer information as soon as you select the customer ID associated with the order.

Modifying the Datasheet View of a Query

Access enables you to customize the datasheet view of a query, enabling you to view the data in the most effective manner possible. You can modify the column widths, row heights, font, font color, background color, and more.

To modify the width of a column in the datasheet view of a query, you must place your mouse pointer within the column headings on the line that separates two of the columns. Your mouse pointer appears as a double-headed arrow with a line through it.

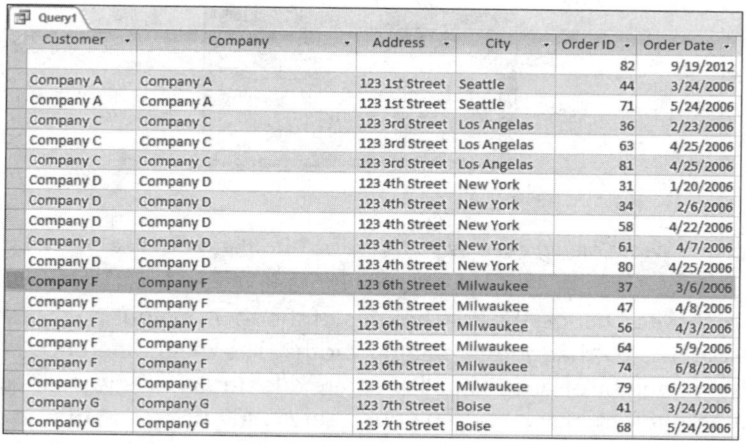

Customer	Company	Address	City	Order ID	Order Date
				82	9/19/2012
Company A	Company A	123 1st Street	Seattle	44	3/24/2006
Company A	Company A	123 1st Street	Seattle	71	5/24/2006
Company C	Company C	123 3rd Street	Los Angelas	36	2/23/2006
Company C	Company C	123 3rd Street	Los Angelas	63	4/25/2006
Company C	Company C	123 3rd Street	Los Angelas	81	4/25/2006
Company D	Company D	123 4th Street	New York	31	1/20/2006
Company D	Company D	123 4th Street	New York	34	2/6/2006
Company D	Company D	123 4th Street	New York	58	4/22/2006
Company D	Company D	123 4th Street	New York	61	4/7/2006
Company D	Company D	123 4th Street	New York	80	4/25/2006
Company F	Company F	123 6th Street	Milwaukee	37	3/6/2006
Company F	Company F	123 6th Street	Milwaukee	47	4/8/2006
Company F	Company F	123 6th Street	Milwaukee	56	4/3/2006
Company F	Company F	123 6th Street	Milwaukee	64	5/9/2006
Company F	Company F	123 6th Street	Milwaukee	74	6/8/2006
Company F	Company F	123 6th Street	Milwaukee	79	6/23/2006
Company G	Company G	123 7th Street	Boise	41	3/24/2006
Company G	Company G	123 7th Street	Boise	68	5/24/2006

FIGURE 11.7

A query result before another customer ID is selected.

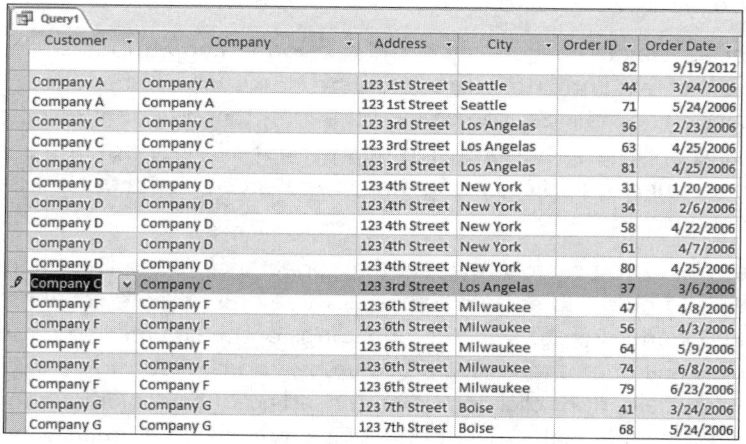

Customer	Company	Address	City	Order ID	Order Date
				82	9/19/2012
Company A	Company A	123 1st Street	Seattle	44	3/24/2006
Company A	Company A	123 1st Street	Seattle	71	5/24/2006
Company C	Company C	123 3rd Street	Los Angelas	36	2/23/2006
Company C	Company C	123 3rd Street	Los Angelas	63	4/25/2006
Company C	Company C	123 3rd Street	Los Angelas	81	4/25/2006
Company D	Company D	123 4th Street	New York	31	1/20/2006
Company D	Company D	123 4th Street	New York	34	2/6/2006
Company D	Company D	123 4th Street	New York	58	4/22/2006
Company D	Company D	123 4th Street	New York	61	4/7/2006
Company D	Company D	123 4th Street	New York	80	4/25/2006
Company C	Company C	123 3rd Street	Los Angelas	37	3/6/2006
Company F	Company F	123 6th Street	Milwaukee	47	4/8/2006
Company F	Company F	123 6th Street	Milwaukee	56	4/3/2006
Company F	Company F	123 6th Street	Milwaukee	64	5/9/2006
Company F	Company F	123 6th Street	Milwaukee	74	6/8/2006
Company F	Company F	123 6th Street	Milwaukee	79	6/23/2006
Company G	Company G	123 7th Street	Boise	41	3/24/2006
Company G	Company G	123 7th Street	Boise	68	5/24/2006

FIGURE 11.8

The result of an autolookup after the customer ID is changed.

Click and drag to make the column to the left of the mouse pointer wider or narrower. If you prefer, you can right-click a column heading and select Field Width. The Column Width dialog appears (see Figure 11.9). Here you can either enter a column width or select Best Fit to size the column to the width of the widest data in the column. Finally, if you want to get the best fit with the mouse, double-click the line between two column headings. As with the Best Fit option in the Column Width dialog, the column width adjusts to fit the widest data in the column.

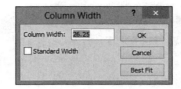

FIGURE 11.9

The Column Width dialog enables you to customize the width of a column in your datasheet.

The process to change the row heights of the rows in your query result is similar to the process to change the column widths. The main difference is that when you modify the height of one row, all rows are affected. This surprises some people. To modify the height of the rows in your query result using the mouse, you can place your mouse pointer on the line between any two rows. Then simply click and drag to row to the wanted size. Alternatively, you can right-click any rows selector in the query result and select Row Height. The Row Height dialog appears. Enter the height of your choice, and click OK.

The easiest way to change any of the text formatting attributes of a query result is using the Text Formatting group on the Home tab on the Ribbon. Here you can bold, underline, italicize, and change the font, font size, font color, background color, and gridlines. The surprising thing about all these options is that they affect the *entire* query grid. For example, if you select bold, Access bolds every cell in the query grid.

Another thing you can do to affect the appearance of the Datasheet view of your queries is to hide and show columns. To hide one or more columns in the query result, click and drag to select the headings of the columns you want to hide. Then right-click any one of the selected columns, and choose Hide Fields. To show the column(s) again, right-click the column heading of any column in the query result and select Unhide Fields. The Unhide Columns dialog appears (see Figure 11.10).

FIGURE 11.10

The Unhide Columns dialog enables you to show hidden columns.

Notice that the hidden columns are unchecked. Click to select the columns you want to show, and click OK to complete the process. The columns reappear.

A powerful feature you can select in Datasheet view of a query is Freeze Fields. To use this feature, you first click and drag to select the headings of the columns you want to freeze. You then select Freeze Fields. If the select columns are not on the far left side of the datasheet, Access moves them to the left. As you view the columns in the table, the frozen columns remain on the screen. If you want to "unfreeze" the columns, simply right-click any column and select Unfreeze All Fields.

The last thing to be aware of when modifying attributes of the query grid is whether you want to save those attributes. If you have made changes to the appearance of the query grid, Access prompts you to save when you close the query. The message that Access generates appears in Figure 11.11. Notice that Access asks you whether you want to save the layout of the query. This is different from the design of the query. The design of the query refers to the structural aspects of the query, such as which columns and expressions appear in the query result.

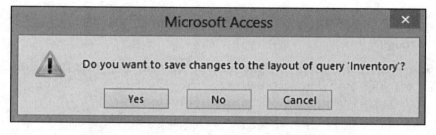

FIGURE 11.11

Access prompts you to save the changes you have made to the layout of the query.

Printing Query Results

After you modify the datasheet view of your query, you may want to send the query results to the printer. Access is a WYSIWYG (what you see is what you get) environment. This means that your datasheet prints complete with any modifications you have made to Datasheet view (font, column widths, and so on). To print a query result

1. Click to select the File tab on the Ribbon.

2. Select Print from the list of options that appear. Your screen appears as in Figure 11.12.

3. Select Quick Print to send the query result to the printer without any further interaction. Access uses default margins and other settings.

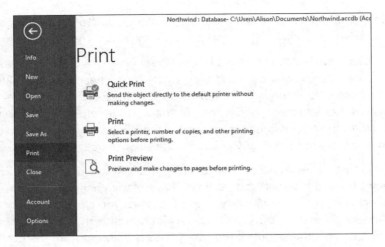

FIGURE 11.12

When you select Print, three options appear.

4. Select Print Preview to view what your query results look like when you print them.

5. Select Print to open the Print dialog. Here you can opt to print a range of pages or to print just selected records (see Figure 11.13). You can also designate the number of copies you want to print.

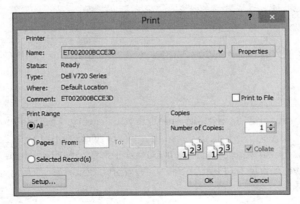

FIGURE 11.13

The Print dialog enables you to designate options such as which pages to print.

6. If you want to further refine your print options, click Setup. Here you can specify the margins and whether you want to print headings.

7. Click OK to close the Print Setup dialog.

8. Click Properties to open the Printing Preferences dialog. The Printing Preferences dialog, pictured in Figure 11.14, varies depending on the printer you have selected. It enables you to specify many print options such as the orientation (portrait or landscape) of the printout.

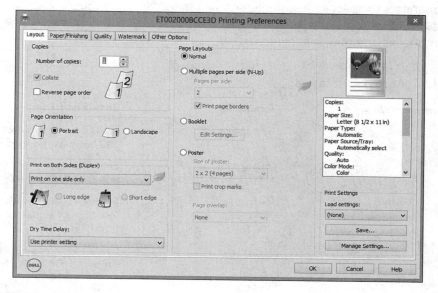

FIGURE 11.14

The Printing Preferences dialog enables you to further refine the look of the printout.

9. Click OK to close the Printing Preferences dialog.

10. Click OK again to send your query result to the printer.

NOTE Moving a column in Datasheet view doesn't modify the query's underlying design. If you move a column in Datasheet view, subsequent reordering in Design view isn't reflected in Datasheet view. In other words, Design view and Datasheet view are no longer synchronized, and you must reorder both manually. This actually serves as an advantage in most cases. For example, if you want to sort by the Country field and then by the CompanyName field, the Country field must appear to the left of the CompanyName field in the design of the query. If you want the CompanyName field to appear to the left of the Country field in the query's result, you must make that change in Datasheet view. Because Access maintains the order of the columns separately in both views enables you to easily accomplish both objectives.

Refining a Query by Using Criteria

One of the important features of queries is the ability to limit output by using selection criteria. Access enables you to combine criteria by using several operators to specify the criteria for multiple fields. In Chapter 4, you learned the basics of working with query criteria. Table 11.1 covers the operators you can use in queries and their meanings.

TABLE 11.1 Access Operators

Operator	Meaning	Example	Result of Example
=	Equal to.	="Sales"	Finds only records with "Sales" as the field value.
<	Less than.	<100	Finds all records with values less than 100 in that field.
<=	Less than or equal to.	<=100	Finds all records with values less than or equal to 100 in that field.
>	Greater than.	>100	Finds all records with values greater than 100 in that field.
>=	Greater than or equal to.	>=100	Finds all records with values greater than or equal to 100 in that field.
<>	Not equal to.	<>"Sales"	Finds all records with values other than Sales in the field.
And	Both conditions must be true.	Created by adding criteria on the same line of the query design grid to more than one field	Finds all records where the conditions in both fields are true.
Or	Either condition can be true.	"CA" or "NY" or "UT"	Finds all records with the value "CA", "NY", or "UT" in the field.
Like	Compares a string expression to a pattern.	Like"Sales*"	Finds all records with the value "Sales" at the beginning of the field. (The asterisk is a wildcard character.)
Between	Finds a range of values.	Between 5 and 10	Finds all records with the values 5—10 (inclusive) in the field.
In	Same as Or.	In("CA","NY","UT")	Finds all records with the value "CA", "NY", or "UT" in the field.

TABLE 11.1 (continued)

Operator	Meaning	Example	Result of Example
Not	Same as <>.	Not "Sales"	Finds all records with values other than Sales in the field.
Is Null	Finds nulls	Is Null	Finds all records where no data has been entered in the field.
Is Not Null	Finds all records that are not null	Is Not Null	Finds all records where data has been entered into the field.

Criteria entered for two fields on a single line of the query design grid are considered an **And** condition, which means that both conditions need to be true for the record to appear in the query output. Entries made on separate lines of the query design grid are considered an **Or** condition, which means that either condition can be true for Access to include the record in the query output. Take a look at the example in Figure 11.15; this query would output all records in which the Job Title field begins with either Accounting or Purchasing, regardless of the customer ID. It outputs the records in which the Job Title field begins with Owner only for the customers whose IDs are greater than or equal to 10. Notice that the word *Owner* is immediately followed by the asterisk. This means that customer would be included in the output. On the other hand, *Accounting* and *Purchasing* are both followed by spaces. That means that only entries that begin with Marketing or Owner followed by a space are included in the output.

Field:	ID	Company	Last Name	First Name	Job Title	Busin
Table:	Customers	Customers	Customers	Customers	Customers	Custo
Sort:						
Show:	✔	✔	✔	✔	✔	
Criteria:					Like "Accounting *" Or Like "Purchasing *"	
or:	>=10				Like "Owner*"	

FIGURE 11.15

Adding And and Or conditions to a query.

Working with Dates in Criteria

Access gives you significant power for adding date functions and expressions to query criteria. Using these criteria, you can find all records in a certain month, on a specific weekday, or between two dates. Table 11.2 lists the date criteria expressions and examples.

TABLE 11.2 Date Criteria Expressions

Expression	Meaning	Example	Result
Date()	Current date	Date()	Records the current date within a field
Day(Date)	The day of a date	Day ([OrderDate])=1	Records the order date on the first day of the month
Month(Date)	The month of a date	Month ([OrderDate])=1	Records the order date in January
Year(Date)	The year of a date	Year ([OrderDate])=2011	Records the order date in 2011
Weekday(Date)	The weekday of a date	Weekday ([OrderDate])=2	Records the order date on a Monday
Between Date And Date	A range of dates	Between #1/1/2011# and #12/31/2011#	Finds all records in 2011
DatePart (Interval, Date)	A specific part of a date	DatePart ("q", [OrderDate])=2	Finds all records in the second quarter

The Weekday(Date, [FirstDayOfWeek]) function works based on your locale and how your system defines the first day of the week. Weekday() used without the optional FirstDayOfWeek argument defaults to vbSunday as the first day. A value of 0 defaults FirstDayOfWeek to the system definition. Other values can be set, too.

Figure 11.16 illustrates the use of a date function. Notice that DatePart ("q",[Order Date]) is entered as the expression, and the value 2 is entered for the criterion. Year([Order Date)] is entered as another expression, with the number 2012 as the criterion. Therefore, this query outputs all records in which the order date is in the second quarter of 2012.

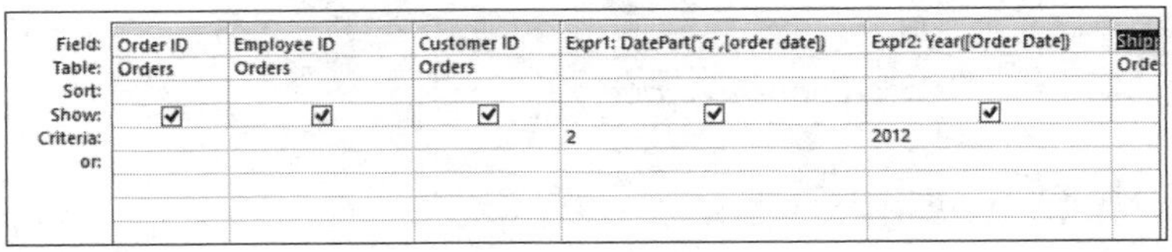

FIGURE 11.16

Using the DatePart() and Year() functions in a query.

THE ABSOLUTE MINIMUM

One of the most important concepts covered in this chapter involves the update-ability of query results. You must understand that when you modify data in a query result, the underlying table(s) are affected. This concept is particularly important to comprehend when you are updating one side of a query based on tables joined in a one-to-many relationship. It may appear to you as if you are affecting only the row that it appears that you are modifying. In actuality, that row on the one side of the relationship is associated with many child rows. So if, for example, you modify the city in the Customer table associated with an order, you are actually modifying the city associated with all orders related to that customer.

Access gives you the ability to modify the datasheet associated with a query result. You can easily change font attributes (such as bold, italic, font, and size), as well as modify the width of columns. You can hide and show columns, as well as freeze columns so that they remain on the screen as you scroll left and right in a record.

When your query result appears exactly as you want it to appear, you may want to send the result to your printer. Remember that what you see in Datasheet view is what you will get when you print. Access gives you quite a bit of flexibility when printing your query result. You can designate the margins, number of copies, orientation, and much more. The specific options available vary based on the printer that you select.

You can accomplish quite a bit when working with queries if you become familiar with the criteria options available to you. After learning about all the basic query operators (=, <=, >=, <>, And, Or, Like, Between, In, Not, and Is Null), you saw several examples of working with criteria involving dates. When you are comfortable with query criteria, you can view just the data you need exactly when you need it.

Queries are the most important objects available in Access. This chapter greatly expanded your knowledge of queries. Chapter 12, further enhances your knowledge of queries and how you can use them to view and update the information in your database exactly as you need to.

12

ADVANCED QUERY TECHNIQUES

You will probably agree from your experience with queries thus far that Access queries are very powerful. This chapter takes Access queries to a whole new level.

You begin by creating calculated fields. You can create calculated fields that multiply the price of an item by the quantity, or you can concatenate (combine) a customer's first and last name. An Expression Builder tool facilitates the process to build calculated expressions in your queries.

You spend the last portion of the chapter learning how to build queries that insert, update, and delete table data, as well as queries that make new tables. All four of these types of queries are easy to design but powerful.

Yet another important query technique is the ability to summarize table data. After reading this section, you can find the information such as the total sales in each state.

Finally, you learn about outer joins. So far you have worked only with inner joins. With an inner join, the result of joining the customers table and the orders table renders only customers with orders. Using outer joins, you can view all customers regardless of whether they have orders. You can also view only customers who don't have orders. You can even view orders not associated with existing customers. Outer joins give you an immense amount of flexibility as to what you see in the results of the queries that you build.

Creating Calculated Fields

One of the rules of data normalization is that you shouldn't include the results of calculations in a database. You can output the results of calculations by building those calculations into queries, and you can display the results of the calculations on forms and reports by making the query the foundation for a form or report. You can also add to forms and reports controls that contain the calculations you want. In certain cases, this can improve performance.

The columns of a query result can hold the result of any valid expression. This makes queries extremely powerful. For example, you can enter the following expression:

```
Left([First Name],1) & "." & Left([Last Name],1) & "."
```

This expression gives you the first character of the first name, followed by a period, the first character of the last name, and another period. An even simpler expression would be this one:

```
[Unit Price]*[Quantity]
```

This calculation would simply multiply the Unit Price field by the Quantity field. In both cases, Access would automatically name the resulting expression. For example, Figure 12.1 shows the calculation that results from concatenating the first and last initials. Notice in the figure that Access gives the expression a name (often referred to as an *alias*). To give the expression a name, such as Initials, you must enter it as follows:

```
Initials:Left([First Name],1) & "." & Left([Last Name],1) & "."
```

The text preceding the colon is the name of the expression—in this case, Initials. If you don't explicitly give an expression a name, the name defaults to Expr1.

FIGURE 12.1

The result of using the expression Left([First Name],1) & "." & Left ([Last Name],1) & "." *in a query.*

NOTE You can enter any valid expression in the Field row of the query design grid. Access automatically surrounds field names included in an expression with square brackets, unless the field name has spaces. If the field name includes any spaces, you must enclose the field name in brackets; otherwise, the query won't run properly. This is just one of the many reasons field and table names shouldn't contain spaces.

Getting Help from the Expression Builder

The Expression Builder is a helpful tool for building expressions in queries and in many other situations in Access. To invoke the Expression Builder, you click the Field cell of the query design grid and then click Build on the toolbar. The Expression Builder appears (see Figure 12.2). Notice that the Expression Builder is divided into three columns. The left column shows the objects in the database. After you select an element in the left column, select the elements you want to paste from the middle and right columns.

The example in Figure 12.3 shows Functions selected in the left column. Within Functions, both user-defined and built-in functions are listed. Here, the Functions object is expanded with Built-In Functions selected. In the center column, Date/Time is selected. After you select Date/Time, all the built-in date and time functions appear in the right column. If you double-click a particular function—in this case, the DatePart function—Access places the function and its parameters in the text box at the top of the Expression Builder window. The DatePart function has four parameters: Interval, Date, FirstWeekday, and FirstWeek. If you know what needs to go into each of these parameters, you can simply replace the parameter placeholders with your own values. If you need more information, you can invoke Help on the

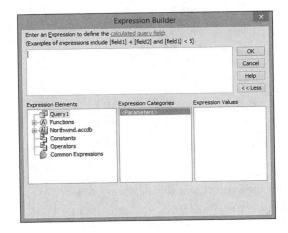

FIGURE 12.2

The Expression Builder.

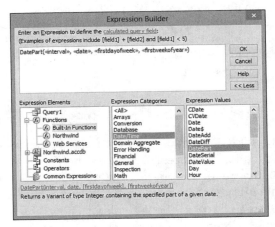

FIGURE 12.3

The Expression Builder with the DatePart *function selected and pasted in the expression box.*

selected function to learn more about the required parameters. Figure 12.4 shows two parameters filled in: the interval and the name of the field evaluated (OrderDate from the Orders table). After you click OK, Access places the expression in the Field cell of the query.

Creating and Running Parameter Queries

You might not always know the parameters for the query output when you design a query—and your application's users also might not know the parameters. *Parameter queries* enable you to specify specific criteria at runtime so that you don't need to modify the query each time you want to change the criteria.

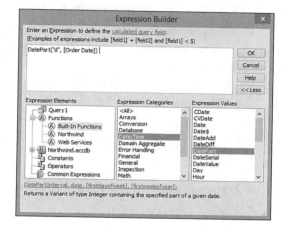

FIGURE 12.4

A function pasted by the Expression Builder, with the parameters updated with appropriate values.

For example, imagine you have a query, as shown in Figure 12.5, for which you want users to specify the date range they want to view each time they run the query. You have entered the following clause as the criterion for the Order Date field:

```
Between [Enter Starting Date] And [Enter Ending Date]
```

This criterion causes two dialog boxes to appear when the user runs the query. The first one, as shown in Figure 12.6, prompts the user with the text

FIGURE 12.5

A Parameter query that prompts for a starting date and an ending date.

FIGURE 12.6

A dialog box that appears when a Parameter query is run.

in the first set of brackets. Access substitutes the text the user types for the bracketed text. A second dialog box appears, prompting the user for whatever is in the second set of brackets. Access uses the user's responses as criteria for the query.

It is best to declare the parameters you include in your query in the Parameters dialog. This way Access knows what type of data to expect when you are entering the parameter values. To access the Parameters dialog:

1. Click Parameters in the Show/Hide group of the Design tab of the ribbon. The Query Parameters dialog appears.

2. Enter the parameters exactly as they appear in the square brackets within the query (see Figure 12.7).

3. Specify the type of data that will be contained in the parameters.

4. Click OK to complete the process.

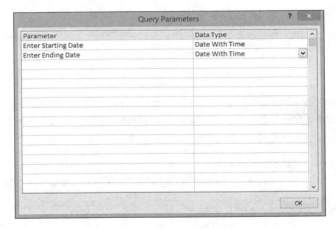

FIGURE 12.7

Use the Parameters dialog to declare the query parameters.

Creating and Running Action Queries

With Action queries, you can easily automate the process to update table data. Actually, using Action queries is often a more efficient method to modify table data than updating it manually. Four types of Action queries are available: Update, Delete, Append, and Make Table. You use Update queries to modify data in a table, Delete queries to remove records from a table, Append queries to add records to an existing table, and Make Table queries to create an entirely new table. The following sections explain these query types and their appropriate uses.

Creating and Running Update Queries

Use Update queries to modify all records or any records that meet specific criteria. You can use an Update query to modify the data in one field or several fields (or even tables) at one time. For example, you could create a query that increases the salary of everyone in California by 10%. As mentioned previously, using Action queries, including Update queries, is usually more efficient than performing the same task manually, so you can consider Update queries a viable way to modify table data.

Build an Update Query

To build an Update query, follow these steps:

1. Select Query Design from the Queries group on the Create tab in the Ribbon. The Show Table dialog box appears.

2. In the Show Table dialog box, select the tables or queries that will participate in the Update query and click Add. Click Close when you want to continue.

3. To let Access know you're building an Update query, select Update from the Query Type group on the Design tab on the Ribbon.

4. Add to the query fields that either you will use for criteria or Access will update as a result of the query. In Figure 12.8, `Ship State/Province` is included on the query grid because you use it as a criterion for the update. `Shipping Fee` is included because it's the field that Access updates. You can find both of those fields in the Orders table.

5. Add any further criteria, if you want. In Figure 12.8, the criterion for `Ship State/Province` is `CA`.

FIGURE 12.8

An Update query that increases Shipping Fee for all clients in California.

6. Add the appropriate Update expression. The example illustrated in Figure 12.8 increases `DefaultRate` by 10%.

7. Click Run in the Results group on the Design tab of the Ribbon. The message box shown in Figure 12.9 appears. Click Yes to continue. Access updates all records that meet the selected criteria.

FIGURE 12.9

The confirmation message you see when you run an Update query.

You should name Access Update queries with the prefix *qupd*. You should give each type of Action query a prefix indicating what type of query it is. This makes your application easier to maintain. Table 12.1 lists all the commonly accepted prefixes for Action queries.

TABLE 12.1 Naming Prefixes for Action Queries

Type of Query	Prefix	Example
Update	qupd	qupdShippingFee
Delete	qdel	qdelOldTimeCards
Append	qapp	qappArchiveTimeCards
Make Table	qmak	qmakTempSales

NOTE Access displays each type of Action query in the Navigation Pane with a distinctive icon.

Access stores all queries as Structured Query Language (SQL) statements. You can display the SQL for a query by selecting SQL View from the View drop-down list on the toolbar. The SQL behind an Access Update query looks like this:

```
UPDATE tblClients SET tblClients._
   DefaultRate = [DefaultRate]*1.1
      WHERE (((tblClients.StateProvince)="CA"));
```

CAUTION You cannot reverse the actions taken by an Update query or by any Action queries. You must therefore exercise extreme caution when running any Action query.

NOTE If you have turned on the Cascade Update Related Fields Referential Integrity setting and the Update query tries to modify a primary key field, Access updates the foreign key of each corresponding record in related tables. If you have not turned on the Cascade Update Related Fields setting and you have enforced referential integrity, the Update query doesn't allow you to modify the offending records.

Creating and Running Delete Queries

Rather than just modify table data, Delete queries permanently remove from a table any records that meet specific criteria; they're often used to remove old records. You might want to use a Delete query to delete all orders from the previous year, for example.

Build a Delete Query

To build a Delete query, follow these steps:

1. While in a query's Design view, select Delete from the Query Type group on the Design tab on the Ribbon.

2. Add to the query grid the criteria you want. The query shown in Figure 12.10 deletes all orders with a **Status ID** of 3 (closed).

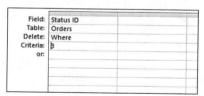

FIGURE 12.10

A Delete query used to delete all time cards entered more than a year ago.

3. Click Run in the Results group on the Design tab on the Ribbon. The message box shown in Figure 12.11 appears.

FIGURE 12.11

The Delete query confirmation message box.

4. Click Yes to permanently remove the records from the table.

The SQL behind a Delete query looks like this:

```
DELETE Orders.[Status ID]
    FROM Orders
    WHERE (((Orders.[Status ID]))=3));
```

NOTE   Remember that if you turn on the Cascade Delete Related Records Referential Integrity setting, Access deletes all corresponding records in related tables. If you do not turn on the Cascade Delete Related Records setting and you do enforce referential integrity, the Delete query doesn't enable you to delete the offending records. If you want to delete the records on the one side of the relationship, first you need to delete all the related records on the many side.

NOTE   It's often useful to view the results of an Action query before you actually affect the records included in the criteria. To view the records affected by an Action query, click the View button in the Results group on the Design tab of the Ribbon before you select Run. All records that will be affected by the Action query appear in Datasheet view. If necessary, you can temporarily add key fields to the query to get more information about the records that are about to be affected.

Creating and Running Append Queries

You can use Append queries to add records to existing tables. You often perform this function during an archive process. You use an archive process in a situation such as when a customer becomes inactive. Remember that deletions are permanent. Deletions cannot be undone. This is just one reason why archiving data, rather than deleting it, is a good idea. To archive table data, first you append to the history table the records that need to be archived by using an

Append query. So, for our example you would append the inactive customers to the history table. Next, you remove the records from the master table by using a Delete query. For our example you would delete the inactive customers from the main customers table.

Build an Append Query

To build an Append query, follow these steps:

1. While in Design view of a query, select Append from the Query Type group on the Design tab on the Ribbon. The dialog box shown in Figure 12.12 appears.

2. Select the table to which you want Access to append the data.

FIGURE 12.12

The dialog box in which you identify the table to which data will be appended and the database containing that table.

3. Drag all the fields whose data you want included in the second table to the query grid. If the field names in the two tables match, Access automatically matches the field names in the source table to the corresponding field names in the destination table (see Figure 12.13). If the field names in the two tables don't match, you need to explicitly designate which fields in the source table match which fields in the destination table.

Field:	Order ID	Employee ID	Customer ID	Order Date
Table:	Orders	Orders	Orders	Orders
Sort:				
Append To:	Order ID	Employee ID	Customer ID	Order Date
Criteria:				Between #1/1/2006# And #3/31/2006#
or:				

FIGURE 12.13

An Append query that appends to an Orders Archive table the Order ID, Employee ID, Customer ID, and Order Date of each order with an order date between 1/1/2006 and 3/31/2006.

4. Enter any criteria in the query grid. Figure 12.12 appends to the destination table all records with an order date between 1/1/2006 and 3/31/2006.

5. To run the query, click Run in the Results group on the Design tab on the Ribbon. The message box shown in Figure 12.14 appears.

FIGURE 12.14

The Append query confirmation message box.

6. Click Yes to finish the process.

The SQL behind an Append query looks like this:

```
INSERT INTO [Orders Archive] ( [Order ID], [Employee ID],
[Customer ID], [Order Date] )
SELECT Orders.[Order ID], Orders.[Employee ID], Orders.
[Customer ID], Orders.[Order Date]
FROM Orders
WHERE (((Orders.[Order Date]) Between #1/1/2006#
And #3/31/2006#));
```

Append queries don't enable you to introduce any primary key violations. If you append any records that duplicate a primary key value, the message box shown in Figure 12.15 appears. If you continue with the append process, Access appends to the destination table only records without primary key violations.

FIGURE 12.15

The warning message you see when an Append query and conversion, primary key, lock, or validation rule violation occurs.

Creating and Running Make Table Queries

Whereas an Append query adds records to an existing table, a Make Table query creates a new table, which is often a temporary table used for intermediary processing. You might want to create a temporary table, for example, to freeze data while you are running a report. By building temporary tables and running a report from those tables, you make sure users can't modify the data underlying the report during the reporting process. Another common use of a Make Table query is to supply a subset of fields or records to another user.

Build a Make Table Query

To build a Make Table query, follow these steps:

1. While in the query's Design view, select Make Table from the Query Type group on the Design tab on the Ribbon. The dialog box shown in Figure 12.16 appears.

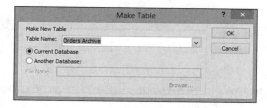

FIGURE 12.16

The dialog box in which you enter a name for a new table and selecting which database to place it in.

2. Enter the name of the new table, and click OK.

3. Move all the fields you want included in the new table to the query grid (see Figure 12.17). You often include the result of an expression in the new table.

4. Add to the query the criteria you want.

5. Click Run on the toolbar to run the query. The message shown in Figure 12.18 appears.

6. Click Yes to finish the process.

FIGURE 12.17

Adding an expression to a Make Table query.

FIGURE 12.18

The Make Table query confirmation message box.

If you try to run the same Make Table query more than one time, Access permanently deletes the table with the same name as the table you're creating. (See the warning message in Figure 12.19.)

FIGURE 12.19

The Make Table query warning message displayed when an existing table already has the same name as the table to be created.

The SQL for a Make Table query looks like this:

```
SELECT Orders.[Order ID], Orders.[Employee ID], Orders.[Cus-
tomer ID],
Orders.[Order Date], Orders.[Shipped Date], Orders.[Shipper
ID], Date() AS ArchiveDate INTO [Orders Archive]
FROM Orders
WHERE (((Orders.[Order Date]) Between #1/1/2006# And
#3/31/2006#));
```

Using Aggregate Functions to Summarize Numeric Data

By using aggregate functions, you can easily summarize numeric data. You can use aggregate functions to calculate the sum, average, count, minimum, maximum, and other types of summary calculations for the data in a query result. These queries let you calculate one value for all the records in a query result or group the calculations as wanted. For example, you could determine the total sales for every record in the query result, as shown in Figure 12.20, or you could output the total sales by ship country/region and ship city, as shown in Figure 12.21. You could also calculate the total, average, minimum, and maximum sales amounts for all customers in the United States. The possibilities are endless.

FIGURE 12.20

Total sales for every record in a query result.

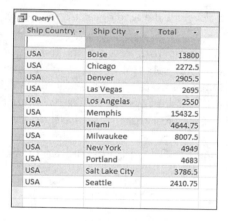

FIGURE 12.21

Total sales by Ship Country/Region and Ship City.

Creating Totals Queries

To create a Totals query, follow these steps:

1. Add to the query grid the fields or expressions you want to summarize. You must add the fields in the order in which you want them grouped. For example, Figure 12.22 shows a query grouped by country and then by city.

2. Click Totals in the Show/Hide group on the Design tab on the Ribbon to add a Total row to the query. By default, each field in the query has `Group By` in the Total row.

3. Click the Total row on the design grid.

4. Open the combo box, and choose the calculation you want, as shown in Figure 12.22.

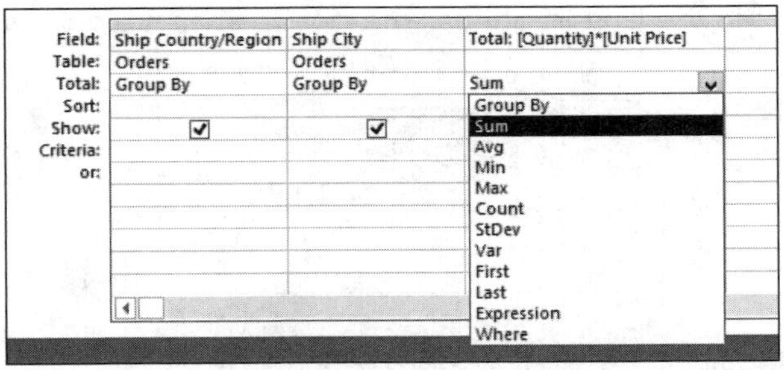

FIGURE 12.22

Selecting from a drop-down list the type of calculation for the Total row.

5. Leave `Group By` in the Total row for any field you want to group by, as shown in Figure 12.22. Remember to place the fields in the order in which you want them grouped. For example, if you want the records grouped by country and then by sales representative, you must place the Country field to the left of the Sales Representative field on the query grid. On the other hand, if you want records grouped by sales representative and then by country, you must place the Sales Representative field to the left of the Country field on the query grid.

6. Add to the query the criteria you want.

Figure 12.23 shows the design of a query that finds the total, minimum, maximum, and average sales by country and city; Figure 12.24 shows the results of running the query. As you can see, aggregate functions can give you valuable information.

If you save this query and reopen it, you should see that Access has made some changes to its design. Access changes the Total cell for `Sum` to `Expression`, and it changes the Field cell to the following:

```
Total: Sum([Unit Price]*[Quantity])
```

If you look at the Total cell for `Avg`, you should see that Access changes it to `Expression`. Access changes the Field cell to the following:

```
Average: Avg([Unit Price]*[Quantity])
```

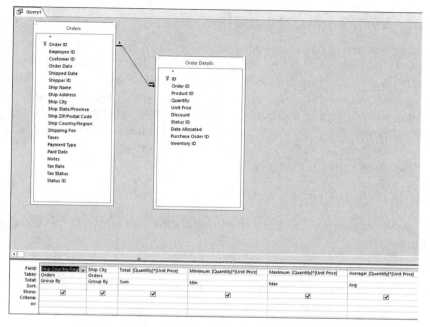

FIGURE 12.23

A query that finds the total, minimum, maximum, and average sales by country and city.

Ship Country	Ship City	Total	Minimum	Maximum	Average
USA	Boise	13800	13800	13800	13800
USA	Chicago	2272.5	52.5	660	284.0625
USA	Denver	2905.5	127.5	1560	968.5
USA	Las Vegas	2695	105	1400	673.75
USA	Los Angelas	2550	0	1930	510
USA	Memphis	15432.5	230	13800	3858.125
USA	Miami	4644.75	70	2250	663.535714285714
USA	Milwaukee	8007.5	127.5	4200	1334.58333333333
USA	New York	4949	35	3240	707
USA	Portland	4683	230	1392	780.5
USA	Salt Lake City	3786.5	96.5	1950	1262.16666666667
USA	Seattle	2410.75	74.75	1150	602.6875

FIGURE 12.24

The result of running a query that has many aggregate functions.

Access modifies the query in this way when it determines that you're using an aggregate function on an expression that has more than one field. You can enter the expression either way. Access stores and resolves the expression as noted.

Working with Outer Joins

Outer joins are used when you want the records on the one side of a one-to-many relationship to be included in the query result, regardless of whether there are matching records in the table on the many side. With a Customers table and an Orders table, for example, users often want to include only customers with orders in the query output. An *inner join* (the default join type) does this. In other situations, users want all customers to be included in the query result, regardless of whether they have orders. This is when an outer join is necessary.

Establish an Outer Join

To establish an outer join, you must modify the join between the tables included in the query:

1. Double-click the line joining the tables in the query grid.

2. The Join Properties window appears (see Figure 12.25). Select the type of join you want to create. To create an outer join between the tables, select Option 2 or Option 3. Notice in Figure 12.25 that the description is Include All Records from Orders and Only Those Records from Order Details Where the Joined Fields Are Equal.

FIGURE 12.25

Establishing a left outer join.

3. Click OK to accept the join. An outer join should be established between the tables. Notice that the line joining the two tables now has an arrow pointing to the many side of the join.

The SQL statement produced when this change is made looks like this:

```
SELECT Customers.CustomerID, Customers.CompanyName

FROM Customers

LEFT JOIN Orders ON Customers.CustomerID = Orders.CustomerID;
```

You can use an outer join to identify all the records on the one side of a join that don't have any corresponding records on the many side. To do this, simply enter `Is Null` as the criteria for any required field on the many side of the join. A common solution is to place the criteria on the foreign key field. In the query shown in Figure 12.26, only customers without orders are displayed in the query result.

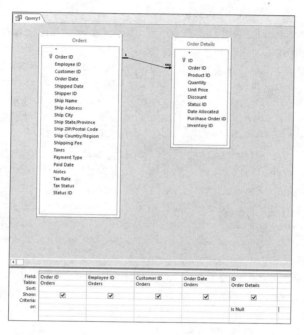

FIGURE 12.26

A query showing orders without order details.

THE ABSOLUTE MINIMUM

Congratulations! You have just successfully completed the chapter on Advanced Query Techniques. You now know much of what there is to know about queries. It's time to put it all to practice.

The ability to add calculated fields to the queries that you build gives you an immense amount of flexibility and power. As you can see, there is no need to store the product of the price and quantity in a table. Actually, you wouldn't want to do so because you would worry about updating the product each time that someone updates the contents of the price or the quantity field. Instead, you include the product in your query result. You can treat that product like a field in subsequent queries, and on forms and reports.

If a calculation seems daunting to build, you can elicit the help of the expression builder. This powerful tool enables you to build the expressions in your query graphically.

Parameters enable you to add further flexibility into the queries that you build. Using parameter queries, you can allow the person running the query to enter criteria values as the query runs. This means, for example, if your query requires a date range for the order date, you can provide dialog boxes for the person running the query to enter the start and end dates dynamically.

Four types of Action queries exist: Update, Delete, Insert, and Make Table. Each of these types of queries serves an important purpose. They all provide a great way to affect your table data in an automated fashion.

Totals queries enable you to summarize your table data. Using a Totals query, you can quickly and easily find the minimum, maximum, average, total, count, and the result of other aggregate functions. Where this becomes particularly powerful is when you aggregate the result of a calculated field. For example, you can find the total of the price times the quantity by city and state!

The concept of outer joins is difficult for many people to understand. Just remember that with the default join type, an inner join, you get only customers who have orders in the query result. When you change to an outer join, you can view customers whether they have orders. You then learned an added twist where you saw how to retrieve only customers who do not have orders.

Armed with the knowledge you attained in this chapter, you should efficiently and effectively use the data entered into the tables in the databases that you build. With practice, the techniques covered in the chapter will become second nature!

13

IN THIS CHAPTER

- What are form controls and how do I work with them?
- What is conditional formatting, and how do I use it?
- What form properties are available, and why are they useful?
- What control properties are available, and why are they important?

BUILDING POWERFUL FORMS

Forms enable you to display the information stored in your database. In Chapter 5, "Using Forms to Display and Modify Information," you learned the basics to work with forms. Here you expand on your knowledge. You begin by working with controls. You then learn about conditional formatting where Access displays data in a control differently depending on the value associated with the control. Finally, you cover how to customize the behavior of both forms and controls using form and control properties.

Power Control Techniques

To work with a form effectively, you must first learn how to manipulate its controls. A *control* is an object that you add to a form or report. Types of controls include text boxes, combo boxes, list boxes, and check boxes.

The following sections cover the processes to add controls to a form, and then select, move, size, delete, and align those controls. The text also includes the process to change control properties and change the tab order of the controls on a form.

Add Fields to a Form

You can use the Field List window to easily add controls to a form. The Field List window contains all the fields that are part of the form's record source. The *record source* for a form is the table, query, or embedded Structured Query Language (SQL) statement that produces the data for the form. For example, in Figure 13.1, the form's record source is the Customers table. The fields listed in the Field List window are the fields that make up the Customers table. To add controls to a form, you drag and drop fields from the Field List onto the form. Each field becomes a control on the form with the control type appropriate for that field. For example, whereas a Text field appears as a text box, a

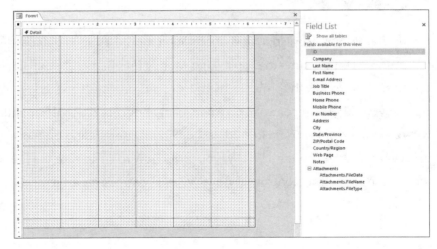

FIGURE 13.1

A form based on the Customers table.

Yes/No field appears as a check box. Follow these two steps to add a control to your form:

1. Build a form in Design view with the Customers table as the record source.

2. Make sure the Field List window is visible. If it isn't, click the Add Existing Fields button in the Tools group on the Design tab on the Ribbon.

3. Locate the field you want to add to the form; then click and drag the field from the field list to the place on the form where you want it to appear. The location you select becomes the upper-left corner of the text box, and the attached label appears to the left of where you dropped the control.

Add Multiple Fields to a Form at the Same Time

To add multiple fields to a form at the same time, complete the following steps:

1. Select several fields from the field list.

2. Hold down the Ctrl key to select noncontiguous (not together) fields or the Shift key to select contiguous (together) fields. For example, if you hold down the Ctrl key and click three noncontiguous fields, each of these three fields is selected. If you click a field, hold down the Shift key, and click another field, all fields between the two selected fields are selected. If you want to select all the fields in a list, double-click the field list title bar, and then click and drag any one of the selected fields to the form; all the fields are then added to the form simultaneously.

Selecting, Moving, Aligning, and Sizing Form Objects

You must know several important tricks of the trade to select, move, align, and size form objects. These tips can save you hours of frustration and wasted time.

Selecting Form Objects

The easiest way to select a single object on a form is to click it. After you have selected the object, you can move it, size it, or change any of its properties. Selecting multiple objects is a bit trickier, but you can accomplish it in several ways. Different methods are more efficient in different situations.

You must understand which objects you've actually selected. Figure 13.2 shows a form with four selected objects. The ID text box, the Company label, and the Address label and Address text box are all selected; however, the Customer ID label and CompanyName text box aren't selected. If you look closely at the figure, you can see that the selected objects are completely surrounded by selection handles. The ID label and Company text box each has just a single

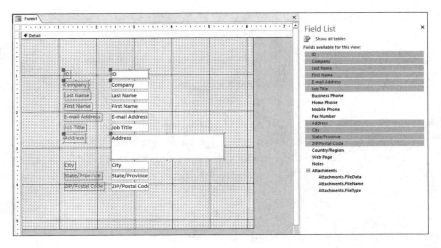

FIGURE 13.2

Selecting objects on a form.

selection handle because each is attached to an object that is selected. If you changed any properties of the selected objects, the ID label and Company text box would be unaffected.

One way to select multiple objects is to hold down the Shift key and click each object you want to select. Access surrounds each selected object with selection handles, indicating that you have selected it.

You can also select objects by lassoing them. Objects to be lassoed must be adjacent to one another on the form. To lasso objects, you place the mouse pointer on a blank area of the form (that is, not over any objects) and then click and drag the mouse pointer around the objects you want to select. You can see a thin line around the objects the mouse pointer is encircling. When you let go of the mouse button, any objects that were within the lasso, including those only partially surrounded, are selected. If you want to deselect any of the selected objects to exclude them, you hold down the Shift key and click the objects you want to deselect.

One of my favorite ways to select multiple objects is to use the horizontal and vertical rulers that appear at the edges of the Form Design window. You click and drag within the ruler, and as you do this, two horizontal lines appear, indicating which objects are selected. As you click and drag across the horizontal ruler, two vertical lines appear, indicating the selection area. When you let go of the mouse button, any objects within the lines are selected. As with the process of lassoing, to remove any objects from the selection, you hold down the Shift key and click the objects you want to deselect.

TIP You can use the Ctrl+A keystroke combination to select all controls on a form. After you select them, you can move them, size them, or change any of their other properties as a unit.

Moving Things Around

To move a single control with its attached label, you don't need to select it first. You place the mouse over the object and click and drag. An outline appears, indicating the object's new location. When the object reaches the position you want, you release the mouse. The attached label automatically moves with its corresponding control.

To move more than one object at a time, you must first select the objects you want to move. You select the objects by using one of the methods outlined in the previous section. When you place the mouse over any of the selected objects and click and drag, an outline appears, indicating the proposed new position for the objects. You release the mouse when you have reached the position you want for the objects.

Sometimes you want to move a control independently of its attached label, and this requires a special technique. If you click a control, such as a text box, as you move the mouse over the border of the control, a hand icon with five fingers pointing upward appears. If you click and drag, both the control and the attached label move as a unit, and the relationship between them is maintained. Figure 13.3 shows the label and text box before they've been moved as a unit.

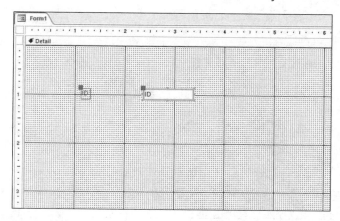

FIGURE 13.3

Objects before moving.

Figure 13.4 shows them after they've been moved as a unit. If you place the mouse pointer over the larger handle in the upper-left corner of the object, the mouse pointer appears as a hand with only the index finger pointing upward. If you click and drag here, the control moves independently of its attached label, and the relationship between the objects changes. Figure 13.5 depicts objects after they've been moved independently.

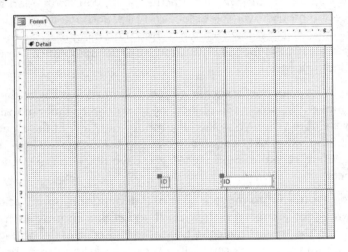

FIGURE 13.4

Objects after moving as a unit.

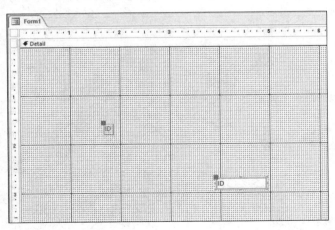

FIGURE 13.5

Objects after moving independently.

Aligning Objects to One Another

Access makes it easy to align objects. Figure 13.6 shows several objects that aren't aligned. Notice that the attached labels of three of the objects are selected. If you align the attached labels, the controls (in this case, text boxes) remain in their original positions. If you also select the text boxes, the text boxes try to align with the attached labels. Because Access doesn't allow the

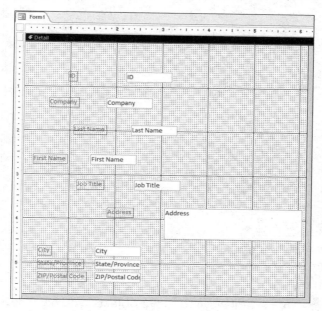

FIGURE 13.6

A form before objects are aligned.

objects to overlap, the text boxes end up immediately next to their attached labels. To left-align any objects (even objects of different types), you select the objects you want to align and then choose Left from the Align drop-down in the Sizing & Ordering group on the Arrange tab on the Ribbon. Access aligns the selected objects (see Figure 13.7). You can align the left, right, top, or bottom edges of any objects on a form.

 NOTE You shouldn't confuse the Align feature on the Arrange tab on the Ribbon with the Align tools (that is, Align Left, Center, and Align Right) on the Home tab on the Ribbon. Whereas the Align feature on the Arrange tab of the Ribbon aligns objects one to the other, the Align tools on the Home tab on the Ribbon justify the text inside an object.

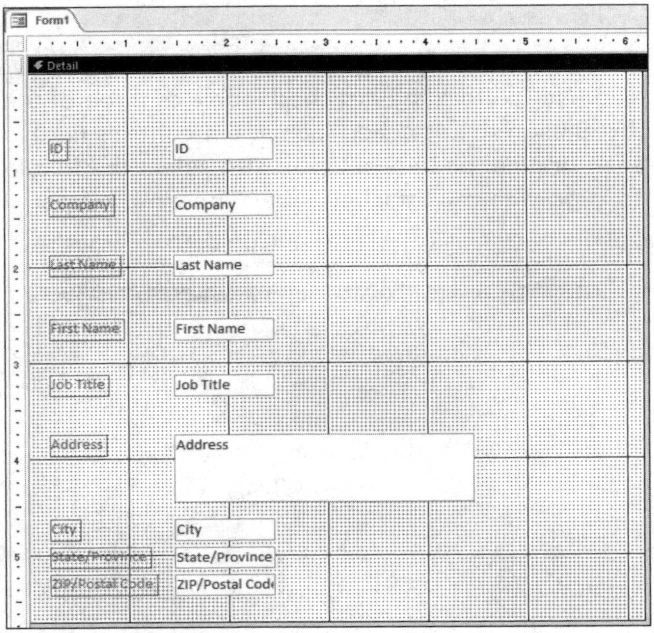

FIGURE 13.7

A form after objects are aligned.

Sizing Your Controls

Just as there are several ways to move objects, you have several options for sizing objects. When you select an object, you can use each handle, except for the handle in the upper-left corner of the object, to size the object. The handles at the top and bottom of the object enable you to change the object's height, and the handles at the left and right of the object enable you to change the object's width. You can use the handles in the upper-right, lower-right, and lower-left corners of the object to change the width and height of the object simultaneously. To size an object, you place the mouse pointer over a sizing handle, click, and drag. You can select several objects and size them all simultaneously. Each of the selected objects increases or decreases in size by the same percentage; their relative sizes stay intact. You use the upper-left handle to move an object independent of its attached label. This means, for example, that you can place the label associated with a text box above the text box, rather than to its left.

Access offers several powerful methods to size multiple objects, which you access by selecting Size/Space from the Sizing & Ordering group on the Arrange tab on the Ribbon:

- **To Fit**—Sizes the selected objects to fit the text within them

- **To Grid**—Sizes the selected objects to the nearest gridlines

- **To Tallest**—Sizes the selected objects to the height of the tallest object in the selection

- **To Shortest**—Sizes the selected objects to the height of the shortest object in the selection

- **To Widest**—Sizes the selected objects to the width of the widest object in the selection

- **To Narrowest**—Sizes the selected objects to the width of the narrowest object in the selection

Probably the most confusing of the options is To Fit. This option is somewhat deceiving because it doesn't perfectly size text boxes to the text within them. In today's world of proportional fonts, it isn't possible to perfectly size a text box to the largest possible entry it contains. Generally, however, you can visually size text boxes to a sensible height and width. You use a field's Size property to limit what's typed in the text box. If the entry is too large to fit in the allocated space, the user can scroll to view the additional text. As the following tip indicates, the To Fit option is much more appropriate for labels than it is for text boxes.

Controlling Object Spacing

Access provides excellent tools for spacing the objects on a form an equal distance from one another. Notice in Figure 13.8 that the ID, Company, Address, and City text boxes aren't equally spaced vertically from one another. To make the vertical distance between selected objects equal, you choose Equal Vertical from the Size/Space drop-down in the Arrange tab on the Ribbon. In Figure 13.9, you can see the result of using this command on the selected objects.

You can make the horizontal distance between objects equal by choosing Equal Horizontal from the Size/Space drop-down. Other related commands on the same drop-down are Increase Vertical (or Decrease) and Increase Horizontal (or Decrease). These commands maintain the relationships between objects while proportionally increasing or decreasing the distances between them.

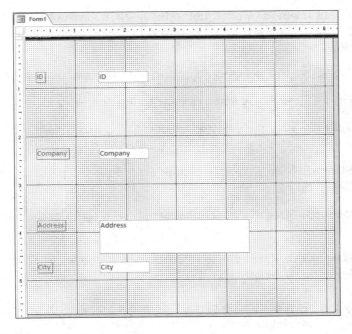

FIGURE 13.8

A form before vertical spacing is modified.

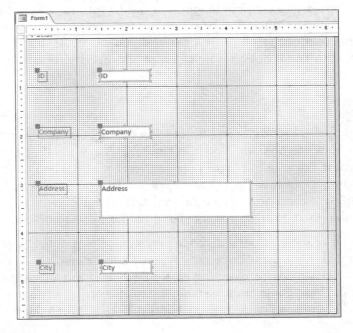

FIGURE 13.9

A form after vertical spacing is modified.

TIP To quickly size a label to fit the text within it, you can select the label and then double-click any of its sizing handles, except the sizing handle in the upper-left corner of the label.

Modifying Object Tab Order

Access bases the tab order for the objects on a form on the order in which you add the objects to the form. However, this order isn't necessarily appropriate for the user. You might need to modify the tab order of the objects on a form. To do so, you select Tab Order from the Tools group on the Design tab on the Ribbon. The Tab Order dialog box, as shown in Figure 13.10, appears. This dialog box offers two options. First, you can click the Auto Order button to tell Access to set the tab order based on each object's location in a section on the form. Second, if you want to customize the order of the objects, you click and drag the gray buttons to the left of the object names listed under the Custom Order heading to specify the objects' tab order.

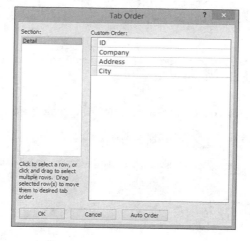

FIGURE 13.10

The Tab Order dialog box, where you select the tab order of the objects in each section of a form.

Conditional Formatting

With conditional formatting, data meeting specified criteria displays differently than does data meeting other criteria. For example, you can use conditional formatting to display sales higher than a certain amount in one color and sales lower than that amount in another color.

Conditionally Format Data

To conditionally format data displayed within a control, follow these steps:

1. Select the control you want to conditionally format.

2. Select Conditional Formatting from the Control Formatting group on the Format tab on the Ribbon. The Conditional Formatting Rules Manager dialog box appears (see Figure 13.11).

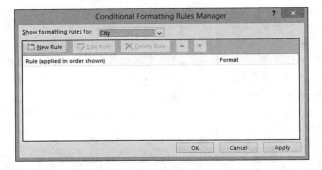

FIGURE 13.11

The Conditional Formatting dialog enables you to display data in a control differently based on a specific condition.

3. Click New Rule. The New Formatting Rule dialog appears (see Figure 13.12).

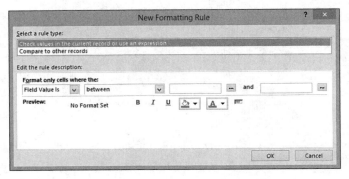

FIGURE 13.12

The New Formatting Rule dialog enables you to designate the specifics for a formatting rule.

4. Select Check Values in the Current Record or Use Expression.

5. Select Field Value Is, Expression Is, or Field Has Focus from the first combo box in the Formatting dialog box. Select Field Value Is when you want to select from a predefined set of operators such as between, not between, equal to, and so

on. Select Expression when you want to build your own conditional expression that Access will evaluate at runtime. Finally, select Field Has Focus if you want Access to apply the conditional format only when that field has the focus.

   6. Select the appropriate operator from the second combo box in the dialog box.

   7. Enter the values you are testing for in the text boxes that appear on the right of the dialog box.

   8. Select the special formatting (bold, italic, background color, and so on) that you want to apply when the conditional criteria are met.

   9. Click OK to return to the Conditional Formatting Rules Manager.

Form Properties and Why Should You Use Them

Forms have many properties that you can use to affect their look and behavior. The properties are broken down into categories: Format, Data, Event, and Other.

To view a form's properties, you must first select the form. To do that, click the form selector (the small gray button at the intersection of the horizontal and vertical rulers).

You must understand how to work with form properties. The following sections begin by focusing on the Properties window. They then hone in on a discussion of some of the important form properties.

Working with the Properties Window

After you select a form, you can click the Properties button on the toolbar to view its properties. The Properties window, as shown in Figure 13.13, consists of five tabs: Format, Data, Event, Other, and All. Many developers prefer to view all properties at once on the All tab, but a form can have a total of 115 properties! Instead of viewing all 115 properties at once, you should try viewing the properties by category. The Format category includes all the physical attributes of the form—the ones that affect the form's appearance, such as background color. The Data category includes all the properties of the data that the form is bound to, such as the form's underlying record source. The Event category contains all the Windows events to which a form can respond. For example, you can write code that executes in response to the form being loaded, becoming active, displaying a different record, and so on. The Other category holds a few properties that don't fit into the other three categories.

FIGURE 13.13

Viewing the Format properties of a form.

Working with the Important Form Properties

As mentioned in the preceding section, a form has 115 properties. Of those 115 properties, 52 are Event properties, and they are covered in most books focused on Access programming. The following sections cover the Format, Data, and Other properties of forms.

The Format Properties of a Form

The Format properties of a form affect its physical appearance. A form has 37 Format properties. The most important ones are described in the following sections.

The Caption Property

The Caption property sets the text that appears on the form's title bar.

The Default View Property

The Default View property enables you to select from five available options:

- **Single Form**—Enables only one record to be viewed at a time

- **Continuous Forms**—Displays as many records as will fit within the form window at one time, presenting each as the detail section of a single form
- **Datasheet**—Displays the records in a spreadsheet-like format, with the rows representing records and the columns representing fields
- **PivotTable**—Displays the records in a Microsoft Excel-type pivot table format
- **PivotChart**—Displays the records in a Microsoft Excel-type pivot chart format

The selected option becomes the default view for the form.

The `Scroll Bars` Property

The `Scroll Bars` property determines whether scrollbars appear if the controls on a form don't fit within the form's display area. You can select from both vertical and horizontal scrollbars, neither vertical nor horizontal scrollbars, just vertical scrollbars, or just horizontal scrollbars.

The `Record Selectors` Property

A record selector is the gray bar to the left of a record in Form view, or the gray box to the left of each record in Datasheet view. It's used to select a record to be copied or deleted. The `Record Selectors` property determines whether the record selectors appear. If you give the user a custom menu, you can opt to remove the record selector to make sure the user copies or deletes records using only the features specifically built into the application.

The `Navigation Buttons` Property

Navigation buttons are the controls that appear at the bottom of a form; they allow the user to move from record to record within a form. The `Navigation Buttons` property determines whether the navigation buttons are visible. You should set it to No for any dialog box forms, and you might want to set it to No for data-entry forms, too, and add your own toolbar or command buttons to enhance or limit the functionality of the standard buttons. For example, in a client/server environment, you might not want to give users the ability to move to the first or last record because that type of record movement can be inefficient in a client/server architecture.

The `Dividing Lines` Property

The `Dividing Lines` property indicates whether you want a line to appear between records when the default view of the form is set to `Continuous Forms`. It also determines whether Access places dividing lines between the form's sections (that is, header, detail, and footer).

The `Auto Resize` Property

The `Auto Resize` property determines whether Access automatically sizes a form to display a complete record.

The `Auto Center` Property

The `Auto Center` property specifies whether a form should automatically be centered within the Application window whenever it's opened.

The `Border Style` Property

The `Border Style` property is far more powerful than its name implies. The options for the `Border Style` property are None, Thin, Sizable, and Dialog. The `Border Style` property is often set to None for splash screens, in which case the form has no border. When the `Border Style` property is set to Thin, the border is not resizable and the Size command isn't available in the Control menu. This setting is a good choice for pop-up forms, which remain on top even when other forms are given the focus. The Sizable setting is standard for most forms; it includes all the standard options in the Control menu. The Dialog setting creates a border that looks like the border created by the Thin setting. A form with the `Border Style` property set to Dialog can't be maximized, minimized, or resized; when the border style of a form is set to Dialog, the Maximize, Minimize, and Resize options aren't available in the form's Control menu. The Dialog setting is often used along with the `Pop Up` and `Modal` properties to create custom dialog boxes.

The `Close Button` Property

The `Close Button` property determines whether the user can close the form by using the Control menu or double-clicking the Control icon. If you set the value of this property to No, you must give the user another way to close the form; otherwise, the user might have to reboot his or her computer to close the application.

The `SubdatasheetHeight` Property

The `SubdatasheetHeight` property is used to designate the maximum height for a subdatasheet.

The `SubdatasheetExpanded` Property

The `SubdatasheetExpanded` property enables you to designate whether a subdatasheet is initially displayed in an expanded format. When this property is set to False, the subdatasheet appears collapsed. When it is set to True, the subdatasheet appears in expanded format.

The *Moveable* Property

The `Moveable` property determines whether the user can move the form window around the screen by clicking and dragging the form by its title bar.

The `Data` Properties of a Form

You use the `Data` properties of a form to control the source for the form's data, what sort of actions the user can take on the data in the form, and how the data in the form is locked in a multiuser environment. A form has 14 `Data` properties (several of which we cover here).

The *Record Source* Property

The `Record Source` property indicates the table, stored query, or SQL statement on which the form's records are based. After you have selected a record source for a form, the controls on the form can be bound to the fields in the record source.

 NOTE The Field List window is unavailable until you have set the Record Source property of the form.

The *Filter* Property

Use the `Filter` property to automatically load a stored filter along with the form. You might prefer to base a form on a query that limits the data displayed on the form. You can pass the query parameters at runtime to customize exactly what data Access displays.

The *Order By* Property

The `Order By` property specifies in what order the records on a form appear. You can modify this property at runtime.

The *Allow_Filters* Property

The `Allow_Filters` property controls whether you can filter records at runtime. When this option is set to No, all filtering options become disabled to the user.

The *Allow Edits*, *Allow Deletions*, and *Allow Additions* Properties

The `Allow Edits`, `Allow Deletions`, and `Allow Additions` properties let you specify whether the user can edit data, delete records, or add records from within a form. These options can't override any permissions that you have set for the form's underlying table or queries

The Data Entry Property

The Data Entry property determines whether users can add only records within a form. You should set this property to Yes if you don't want users to view or modify existing records but want them to add new records.

The Other Properties of a Form

Format properties affect the appearance of a form. Data properties affect the data underlying a form. This section focuses on the Other properties of a form. As you'll see, although these properties don't fit neatly into the Format and Data categories, they are extremely robust and powerful properties. The most commonly used properties are covered here.

- Pop Up—The Pop Up property indicates whether a form always remains on top of other windows. You often set this property, along with the Modal property (discussed next), to Yes when creating custom dialog boxes.

- Modal—The Modal property indicates whether the user can remove focus from a form while it's open. When the Modal property is set to Yes, the user must close the form before he or she can continue working with the application. As mentioned earlier, this property is used with the Pop Up property to create custom dialog boxes.

- Cycle—The Cycle property controls the behavior of the Tab key in a form. The settings are All Records, Current Record, and Current Page. When you set the Cycle property to All Records, users move to the next record on a form when they presses Tab from the last control on the previous record. When the property is set to Current Record, users move from the last control on a form to the first control on the same record. The Current Page option refers only to multipage forms; when you set the Cycle property to Current Page, users tab from the last control on the page to the first control on the same page. All three options are affected by the tab order of the objects on the form.

- Tag—The Tag property is used to store miscellaneous information about a form. This property is often set and monitored at runtime to store necessary information about a form. You could use the Tag property to add a tag to each of several forms that should be unloaded as a group.

- Allow Design Changes—The Allow Design Changes property determines whether changes can be made to the design of a form while you're viewing form data. If this property is set to All Views, the Properties window is available in Form view, and changes made to form properties while you're in Form view are permanent if the form is saved.

Control Properties and Why to Use Them

Available control properties vary quite a bit, depending on the type of control. The following sections cover the most common properties. To view the properties of a control, select the control, and then open the Properties window.

The Format Properties of a Control

The Format properties of a control affect the appearance of the control. You use these properties to change the color, size, font, and other physical attributes of the control. To view the Format properties of a control, with the control already selected, and the Properties window open, click the Format tab (see Figure 13.14). The text that follows discusses many of these properties and their uses.

FIGURE 13.14

The Format properties of a control.

- Format—The Format property of a control determines how Access displays the data in the control. A control's format is automatically inherited from its underlying data source. Access enables you to use this property in three situations: when the Format property is not set for the underlying field, when you want to override the existing Format setting for the field, and when you want to apply a format to an unbound control. You can select from a multitude of predefined values for a control's format, or you can create a custom format. The author often modifies the Format property at runtime to vary the format of a control, depending on a certain condition. For example, the format for a Visa card number is different from the format for an ATM card number.

- Decimal Places—The Decimal Places property specifies how many decimal places you want to appear in the control. This property is used with the Format property to determine the control's appearance.

- Caption—You use the Caption property to specify information that is helpful to the user. It's available for labels, command buttons, and toggle buttons.

- Visible—The Visible property indicates whether a control is visible. This property can be toggled at runtime, depending on specific circumstances. For example, a question on the form might apply only to records in which the gender is set to Female; if the gender is set to Male, the question isn't visible.

- Display When—The Display When property is used when you want certain controls on a form to be sent only to the screen or only to the printer. The three settings for this property are Always, Print Only, and Screen Only. An example of the use of the Display When property is for a label containing instructions. You can use the Display When property to have the instructions appear onscreen but not on the printout.

- Scroll Bars—The Scroll Bars property determines whether scrollbars appear when the data in a control doesn't fit within the control's size. The options are None and Vertical. The author often sets the Scroll Bars property to Vertical when the control is used to display data from a memo field. The scrollbar makes it easier for the user to work with a potentially large volume of data in the memo field.

- Back Style and Back Color—You can set the Back Style property to Normal or Transparent. When this property is set to Transparent, the form's background color shows through the control. This is often the preferred setting for an option group. The control's Back Color property specifies the background color (as opposed to text color) for the control.

 NOTE If the Back Style property of a control is set to Transparent, the control's Back Color property is ignored.

- Special Effect—The Special Effect property adds 3D effects to a control. The settings for this property are Flat, Raised, Sunken, Etched, Shadowed, and Chiseled. Each of these effects gives a control a different look.

- Border Style, Border Color, and Border Width—The Border Style, Border Color, and Border Width properties affect the look, color, and thickness of a control's border. The settings for the `Border Style` property are Transparent, Solid, Dashes, Short Dashes, Dots, Sparse Dots, Dash Dot, and Dash Dot Dot. The `Border Color` property specifies the color of the border; you can select from a variety of colors. The `Border Width` property can be set to one of several point sizes.

- `Fore Color, Font Name, Font Size, Font Weight, Font Italic, and Font Underline`—The `Fore Color`, `Font Name`, `Font Size`, `Font Weight`, `Font Italic`, and `Font Underline` properties control the appearance of the text in a control. As their names imply, they let you select a color, font, size, and thickness of the text and determine whether the text is italicized or underlined. You can modify these properties in response to a runtime event. For example, you can modify a control's text color if the value in that control exceeds a certain amount. The `Font Weight` property settings generally exceed what is actually available for a particular font and printer—normally, you have a choice of only Regular and Bold in whatever value you select for this property.

NOTE If the Border Style property of a control is set to Transparent, Access ignores the control's Border Color and Border Width properties.

- `Text Align`—The `Text Align` property is often confused with the ability to align controls, but the `Text Align` property affects how the data is aligned *within* a control.

- `Left Margin, Top Margin, Right Margin, and Bottom Margin`—The `Left Margin`, `Top Margin`, `Right Margin`, and `Bottom Margin` properties determine how far the text appears from the left, top, right, and bottom of the control. They are particularly useful with controls such as text boxes based on memo fields, which are generally large controls.

- `Line Spacing`—The `Line Spacing` property is used to determine the spacing between lines of text in a multiline control. This property is most commonly used with text boxes based on memo fields.

Notice Figure 13.15. This TextBox control uses many of the Format properties that you just learned about. The `Scroll Bars` property is set to Vertical so that the control appears with a vertical scroll bar. The `Back Color` property is modified. The `Border Style` is set to Solid, its color modified, and it is now *very* wide. The font is modified and enlarged, with extra bold and italic. Finally, text is aligned so that it is centered within the control. You can see all these changes graphically, as well as the properties that affect the control.

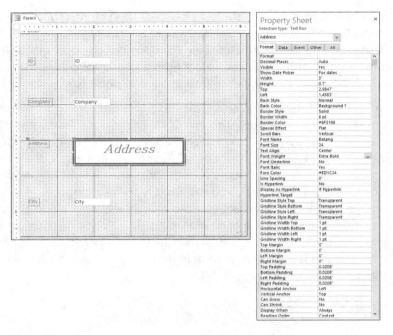

FIGURE 13.15

A TextBox control using many of the Format properties.

The Data Properties of a Control

Whereas `Format` properties affect the appearance of the control, `Data` properties affect the data that displays in the control. In this section, you explore the various `Data` properties. You cover everything from the `Control Source` property that determines what data displays in the control, to the `Input Mask` property that determines what data the user can enter into each character of the control. As you'll see, there's a rich list of `Data` properties for a control. They appear in Figure 13.16, and many are described in the text that follows. To access the data properties of a control, select the control, open the Property Sheet, and click to select the Data tab.

- `Control Source`—The `Control Source` property specifies the field from the record source that's associated with a particular control. The `Control Source` property can also be set to any valid Access expression.

- `Input Mask`—Whereas the `Format` and `Decimal Places` properties affect the appearance of a control, the `Input Mask` property affects what data the user can enter into the control. The input mask of the field underlying the control is automatically inherited into the control. If no input mask is entered as a field property, the input mask can be entered directly in the form. If you entered the

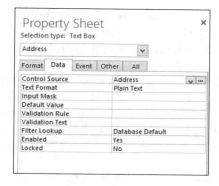

FIGURE 13.16

The Data properties of a control.

input mask for the field, you can use the input mask of the associated control on a form to further restrict what the user enters into that field via the form. If you select the Input Mask property and click the Build button, the Input Mask Wizard appears (see Figure 13.17).

FIGURE 13.17

The Input Mask Wizard.

- Default Value—The Default Value property of a control determines the value assigned to new records entered in a form. You can set this property within the field properties of the underlying table. A default value set at the field level of the table is automatically inherited into the form. The default value set for the control overrides the default value set at the field level of the table.

- Validation Rule and Validation Text—The Validation Rule and Validation Text properties of a control perform the same functions as they do for a field. This means that the Validation Rule enables you to validate the data that users enter into the control, and the `Validation Text` enables you to supply users with the error message that appears when they enter a value that violates the validation rule.

 NOTE Because a validation rule is enforced at the database engine level, the validation rule set for a control can't be in conflict with the validation rule set for the field to which the control is bound. If the two rules conflict, the user can't enter data into the control.

- `Enabled`—The `Enabled` property determines whether you allow a control to get the focus. If this property is set to No, the control appears dimmed.

- `Locked`—The `Locked` property determines whether the user can modify the data in a control. When the `Locked` property is set to Yes, the control can get the focus but can't be edited. The `Enabled` and `Locked` properties of a control interact with one another. Table 13.1 summarizes their interactions. Where you see the Enabled column equal to Yes in the table, that means that the `Enabled` property is set to Yes. Where you see `Locked` property equal to Yes in the table, that means that the `Locked` property is set to Yes. The third column shows the effect of the combination of those two property settings. For example, if you set `Enabled` to Yes and `Locked` to Yes, the control can get the focus and its data can be copied but not modified.

- `Filter Lookup`—The `Filter Lookup` property indicates whether you want the values associated with a bound text box to appear in the Filter by Form window.

TABLE 13.1 How `Enabled` and `Locked` Properties Interact

Enabled	Locked	Effect
Yes	Yes	The control can get the focus; its data can be copied but not modified.
Yes	No	The control can get the focus, and its data can be edited.
No	Yes	The control can't get the focus.
No	No	The control can't get the focus; its data appears dimmed.

Take a look at the example in Figure 13.18. The text box control has its `Control Source` property set to State/Province, indicating that it is bound to the Region field in the underlying data source. Its `Default Value` property is CA. This means that when the user adds a new record, the Region field defaults to CA. The `Validation`

Rule property connotes that the Region must be CA, UT, AZ, NJ, or NY. The `Validation Text` property provides the error message the user will receive if the user violates the validation rule.

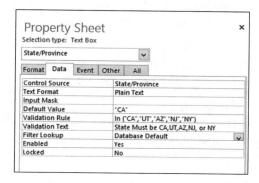

FIGURE 13.18

The `Display Control` property, on the Lookup tab of the Table Design window.

The Other Properties of a Control

The Other properties of a control are properties that did not fit neatly into any other category. This does not mean that they are unimportant. Actually, you can find some of the most important and useful control properties under the Other properties of a control. To access these properties, select the control, invoke the Properties window, and then click the Other tab of the Properties window (see Figure 13.19 where I am viewing the Other properties of the State/Province control). Now take a look.

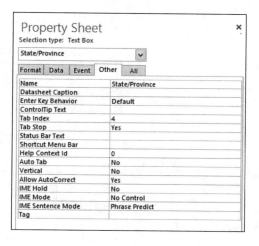

FIGURE 13.19

The Other properties of the State/Province control.

- Name—The Name property enables you to name a control. You use the name that is set in this property when you refer to the control in code, and this name is also displayed in various drop-down lists that show all the controls on a form. Name controls because named controls improve the readability of code and make working with Access forms and other objects easier.

- Status Bar Text—The Status Bar Text property specifies the text that appears in the status bar when a control gets focus. The setting of this property overrides the Description property that you can set in a table's design.

- Enter Key Behavior—The Enter Key Behavior property determines whether the Enter key causes the cursor to move to the next control or to add a new line in the current control. You will often change the setting of this property for text boxes that you use to display the contents of memo fields.

- Allow AutoCorrect—The Allow AutoCorrect property specifies whether the AutoCorrect feature is available in a control. The AutoCorrect feature automatically corrects common spelling errors and typos.

- Vertical—The Vertical property is used to control whether the text in a control is displayed horizontally or vertically. The default setting is No, or horizontal. When you select Yes (vertical display), Access rotates the text in the control 90 degrees (see Figure 13.20).

- Auto Tab—When the Auto Tab property is set to Yes, the cursor automatically advances to the next control when the user enters the last character of an input mask. Some users like this option, and others find it annoying, especially if they must tab out of some fields but not others.

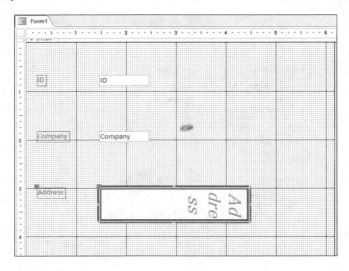

FIGURE 13.20

The Address text box with the Vertical property set to Yes.

- `Default`—The `Default` property applies to a command button or to an ActiveX control and specifies whether the control is the default button on a form.

- `Cancel`—The `Cancel` property applies to a command button or to an ActiveX control. It indicates that you want the control's code to execute when the user presses the Esc key while the form is active.

- `Status Bar Text`—The `Status Bar Text` property specifies the message that appears in the status bar when a control has the focus.

- `Tab Stop`—The `Tab Stop` property determines whether the user can use the Tab key to enter a control. It's appropriate to set this property to No for controls whose values rarely get modified. The user can opt to click in the control when necessary.

- `Tab Index`—The `Tab Index` property sets the tab order for a control. The author generally sets the `Tab Index` property by using the Tab Order button found in the Tools group on the Design tab of the Ribbon rather than by setting the value directly in the control's `Tab Index` property. This enables you to set the tab order graphically, which is more intuitive and easier, and saves a lot of time.

- `ControlTip Text`—The `ControlTip Text` property specifies the ToolTip associated with a control. The ToolTip automatically appears when the user places the mouse pointer over the control and leaves it there for a moment.

- `Tag`—The `Tag` property is used to store information about a control. Your imagination determines how you use this property. The `Tag` property can be read and modified at runtime.

THE ABSOLUTE MINIMUM

The first step to build a custom Access form is generally adding controls to the form. There are lots of tricks and tips that you should know when accomplishing this task. For example, there are many ways to select objects. This chapter covers the various methods you can use to select objects. Knowing when each one is appropriate and best to use is a matter of experience. You need to experiment with each method until you become comfortable with all of them.

There are also many tips and tricks that you should know when aligning, and sizing objects, as well as controlling the spacing between them. After reading this chapter, you are aware of what is available. Again, when to use each technique to your advantage is a matter of experience.

Conditional formatting is one of the more powerful aspects of Access. Using conditional formatting, you can highlight important data. For example, if your form displays sales amounts, you can color-code the display of the data to display sales amounts in various ranges in different colors.

After you learn the basics to work with form controls, it is a good idea to learn about form properties. Form properties enable you to add professional touches to the forms that you build and to control important aspects of the data behind those forms. You learned about Format properties of a form. Format properties affect the appearance of the forms that you build. You then learned about Data properties. The Data properties enable you to filter and order the data behind a form, as well as to control whether the data in the form can be edited or deleted and whether you can insert table data. The Other properties of a form do not fit neatly into any other category. They enable you to affect other aspects of the behavior of the form such as what happens when the user taps the Tab key when on the last control on a form.

You completed the chapter with a discussion of control properties. Whereas Form properties affect the entire form, Control properties affect individual controls on the form. Like form properties, control properties are divided into Format properties, Data properties, and Other properties. Format properties affect the look and appearance of the controls. Using Format properties, you can do everything from hide a control to determine whether it contains scrollbars. Like the Data properties of a form, the Data properties of a control all relate to the data underlying the control. The most important property is the Control Source property. You use the Control Source property to indicate what data you want to associate with the control. Finally, the Other properties of a control are those properties that don't fit neatly into any other category.

You should be fairly comfortable building your own forms. In Chapter 14, "Advanced Form Techniques," you take your knowledge to an advanced level.

14

ADVANCED FORM TECHNIQUES

After reading Chapter 5, "Using Forms to Display and Modify Information," and Chapter 13, "Building Powerful Forms," you should be comfortable working with forms. Here you take your knowledge to the next level. To begin, you learn how to work with combo boxes and list boxes. Then you learn how to generate macros with the Command Button Wizard. Finally, you learn how to build forms based on data stored in more than one table.

Working with Combo Boxes

Combo boxes enable users to select from a list of appropriate choices. Access offers several easy ways to add a combo box to a form. If you have set a field's `Display Control` property to Combo Box, Access adds a combo box to a form when you add the field to the form. The combo box automatically knows the source of its data and all its other important properties.

If a field's `Display Control` property hasn't been set to Combo Box, the easiest way to add a combo box to a form is to use the Control Wizards tool. The Control Wizards tool helps you add combo boxes, list boxes, option groups, and subforms to forms. Although you can manually set all the properties set by the Combo Box Wizard, using the wizard saves both time and energy.

If you want Access to launch the Combo Box Wizard when you add a combo box to the form, you need to make sure you click the Control Wizards tool in the toolbox before you add the combo box. Then select the Combo Box tool in the toolbox, and then click and drag to place the combo box on the form. Doing so launches the Combo Box Wizard. As shown in Figure 14.1, the first step of the Combo Box Wizard gives you three choices for the source of the combo box's data. You use the first option if the combo box will select the data that's stored in a field, such as the state associated with a particular customer. I rarely, if ever, use the second option, which requires that you type the values for the combo box. Populating a combo box this way makes it difficult to maintain. Every time you want to add an entry to the combo box, you must modify the application. You use the third option when you want to use the combo box as a tool to search for a specific record. For example, a combo box can be placed in a form's header to display a list of valid customers. After you select a customer, the user is moved to the appropriate record. This option is available only when the form is bound to a record source.

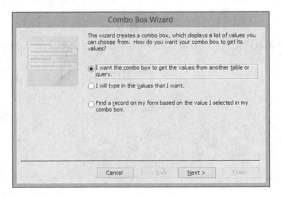

FIGURE 14.1

The first step of the Combo Box Wizard: selecting the source of the data.

If you select to have the combo box look up the values in a table or query, in the second step of the Combo Box Wizard, you select a table or query to populate the combo box and then click Next. In the third step of the wizard (shown in Figure 14.2), you select the fields that appear in the combo box. Use the combo box being built in the example to select the customer associated with the current order. Although the Company field is the only field visible in the combo box, both ID and Company are selected because ID is a necessary element of the combo box. After the user has selected a company name from the combo box, Access stores the ID associated with the company name in the Customer ID field of the Orders table.

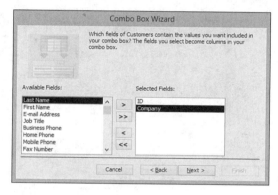

FIGURE 14.2

The third step of the Combo Box Wizard: selecting fields.

The fourth step of the wizard enables you to designate the sort order for the data in the combo box. You can opt to sort on as many as four fields.

The fifth step of the wizard enables you to specify the width of each field in the combo box. Notice in Figure 14.3 that Access recommends that you hide the key

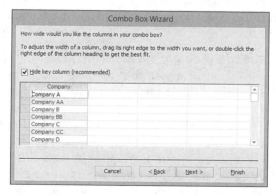

FIGURE 14.3

The fifth step of the Combo Box Wizard: setting column widths.

column ID. The idea is that the user will see the meaningful English description, while Access worries about storing the appropriate key value in the record.

In the wizard's sixth step, you specify whether you want Access to just remember the selected value or store it in a particular field in the table that underlies the form. Figure 14.4 shows that Access will store the selected combo box value in the Customer ID field of the Orders table. The Orders table in this example is the RecordSource of the form.

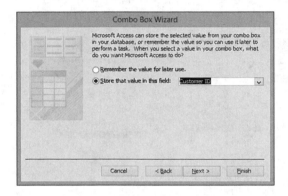

FIGURE 14.4

The sixth step of the Combo Box Wizard: indicating where the selected value will be stored.

The seventh and final step of the Combo Box Wizard prompts for the text that will become the attached label for the combo box. After you click the Finish button, Access completes the process, building the combo box and filling in all its properties with the appropriate values.

Although the Combo Box Wizard is a helpful tool, you must understand the properties it sets. Figure 14.5 shows the Properties window for a combo box. Now take a moment to go over the properties set by the Combo Box Wizard in this example.

The `Control Source` property indicates the field in which the selected entry is stored. In Figure 14.5, you can see that the selected entry will be stored in the Customer ID field of the Orders table. The `Row Source Type` property specifies whether the source used to populate the combo box is a table/query, value list, or field list. In the example, the `Row Source Type` property is set to Table/Query. The `Row Source` property is the name of the actual table or query used to populate the combo box. In the example, the `Row Source` property is a SQL `SELECT` statement that selects the `CustomerID` and `CompanyName` from the Customers table. The `Column Count` property designates how many columns are in the combo box, and the `Column Widths` property indicates the width of each column. In the example, the width of the first column is zero, which renders the column invisible. Finally, the `Bound Column` property specifies which column in the combo box is used to store data in the control source. In the example, this is column 1.

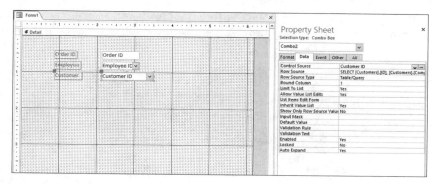

FIGURE 14.5

Properties of a combo box, showing that the Customer ID field has been selected as the control source for the Combo2 combo box.

List Boxes

List boxes are similar to combo boxes, but they differ from them in three major ways:

- They consume more screen space.
- They allow the user to select only from the list that displays. This means the user can't type new values into a list box (as you can with a combo box).
- They can be configured to let the user select multiple items.

If you set the `Display Control` property of a field to List Box, Access adds a list box to the form when the field is clicked and dragged from the field list to the form.

The List Box Wizard is almost identical to the Combo Box Wizard. After you run the List Box Wizard, the list box properties affected by the wizard are the same as the combo box properties.

The Command Button Wizard: Programming Without Typing

With the Command Button Wizard, you can quickly and easily add functionality to forms. The wizard writes the code to perform more than 30 commonly required tasks separated into record navigation, record operations, form operations, report operations, application operations, and other miscellaneous tasks. The Command

Button Wizard is automatically invoked when you add a command button with the Control Wizards tool selected. Here are the steps involved in using the Command Button wizard:

1. The first step of the Command Button Wizard is shown in Figure 14.6. In this dialog box, you specify the category of activity and specific action you want the command button to perform. The subsequent wizard steps vary, depending on the category and action you select.

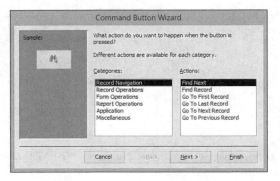

FIGURE 14.6

The first step of the Command Button Wizard.

2. Figure 14.7 shows the second step of the Command Button Wizard when you select the Form Operations category and the Open Form action in the first step. This step asks which form you want to open. After you select a form and click Next, you're asked whether you want Access to open the form and find specific data to display or whether you want Access to open the form and display all the records.

FIGURE 14.7

The Command Button Wizard, requesting the name of a form to open.

3. If you indicate that you want to display only specific records, the dialog box shown in Figure 14.8 appears. This dialog box asks you to select fields related to the two forms. You must select the related fields and then click the <> button to notify Access of the relationship.

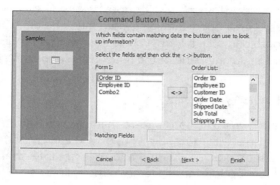

FIGURE 14.8

The Command Button Wizard, asking for the fields that relate to each form.

4. In the next step of the wizard, you select text or a picture for the button.

5. The final step of the wizard asks you to name the button. When you're done, click Finish.

What's surprising about the Command Button Wizard is how much it varies depending on the features you select. It enables you to add somewhat sophisticated functionality to an application without writing a single line of code. Figure 14.9 shows the embedded macro created by the example just outlined. This code will make a lot more sense to you after you read Chapter 17, "Automating Your Database with Macros." After you have the Command Button Wizard generate a macro for you, you can modify it; this means that you can have Access do some of the dirty work for you and then customize the work to your liking.

FIGURE 14.9

Macro created by the Command Button Wizard.

Building Forms Based on More Than One Table

Many forms are based on more than one table; such forms are called *one-to-many forms*. For example, a form that shows a customer at the top and the orders associated with that customer at the bottom is considered a one-to-many form. Forms can also be based on a query that joins more than one table. Rather than see a one-to-many relationship in such a form, you see the two tables displayed as one, with each record on the "many" side of the relationship appearing with its parent's data.

Creating One-to-Many Forms

There are several ways to create one-to-many forms. As with many other types of forms, you can use a wizard to help you, or you can build the form from scratch. Because all the methods for creating a form are helpful to users and developers alike, the available options are covered in the following sections.

Build a One-to-Many Form by Using the Form Wizard

Building a one-to-many form by using the Form Wizard is a simple 10-step process:

1. On the Create tab on the Ribbon, select Form Wizard in the Forms group. The Form Wizard launches.

2. From the Tables/Queries drop-down list, select the table or query that will appear on the "one" side of the relationship. For this example, I have selected the Customers table.

3. Select the fields you want to include from the "one" side of the relationship.

4. Use the Tables/Queries drop-down list to select the table or query that will appear on the "many" side of the relationship. For this example, I have selected the Orders table.

5. Select the fields you want to include from the "many" side of the relationship.

6. Click Next.

7. Select whether you want the parent form to appear with subforms or the child forms to appear as linked forms. This example shows the parent form with sub-forms, so click the Form with Subforms option (see Figure 14.10). Click Next.

8. Indicate whether you want the subform to appear in a tabular format, as a datasheet, as a pivot table, or as a pivot chart. (This option is not available if you select Linked Forms in step 7.) Click Next.

9. Select a style for the form, and then click Next.

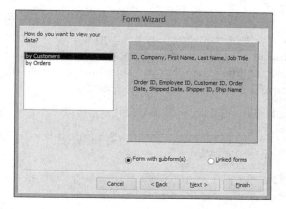

FIGURE 14.10

The Form Wizard, creating a parent form with subforms.

10. Name both the form and the subform, and then click Finish.

The result of this process is a main form that contains a subform. Figure 14.11 shows an example.

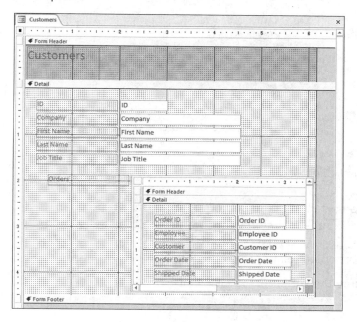

FIGURE 14.11

The result of creating a one-to-many form by using the Form Wizard.

Building a One-to-Many Form by Using the Subform Wizard

You can create a one-to-many form by building the parent form and then adding a Subform/Subreport control from the toolbox. If you want to use the Subform/Subreport Wizard, you need to make sure that you select the Control Wizards tool before you add the Subform/Subreport control to the main form. Then follow these steps:

1. Click to select the Subform/Subreport control.

2. Click and drag to place the Subform/Subreport control on the main form. The Subform/Subreport Wizard appears.

3. Indicate whether you want to use an existing form as the subform or build a new subform from an existing table or query.

4. If you select Use Existing Tables and Queries, the next step of the Subform/Subreport Wizard prompts you to select a table or query and which fields you want to include (see Figure 14.12). Select the fields, and then click Next.

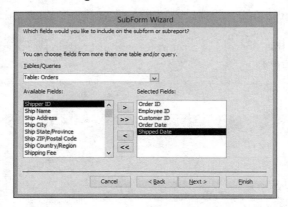

FIGURE 14.12

Selecting fields to include in a subform.

5. The next step of the Subform/Subreport Wizard enables you to define which fields in the main form link to which fields in the subform. You can select from the suggested relationships or define your own (see Figure 14.13). Select the appropriate relationship and click Next.

6. Name the subform and click Finish.

NOTE When the subform display in Datasheet view, the order of the fields in the subform has no bearing on the datasheet that appears in the main form. The order of the columns in the datasheet depends on the tab order of the fields in the subform. You must therefore modify the tab order of the fields in the subform to change the order of the fields in the resulting datasheet.

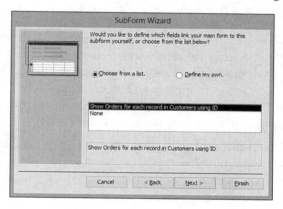

FIGURE 14.13

Defining the relationship between the main form and the subform.

The resulting form should look similar to the form created with the Form Wizard. Creating a one-to-many form this way is simply an alternative to using the Form Wizard.

 TIP Another way to add a subform to a main form is to click and drag a form from the Database window onto the main form. Access then tries to identify the relationship between the two forms.

Working with Subforms

After you add a subform to a form, you need to understand how to work with it. To begin, you need to be familiarize with a few properties of a Subform control:

- `Source Object`—Specifies the name of the form that displays in the control
- `Link Child Fields`—Specifies the fields from the child form that link the child form to the master form
- `Link Master Fields`—Specifies the fields from the master form that link the child form to the master form

NOTE It can be difficult and confusing to understand the difference between the subform and the Subform control. The Subform control *contains* the subform. When you click to select the Subform control, the Source Object, Link Child Fields, and Link Master Fields properties all appear. When you click *within* the Subform control, you are actually selecting the subform, and can manipulate objects within it.

You should also understand how to make changes to a subform. One option is to open a subform in a separate window (as you would open any other form). After you close and save the form, all the changes automatically appear in the parent form. The other choice is to modify a subform from within the main form. With the main form open, the subform is visible. Any changes made to the design of the subform from within the main form are permanent.

The default view of the subform is Datasheet or Continuous Forms, depending on how you added the subform and what options you selected. If you want to modify the default view, you simply change the subform's `Default View` property.

THE ABSOLUTE MINIMUM

Working with combo boxes (drop-downs) and list boxes can be overwhelming at first. With a little practice you can get to know the properties of combo boxes and list boxes, and you will feel quite comfortable working with them. The combo box and list box wizards can help you to get started. It is a good idea to explore the properties that they set. That way you will be prepared if you need to make changes after you have run the wizards. An example of a property that you should be comfortable with is the Row Source property. You use the Row Source property to determine the data that displays in the combo box or list box.

You should also know when to use a combo box and when to use a list box. A list box is most appropriate when you want to allow the user to make multiple selections. An example is a list box that would allow the user to select multiple reports that they want to print. Remember that you must use a combo box if you want to allow the user to type values not in the combo box. List boxes allow you to select only from the listed items.

The Command Button Wizard is a great tool. It can help you with the process to automate the tasks you want to perform in your database. For example, using the Command Button Wizard you can add a command button to the Customer form that opens the Order form. Access builds the underlying macro that performs the necessary tasks. If you want to enhance the macros the Command Button Wizard creates, you can easily modify them. This gives you great power and flexibility.

You must understand how to build forms based on data in more than one table. You can use the Form Wizard and the Subform Wizard, or you can simply drag and drop the child form onto the parent form to create a form based on data from more than one table. The wizards both enable you answer a series of questions to customize the behavior of the form that you are building. The drag and drop method adds the subform with default options. In either case you can easily customize the properties of the subform control to get exactly the results that you need.

IN THIS CHAPTER

- What sections make up a report, and why is each one important?

- What control properties are available on a report, and when should you use them?

- How do you build reports based on data from multiple tables?

- What are subreports, and what do you need to know about them?

BUILDING POWERFUL REPORTS

Reports enable you to preview and print the information stored in your database. In Chapter 7, "Using Reports to Print Information," you learned the basics to work with reports. Here you take your knowledge to the next level. You begin by discussing report bands and how to use them. You then explore report controls and how you can control their behavior by using control properties. You also learn how to create one-to-many reports and how to work with subreports.

The Anatomy of a Report

Reports can have many parts, referred to as *sections* of the report. A new report automatically consists of the following three sections, as shown in Figure 15.1:

- Page Header
- Detail
- Page Footer

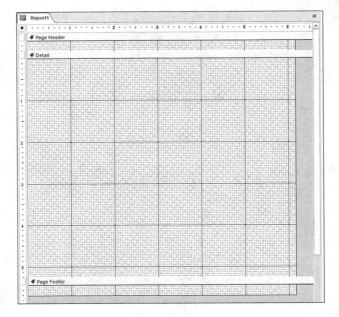

FIGURE 15.1

Sections of a report.

The Detail section is the main section of the report and displays the detailed data of the table or query underlying the report. Certain reports, such as Summary reports, have nothing in the Detail section. Instead, Summary reports contain data in group headers and footers.

The Page Header section automatically prints at the top of every page of the report. It often includes information such as the report's title. The Page Footer section automatically prints at the bottom of every page of the report and usually contains information such as the page number and date. Each report can have only one page header and one page footer.

In addition to the three sections that Access automatically adds to every report, a report can have the following sections:

- Report Header
- Report Footer
- Group Headers
- Group Footers

A Report Header prints once, at the beginning of the report; the Report Footer prints once, at the end of the report. Each Access report can have only one Report Header and one Report Footer. You often use the Report Header to create a cover sheet for a report. It can include graphics or other fancy effects to add a professional look to a report. The most common use of the Report Footer is for grand totals, but it can also include any other summary information for a report.

In addition to Report and Page Headers and Footers, an Access report can have up to 10 group headers and footers. Report groupings separate data logically and physically. The Group Header prints before the detail for the group, and the Group Footer prints after the detail for the group. For example, you can group customer sales by country and city, printing the name of the country or city for each related group of records. If you total the sales for each country and city, you can place the country and city names in the country and city Group Headers and the totals in the country and city Group Footers.

Control Properties and Why to Use Them

Control properties enable you to change the behavior and appearance of a control. You can change most control properties at design time or at runtime; this enables you to easily build flexibility into reports. For example, certain controls are visible only when specific conditions are true. This section begins by discussing the Format properties of a control and then continues by covering the Data and Other properties of a control.

The Format Properties of a Control

The Format properties of a control enable you to customize the appearance of the control. Using the Format properties, you can modify control attributes such as the back color, font, special effect, and text alignment of the control. You can modify many of the Format properties of selected objects by using the Format tab on the Ribbon (see Figure 15.2). If you prefer, you can set the Format properties in the Properties window (see Figure 15.3). The remainder of this section discusses the Format properties available to you.

Format tab

FIGURE 15.2

The Format tab of the Ribbon.

Format tab

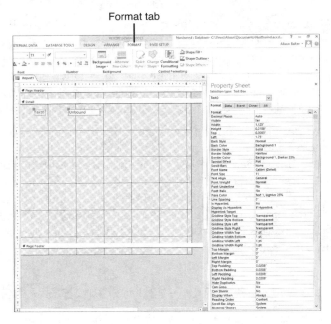

FIGURE 15.3

The Format properties of a control.

- **Format**—The `Format` property determines how Access displays the data in a control. This property is automatically inherited from the underlying field. If you want the control's format on the report to differ from the underlying field's format, you must set the `Format` property of the control. The format options available vary based on the field type of the underlying field. In other words, the formatting options vary if the underlying field is a Text field versus a Number field.

- **Caption**—The `Caption` property specifies the text displayed for labels and command buttons. It does not apply to other controls, such as text boxes. A caption is a string that contains up to 2,048 characters.

- **Decimal Places**—The **Decimal Places** property defines the number of decimal places displayed for numeric values. Decimal places generally apply to text boxes.

- **Visible**—The **Visible** property determines whether a control is visible. You can use this property to toggle the visibility of a control in response to different situations.

- **Hide Duplicates**—The **Hide Duplicates** property hides duplicate data values in a report's Detail section. Duplicate data values occur when one or more consecutive records in a report contain the same value in one or more fields. Figure 15.4 shows a report with the **Hide Duplicates** property set to its default value, False. Notice the duplicate **Order Date** values. Figure 15.5 shows the same report with the **Hide Duplicates** property of the **Order Date** control set to True. The duplicate order date values no longer appear.

- **Can Grow** and **Can Shrink**—When the **Can Grow** property is set to Yes in a control, the control can expand vertically to accommodate all the data in it. The **Can Shrink** property eliminates blank lines when no data exists in a

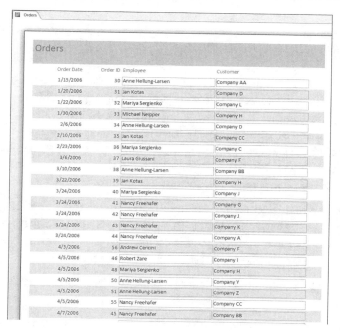

FIGURE 15.4

The Hide Duplicates property set to False.

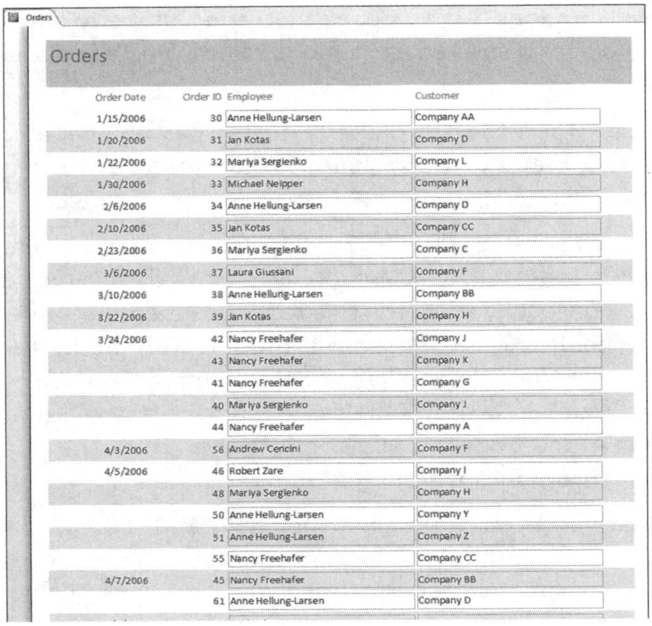

FIGURE 15.5

The Hide Duplicates property set to True.

field for a particular record. For example, if you have a second address line on a mailing label but there's no data in the Address2 field, you don't want a blank line to appear on the mailing label (see Figure 15.6). You must therefore set the `Can Shrink` property for the Address2 control to Yes (see results in Figure 15.7). Likewise, if you have a memo that sometimes has only one line of data but at other times has multiple lines of data, you might want to set the `Can Grow` property to Yes so that the control grows as necessary.

- `Back Style` and `Back Color`—You can set the `Back Style` property to Normal or Transparent. When this property is set to Transparent, the color of the report shows through to the control. When it is set to Normal, the control's `Back Color` property determines the object's color.

- `Special Effect`—The `Special Effect` property adds 3D effects to a control.

- `Border Style`, `Border Color`, and `Border Width`—These properties set the physical attributes of a control's border.

- `Fore Color`—The `Fore Color` property sets the color of the text within a control.

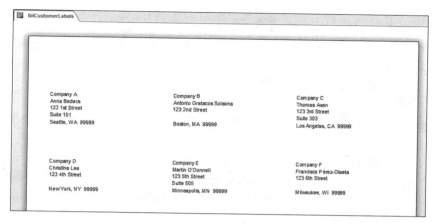

FIGURE 15.6

The *Can Shrink* property set to No.

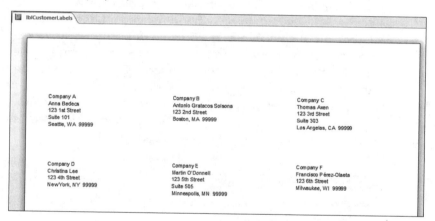

FIGURE 15.7

The *Can Shrink* property set to Yes.

- `Font Color`, `Font Name`, `Font Size`, `Font Weight`, `Font Italic`, and `Font Underline`—These properties affect the appearance of the text within a control.

- `Text Align`—The `Text Align` property sets the alignment of the text within a control. You can set this property to Left, Center, Right, or Distribute. When it is set to Distribute, text is justified

- `Line Spacing`—The `Line Spacing` property is used to control the spacing between lines of text within a control. The `Line Spacing` property is designated in inches.

The Data Properties of a Control

The Data properties of a control described in the following list specify information about the data underlying a particular report control. Using the Data properties, you can designate everything from what data displays in a control, to whether the data sums as it displays:

- `Control Source`—The `Control Source` property specifies the field in the report's record source used to populate the control. An example is FirstName. A control source can also be a valid expression.

- `Running Sum`—The `Running Sum` property (which is unique to reports) is powerful. You can use it to calculate a record-by-record or group-by-group total. You can set it to No, Over Group, or Over All. When set to No, no running sum is calculated. When it is set to Over Group, the value of the text box accumulates from record to record within the group but is reset each time the group value changes. One example is a report that shows deposit amounts for each state, with a running sum for the amount deposited within the state. Each time the state changes, the amount deposited is set to zero. When this property is set to Over All, the sum continues to accumulate over the entire report. Another example is where you set the Control Source property of the control to = 1. As with the previous example, you can then set the `Running Sum` property to Over Group or Over All. When set to Over Group, the control's value starts at one for each new group (see Figure 15.8). When set to Over All, the value continues to increment (see Figure 15.9).

The Other Properties of a Control

The Other properties of a control include properties that don't fit into any other category such as the following:

A common mistake many Access developers and users make is to give controls names that conflict with Access names. This type of error is difficult to track down. You need to make sure you use distinctive names for both fields and controls. Furthermore, you should not give a control the same name as a field within its expression. For example, the expression `= ContactName & ContactTitle` shouldn't have the name **"ContactName"**; that would cause an `#error#` message when you run the report. Finally, you shouldn't give a control the same name as its control source. Access gives a bound control the same name as its field, and you need to change this name to avoid problems. Following these simple warnings will spare you a lot of grief!

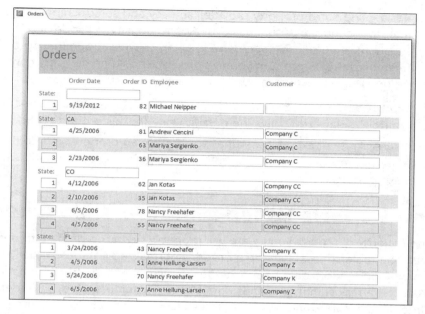

FIGURE 15.8

Running sum with Over Group selected.

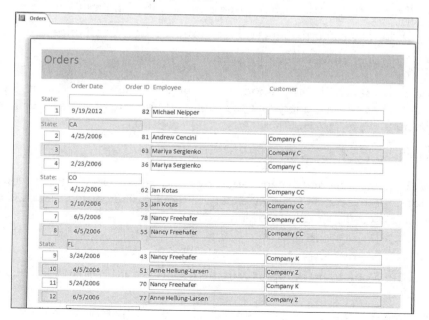

FIGURE 15.9

Running sum with Over All selected.

- **Name**—The **Name** property provides an easy and self-documenting way to refer to a control in Visual Basic for Applications (VBA) code and in many other situations. If you or someone else is going to write programming code that references the controls on your report, you should name every control on the report. This way you can easily identify them in queries, macros, and so on.

- **Vertical**—The **Vertical** property determines whether the text within a control displays vertically. The default value for this property is **No**.

- **Tag**—Like the **Tag** property of a report, the **Tag** property of a control provides a user-defined slot for the control. You can place extra information in the **Tag** property.

Building Reports Based on More Than One Table

The majority of reports you create will probably be based on data from more than one table. This is because a properly normalized database usually requires that you bring table data back together to give users valuable information. For example, a report that combines data from a Customers table, an Orders table, an Order Details table, and a Product table can supply the following information:

- Customer information, such as company name and address

- Order information, such as order date and shipping method

- Order detail information, such as quantity ordered and price

- A product table, including a product description

You can base a multitable report directly on the tables whose data it displays, or you can base it on a query that has already joined the tables, providing a flat table structure.

Creating One-to-Many Reports

You can create a one-to-many report by using the Report Wizard, or you can build a report from scratch. Different situations require different techniques, some of which are covered in the following sections.

Build a One-to-Many Report by Using the Report Wizard

Building a one-to-many report with the Report Wizard is quite easy. You just follow these steps:

1. From the Reports group on the Create tab on the Ribbon, select Report Wizard.

2. From the Tables/Queries drop-down list box, select the first table or query whose data will appear on the report.

3. Select the fields you want to include from that table.

4. Select each additional table or query you want to include on the report, selecting the fields you need from each (see Figure 15.10). For this example select ID, Company, First Name and Last Name from the Customers table, Order ID and Order Date from the Orders table, and Company and Shipping Fee from the Shippers table. Click Next.

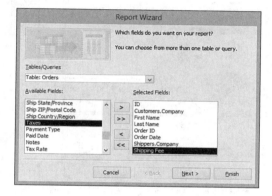

FIGURE 15.10

The first step of the Report Wizard: Select the fields you want on a report.

5. The next step of the Report Wizard asks you how you want to view the data (see Figure 15.11). You can accept Access's suggestion (by Customers), or you can choose from any of the available options (by Customers, by Orders, or by Shippers). Click Next.

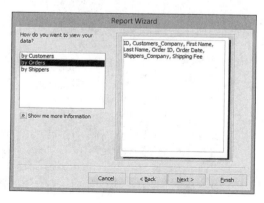

FIGURE 15.11

The second step of the Report Wizard: Designate how you want to view the data.

6. The next step of the Report Wizard asks whether you want to add any grouping levels. You can use grouping levels to visually separate data and to provide subtotals. In the example in Figure 15.12, the report is grouped by Shippers Company. After you select grouping levels, click Next.

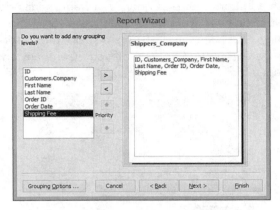

FIGURE 15.12

The third step of the Report Wizard: Select groupings.

7. The next step of the Report Wizard enables you to select how you want the records in the report's Detail section to be sorted. This step of the wizard also enables you to specify any summary calculations you want to perform on the data (see Figure 15.13). Click the Summary Options button to specify the summary calculations. By clicking the Summary Options button, you can even opt to include the percentage of total calculations. Click OK when you finish adding the summary options.

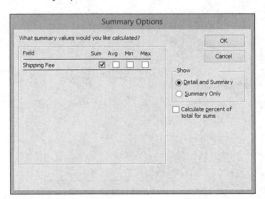

FIGURE 15.13

Add summary calculations.

8. In the next step of the Report Wizard, you select the layout and orientation of the report. Layout options include Stepped, Blocked, Outline 1, Outline 2, Align Left 1, and Align Left 2. You can click the different option buttons to preview how each report looks.

9. In the next step of the Report Wizard, you select a title for the report. The title also becomes the name of the report. You can select an appropriate name and change the title after the wizard finishes. The final step also enables you to determine whether you want to immediately preview the report or see the report's design first. Click Finish when you are ready to complete the process.

The report created in this example is shown in Figure 15.14. The report is sorted and grouped by Shippers Company, OrderDate, and Customers Company. The report's data is in order by OrderDate and Customers Company within a Shippers Company grouping.

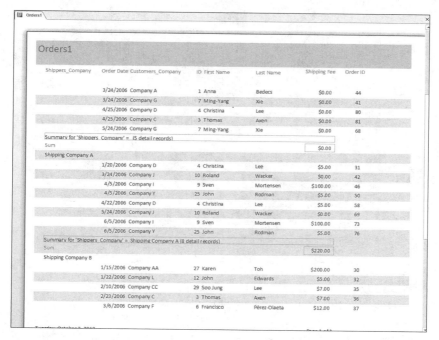

FIGURE 15.14

A completed one-to-many report.

This method to create a one-to-many report is by far the easiest. The background-join technology that the wizards use when they enable you to pick fields from multiple tables—figuring out how to build the complex queries needed for the report or form—is one of the major benefits of Access as a database tool. It's a huge timesaver and helps hide unnecessary complexity from you as you build a report. Although you should take advantage of this feature, you must know what's happening under the covers. The following two sections give you this necessary knowledge.

Building a Report Based on a One-to-Many Query

A popular method to build a one-to-many report is from a one-to-many query. A one-to-many report built in this way is constructed as though it were based on the data within a single table. First, you build the query that underlies the report (see Figure 15.15).

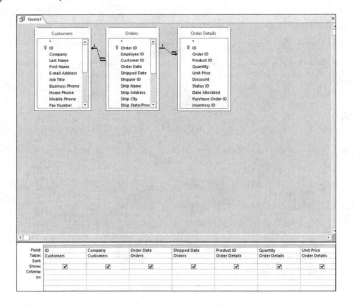

FIGURE 15.15

An example of a query underlying a one-to-many report.

When you finish the query, you can select it rather than select each individual table (as done in the previous section). After you select the query, you follow the same process to create the report as described in the preceding section.

Build a One-to-Many Report with the SubReport Wizard

You can build a one-to-many report by building the parent report and then adding a SubReport control. This is often the method used to create reports such as invoices that show the report's data in a one-to-many relationship rather than in a denormalized format. If you want to use the SubReport Wizard, you must ensure that you select the Control Wizards tool before you add the SubReport control to the main report. Here is the process:

1. Click to select the SubForm/SubReport control tool.

2. Click and drag to place the SubForm/SubReport control on the main report. You usually place the SubForm/SubReport control in the report's Detail section. When you place the SubForm/SubReport control on the report, the SubReport Wizard is invoked.

3. Indicate whether you want to base the subreport on an existing form or report or whether you want to build a new subreport based on a query or table. Click Next.

4. If you select Table or Query, you must select the table or query on which you will base the subreport. You can then select the fields you want to include on the subreport. You can even select fields from more than one table or query. When you finish making selections, click Next.

5. The next step of the SubReport Wizard suggests a relationship between the main report and the subreport (see Figure 15.16). You can accept the selected relationship, or you can define your own. When you finish, click Next.

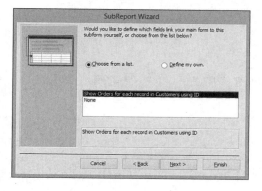

FIGURE 15.16

The SubReport Wizard: Identify the relationship.

6. The final step of the SubReport Wizard asks you to name the subreport. Click Finish when you're done.

As you can see in Figure 15.17, the one-to-many relationship between two tables is clearly highlighted by this type of report. In Figure 15.17, each customer is listed. All the detail records reflecting the orders for each customer are listed immediately following each customer's data.

 NOTE To follow standards, the name should begin with the prefix rsub.

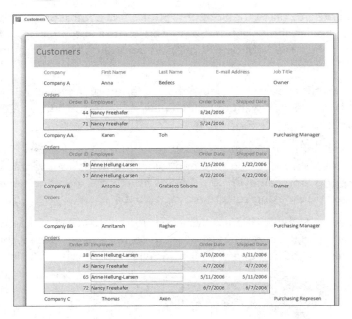

FIGURE 15.17

A one-to-many report created with the SubReport Wizard.

Working with Subreports

When you add a subreport to a report, you must understand what properties the SubReport Wizard sets so that you can modify the SubForm/SubReport control if needed. You should become familiar with the following properties of a SubForm/SubReport control (see Figure 15.18).

- `Source Object`—This control specifies the name of the report or other object that's displayed within the control.

- `Link Child Fields`—This control specifies the fields from the child report that link the child report to the master report.

- `Link Master Fields`—This control specifies the fields from the master report that link the master report to the child report.

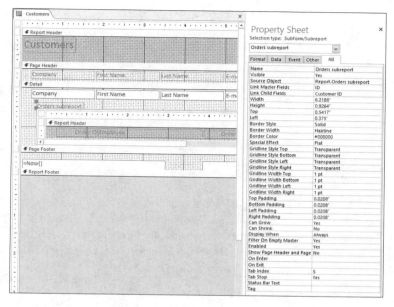

FIGURE 15.18

Properties of the SubForm/SubReport control.

- **Can Grow**—This control determines whether the control can expand vertically to accommodate data in the subreport.

- **Can Shrink**—This control determines whether the control can shrink to eliminate blank lines when no data is found in the subreport.

Not only should you know how to work with the properties of a SubForm/SubReport object, but you should also easily modify the subreport from within the main report. You can always modify the subreport by selecting it from the list of reports in the Database window. To do this, select the report you want to modify, and then click Design. You can also modify a subreport by selecting its objects directly within the parent report.

THE ABSOLUTE MINIMUM

You must understand report bands and the use of each band. When you create a report, you automatically get a Page Header band, a Page Footer band, and a Detail band. Anything that you place in the Page Header band appears at the top of each and every page. A common item to place in the Page Header is a report title. The contents of the Page Footer Band print at the bottom of each page. The most common thing found in the Page Footer is the page number. The Detail band prints once for each record in the data underlying the report. If you want a summary-only report, set the Visible property of the Detail band to False.

You can open a subreport in its own separate Design view window by right-clicking the subreport and selecting Subreport in New Window.

The Report Header band appears once at the beginning of the report, and the contents of the Report Footer band print at the end of the report. Although not as commonly used, the Report Header is usually used for a cover sheet. It is common to include a Report Footer as part of your report. This is where you place grand totals of calculations (such as sales) found on the report.

You can add multiple Group Header and Group Footer bands to the reports that you build. You generally use the Group Header section to display text indicating what will appear in that group. For example, if you group by City, you display the value of the city for that group in the group header (for example, Newbury Park). It is most common to use the Group Footer bands for subtotals. For example, you may display the subtotal sales amount for the city in the group footer (for example, $1,500).

Control properties are divided into Format properties, Data properties, and Other properties. Format properties affect the visual appearance of the control on the form. Like their name implies, Data properties determine what data the control displays. Other properties are miscellaneous properties, such as the Name property, which don't fit neatly into any of the other categories.

Many reports require that you include data from more than one table. You can create one-to-many reports using the Report Wizard and SubReport Wizard or by clicking and dragging the subreport onto the main report. Use the Report Wizard when you have not yet created any part of the report. Use the SubReport Wizard when you have built the main report and want to add data to the report related to the data in the main report. Use the click and drag method to add a subreport when the subreport that you want to tie to the main report already exists.

You can now create powerful reports. Chapter 16, "Advanced Report Techniques," further enhances your knowledge of working with reports.

ADVANCED REPORT TECHNIQUES

This chapter begins by showing you how to sort and group report data. You then learn how to customize the Group Headers and Footers that you create. You then explore the available report properties. You learn about Data properties, Format properties, and Other properties. Finally, you discuss the process to base a report on a stored query versus a SQL statement and cover the pros and cons of each.

Working with Sorting and Grouping

Unlike sorting data within a form, sorting data within a report isn't determined by the underlying query. The underlying query affects the report's sort order only when you have not specified a sort order for the report. Any sort order specified in the query is completely overwritten by the report's sort order, which is determined in the report's Group, Sort, and Total window (see Figure 16.1). The sorting and grouping of a report is affected by what options you select when you run the Report Wizard. You can use the Group, Sort, and Total window to add, remove, or modify sorting and grouping options for a report. Sorting simply affects the order of the records in the report. Grouping adds Group Headers and Footers to the report.

Add Sorting and Grouping to a Report

Often, you want to add sorting or grouping to a report. Grouping enables you to add Group Headers and Group Footers to a report, and sorting enables you to designate the sort order within your groups. To add grouping and sorting, follow these steps:

1. Click Group & Sort in the Grouping & Totals group on the Design tab on the Ribbon to open the Group, Sort, & Total window.

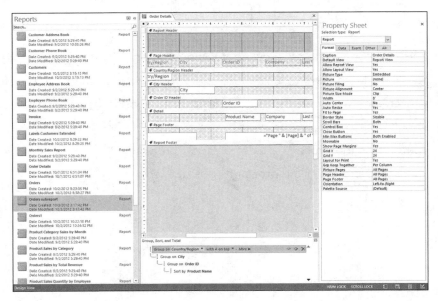

FIGURE 16.1

The Sorting and Grouping window, showing grouping by Country, City, and OrderID and sorting by product name.

2. Select Add a Group to add a grouping to the report, or select Add a Sort to add an additional sorting level to the report.

3. Select the field on which you want to sort or group (see Figure 16.2).

4. Click and drag the group or sort level until it appears in the appropriate position in the Group, Sort, and Total window.

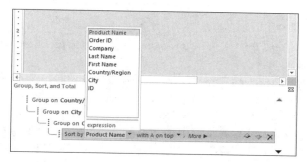

FIGURE 16.2

Inserting a sorting or grouping level.

5. Set the properties to determine the nature of the sorting or grouping (see the next section, "Sorting and Grouping Properties"). Close the Group, Sort, and Total window, if wanted.

 TIP To remove a sorting or grouping that you have added, you click the X for the appropriate field in the Group, Sort, and Total window that you want to delete. Access warns you that any controls in the group header or footer will be lost.

Sorting and Grouping Settings

Each grouping in a report has settings that define the group's attributes. The settings determine things such as whether the field or expression is used for sorting, grouping, or both. They are also used to specify details about the grouping options. To view the sorting and grouping settings, click More on one of the fields available in the Group, Sort, and Total window. The band expands, as shown in Figure 16.3. You can set the following attributes:

- `Sort Direction`—The `Sort Direction` setting specifies whether you want to sort in ascending or descending order.

- `By Entire Value`—The `By Entire Value` setting specifies whether you want to group by an entire value or by a specific number of starting characters of the value (for example, the first two characters).

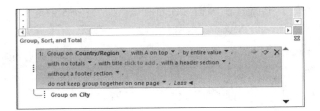

FIGURE 16.3

The Group, Sort, and Total window, showing the expanded list of sorting and grouping settings.

- **With No Totals**—The **With No Totals** setting specifies what fields you want to total. If you opt to total a field, you can specify the type of calculation you want to perform (sum, average, count, and so on). You can also designate whether you want to show the grand total, show a group subtotal as a percentage of the grand total, and whether you want subtotals in the Group Header and Footer (see Figure 16.4).

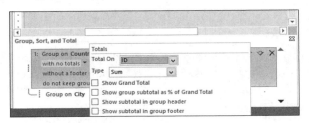

FIGURE 16.4

Including totals in a header or footer.

- **With Title**—You use the **With Title** setting to create a title for the grouping and to designate a font for that title.

- **With a Header Section**—You use the **With a Header Section** setting to designate whether you want to include a Group Header.

- **With a Footer Section**—You use the **With a Footer Section** setting to designate whether you want to include a Group Footer.

- **Do Not Keep Together on One Page**—The **Do Not Keep Together on One Page** setting determines whether Access tries to keep an entire group together on one page, whether it prints the Group Header on a page only if it can also print the first detail record on the same page, or whether it makes no attempt to keep the header together with the detail section.

NOTE If you select Keep Whole Group Together on One Page, and the group is too large to fit on a page, Access ignores the property setting. Furthermore, if you select Keep Header and First Record Together on One Page and either the group header or the detail record is too large to fit on one page, that setting is ignored, too.

Group Header and Footer Properties and Why to Use Them

Each Group Header and Footer has its own properties that determine the behavior of the Group Header or Footer (see Figure 16.5).

- **Force New Page**—You can set the **Force New Page** property to None, Before Section, After Section, or Before & After. If it is set to None, no page break occurs either before or after the report section. If it is set to Before Section, a page break occurs before the report section prints. If it is set to After Section, a page break occurs after the report section prints. If it is set to Before & After, a page break occurs before the report section prints and after it prints.

- **New Row or Col**—The **New Row or Col** property determines whether a column break occurs whenever the report section prints. This property applies only to multicolumn reports. The settings are None, Before Section, After Section, and Before & After. Like the **Force New Page** property, this property determines whether the column break occurs before the report section prints, after it prints, or before and after, or whether it's affected by the report section break.

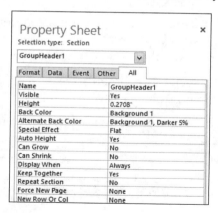

FIGURE 16.5

Group Header and Footer properties.

- `Keep Together`—The `Keep Together` property specifies whether you want Access to try to keep an entire report section together on one page. If this property is set to Yes, Access starts printing the section at the top of the next page if it can't print the entire section on the current page. When this property is set to No, Access prints as much of the section as possible on the current page, inserting page breaks as necessary. If a section exceeds the page length, Access starts printing the section on a new page and continues printing it on the following page.

- `Visible`—The `Visible` property indicates whether the section is visible. It's common to hide the visibility of a particular report section at runtime in response to different situations. You can easily accomplish this by changing the value of the report section's `Visible` property with a macro or VBA code, usually on the Format event.

- `Can Grow` and `Can Shrink`—The `Can Grow` property determines whether you want the section to stretch vertically to accommodate the data in it. The `Can Shrink` property specifies whether you want the section to shrink vertically, eliminating blank lines.

- `Repeat Section`—The `Repeat Section` property is a valuable property that lets you specify whether Access repeats the Group Header on subsequent pages if a report section needs to print on more than one page.

Report Properties and Why to Use Them

You can modify many different properties on reports to change how the report looks and performs. Like form properties, report properties are divided into categories: Format, Data, Event, and Other. To view a report's properties, you first select the report, rather than a section of the report, in one of two ways:

- Click the report selector (see Figure 16.6), which is the small gray button at the intersection of the horizontal and vertical rulers.

- Select Report from the drop-down list box in the Properties window.

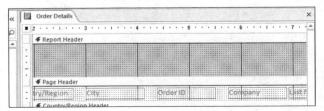

FIGURE 16.6

The report selector.

After you select a report, you can view and modify its properties.

Working with the Properties Window

To select a report and open the Properties window at the same time, you double-click the report selector. When you select a report, the Properties window appears showing all the properties associated with the report. A report has 77 properties available on the Property Sheet (there are additional properties available only from code) broken down into the appropriate categories in the Properties window. Fifty of the properties relate to the report's Format, Data, and the properties on the Other tab; the remaining 27 relate to the events that occur when a report is run. The Format, Data, and Other properties are described here.

The Format Properties of a Report

A report has the following 29 Format properties for changing the report's physical appearance. The text that follows explains many of the Format properties:

- `Caption`—The `Caption` property of a report is the text that appears in the Report window's title bar when the user is previewing the report. You can modify it at runtime to customize it for a particular situation.

- `Default View`—The `Default View` determines whether a report is opened in Report view or Print Preview.

- `Auto Resize`—The `Auto Resize` property determines whether a report is resized automatically to display all the data on the report.

- `Auto Center`—You use the `Auto Center` property to designate whether you want the Report window to automatically be centered on the screen.

- `Page Header` and `Page Footer`—The `Page Header` and `Page Footer` properties determine on what pages the Page Header and Page Footer sections appear. The options are All Pages, Not with Rpt Hdr, Not with Rpt Ftr, and Not with Rpt Hdr/Ftr. You might not want the page header or page footer to print on the report header or report footer pages, and these properties give you control over where those sections print.

- `Grp Keep Together`—In Access, you can keep a group of data together on the same page by using the `Grp Keep Together` property. The Per Page setting forces the group of data to remain on the same page, and the Per Column setting forces the group of data to remain within a column. A *group of data* refers to all the data within a report grouping (for example, all the customers in a city).

- `Border Style`—The `Border Style` property is more powerful than its name implies. The options for the `Border Style` property are None, Thin, Sizable, and Dialog. If the `Border Style` property is set to None, the report has no border. If the `Border Style` property is set to Thin, the border is not resizable; the Size command isn't available in the Control menu. This setting is a good choice for pop-up reports, which remain on top even when other forms or reports are given the focus. Having the `Border Style` property set to Sizable is standard for most reports. It includes all the standard options in the Control menu. The Dialog setting creates a border that looks like the border created by the Thin setting. The user can't maximize, minimize, or resize a report with the `Border Style` property set to Dialog. After you set the `Border Style` property of a report to Dialog, the Maximize, Minimize, and Resize options aren't available in the report's Control menu.

- `Moveable`—The `Moveable` property determines whether the user can move the Report window around the screen by clicking and dragging the report by its title bar.

The Report's Data Properties

A report has the following six Data properties, which are used to supply information about the data underlying a report:

- `Record Source`—The `Record Source` property specifies the table or query whose data underlies the report. You can modify the record source of a report at runtime. This feature of the `Record Source` property makes it easy for you to create generic reports that use different record sources in different situations.

- `Filter`—The `Filter` property enables you to open a report with a specific filter set. You might prefer to base a report on a query rather than apply a filter to it. At some times, however, it's more appropriate to base the report on a query and then apply and remove a filter as required based on the report's runtime conditions.

- `Filter On Load`—The `Filter On Load` property determines whether a report filter is applied. If the `Filter On Load` property is set to No, the `Filter` property of the report is ignored.

- `Order By`—The `Order By` property determines how the records in a report are sorted when the report is opened.

- `Order By On Load`—The `Order By On Load` property determines whether the `Order By` property of the report is used. If the `Order By On Load` property is set to No, the report's `Order By` property is ignored when loading the report.

- **Allow Filters**—The **Allow Filters** property determines whether the report data can be filtered.

Other Properties of a Report

A report has 15 Other properties (see Figure 16.7); these miscellaneous properties, some of which are described in the following text, enable you to control other important aspects of a report:

- **Record Locks**—The **Record Locks** property determines whether Access locks the tables used in producing a report while it runs the report. The two values for this property are No Locks and All Records. No Locks is the default value, which means that no records in the tables underlying the report are locked while the report is run. Users can modify the underlying data as the report runs, which can be disastrous when running sophisticated reports. If users can change the data in a report as the report is being run, figures for totals and percentages of totals are invalid. Although using the All Records option for this property locks all records in all tables included in the report (thereby preventing data entry while the report is run), it might be a necessary evil to produce an accurate report.

- **Date Grouping**—The **Date Grouping** property determines how grouping of dates occurs in a report. The US Defaults setting means that Access uses United States defaults for report groupings; therefore, Sunday is the first day of the week, the first week begins January 1, and so on. The Use System Settings setting means that date groupings are based on the locale set in the Control Panel's Regional Settings, rather than on US Defaults.

FIGURE 16.7

The Other properties of a report.

- **Pop Up**—The **Pop Up** property determines whether a report's Print Preview window opens as a pop-up window. In Microsoft Access, pop-up windows always remain on top of other open windows.

- **Modal**—The **Modal** property instructs Access to open the Report window in a modal or modaless state. The default is No, meaning that the window will not be opened as modal. A modal window retains the application program's focus until the window receives the user input that it requires.

- **Tag**—The **Tag** property stores information defined by the user at either design time or runtime. It is Microsoft Access's way to give you an extra property. Access makes no use of this property; if you don't take advantage of it, it will never be used.

 TIP A couple of the Has Module property's behaviors deserve special attention. This property applies when you, or someone else, adds VBA programming code to your report. When a report is created, the default value for the Has Module property is No. Access automatically sets the Has Module property to Yes as soon as you try to view a report's module. If you set the Has Module property of an existing report to No, Access asks you whether you want to proceed. If you confirm the change, Access deletes the object's class module and all the code it contains.

Basing Reports on Stored Queries or Embedded SQL Statements

Basing Access reports on stored queries offers two major benefits:

- The query underlying the report can be used by other forms and reports.
- Sophisticated calculations need to be built only once—they don't need to be re-created for each report (or form).

In earlier version of Access, reports based on stored queries open faster than reports based on embedded SQL statements. This is because when you build and save a query, Access compiles and creates a query plan. This query plan is a plan of execution that's based on the amount of data in the query's tables and all the indexes available in each table. In early versions of Access, if you run a report based on an embedded SQL statement, the query compiles, and the query plan is built at runtime, slowing the query's execution. With Access 2013, query plans are built for embedded SQL statements when a form or report is saved. Query plans are stored with the associated form or report.

TIP It's easy to save an embedded SQL statement as a query, and doing so allows you to use the Report Wizard to build a report using several tables. You can then save the resulting SQL statement as a query. With the report open in Design view, you bring up the Properties window. After you select the Data tab, click in the Record Source property and click the ellipsis (...). The embedded SQL statement appears as a query. You need to select Save Object As from the File tab, enter a name for the query, and click OK. Then you close the Query window, indicating that you want to update the Record Source property. The query is then based on a stored query instead of an embedded SQL statement.

So what are the benefits of basing a report on a stored query instead of an embedded SQL statement? You may want to build several reports and forms all based on the same information. An embedded SQL statement can't be shared by multiple database objects. At the least, you must copy the embedded SQL statement for each form and report you build. Basing reports and forms on stored queries eliminates this problem. You build the query once and then modify it if changes need to be made to it. Many forms and reports can all use the same query (including its criteria, expressions, and so on).

Reports often contain complex expressions. If a particular expression is used in only one report, nothing is lost by building the expression into an embedded SQL statement. On the other hand, many complex expressions are used in multiple reports and forms. If you build these expressions into queries on which the reports and forms are based, you must create each expression only one time.

Although basing reports on stored queries offers several benefits, it also has downsides. For example, if a database contains numerous reports, the database container becomes cluttered with a large number of queries that underlie those reports. Furthermore, queries and the expressions within them are often specific to a particular report. If that is the case, you should opt to use embedded SQL statements rather than stored queries. As a general rule, if several reports are based on the same data and the same complex calculations, you should base them on a stored query. If a report is based on a unique query with a unique set of data and unique calculations, you should base it on an embedded SQL statement.

THE ABSOLUTE MINIMUM

The ability to sort and group report data makes your reports powerful. By adding report groupings, you can easily show subtotals for each grouping. For example, if you group your report data by state and then within state by city, you can easily display subtotals for each city within a state and then for each state as a whole. You can then display grand totals for all states at the bottom of the report. Within a grouping you can sort data by a field in that grouping or within the Detail section of the report. For example, you can group by state and city and then sort the data within each city by product name. The plethora of sorting and grouping settings available to you provide you with the ability to customize the behavior of each individual group and sort level.

After you add groupings, your report contains Group Headers and/or Footers. Using Group Header and Footer properties, you can easily define how the Group Headers and Footers behave. For example, you can set the Visible property of a header or footer to Yes or No as appropriate. You can also determine whether or not a page break occurs before and after each section.

Access enables you to define properties of the entire report. Like most objects, a report has Format properties, Data properties, and Other properties that you can define. The Format properties affect the visual appearance of the report. Data properties affect the data underlying the report. Other properties are properties that don't neatly fit into the other two categories. An example of a Format property is the Caption property. Using the Caption property, you can designate what appears in a report's title bar. An example of a Data property is the Record Source property. This is where you specify the name of the table or query whose data underlies the report. Finally, an example of the Other properties of a report is the Modal property. Using the Modal property, you can designate whether you want the report to open modally, meaning that you cannot access any other objects in the database until you close the report.

This chapter covered the pros and cons of basing a report on a stored query versus basing it on an embedded SQL statement. Generally, unless you base multiple reports on the same SQL statement, you can base your reports on embedded SQL statements. In this way you don't end up with a multitude of query objects in the database, each only used by one report.

IN THIS CHAPTER

- What are macro actions, and should you work with them?
- What are macro action arguments, and why are they important?
- What is a submacro, and when do you need one?
- How do you control the flow of the macros that you build?
- What are the various ways that you can run an Access macro?
- How do you modify an existing macro?
- What is an embedded macro, and how do you create one.

AUTOMATING YOUR DATABASE WITH MACROS

In this chapter, you learn the basics of creating a macro. You learn how to work with macro actions and how to create submacros. You also learn how to include logic in your macros so that you can control the program flow. You see how easy it is to run an Access macro and how to modify an existing macro. You learn many important techniques such as how to create an embedded macro.

Learning the Basics of Creating and Running a Macro

To create a macro, click the Create tab. Then select Macro from the Macros & Code group. The Macro Design window shown in Figure 17.1 appears. In this window, you can build a program by adding macro actions, arguments, and program flow items to the macro.

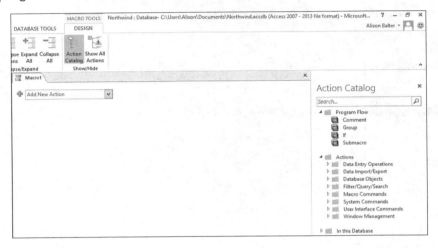

FIGURE 17.1

The Macro Design window, showing the Action Catalog and the Macro Tools Design tab on the Ribbon.

Macro *actions* are like programming commands or functions. They instruct Access to take a specific action (for example, to open a form). Macro *arguments* are like parameters to a command or function; they give Access specifics on the selected action. For example, if the macro action instructs Access to open a form, the arguments for that action tell Access which form should be opened and how it should be opened (Form, Design, Datasheet view, or Print Preview). Program flow items enable you to determine when a specific macro action will execute. For example, you might want one form to open in one situation and a second form to open in another situation.

Working with Macro Actions

As mentioned, macro actions instruct Access to perform a task. You can add a macro action to the Macro Design window in several ways. One way is to click in the macro item and then click to open the drop-down list. A list of all the macro actions appears, as shown in Figure 17.2. Select the one you want from the list, and it's instantly added to the macro. Use this method to select a macro action if you aren't sure of the macro action's name and want to browse the available actions.

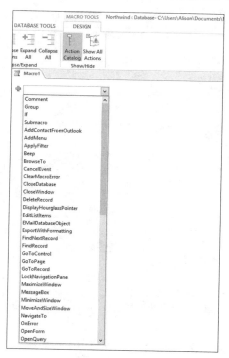

FIGURE 17.2

The Macro Action drop-down list, showing all the available macro actions.

After you work with macros for a while, you will know which actions you want to select. Instead of opening the drop-down list and scrolling through the entire list of actions, you can click a cell in the Action column and then start typing the name of the macro action you want to add. Access finds the first macro action beginning with the characters you type.

Drag and Drop Objects into Macros

The `OpenTable`, `OpenQuery`, `OpenForm`, and `OpenReport` actions open a table, query, form, or report, respectively. These actions and associated arguments can all be filled in easily with a drag-and-drop technique:

1. Scroll through the Navigation Pane until you see the object that you want to add to the macro.

2. Click and drag the object you want to open over to the Macro Design window. The appropriate action and arguments are automatically filled in. Figure 17.3 shows the effects of dragging and dropping the Customer List form onto the Macro Design window.

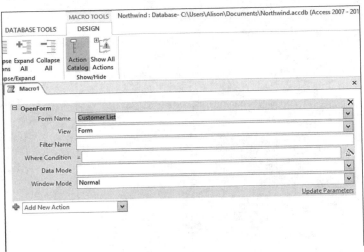

FIGURE 17.3
The Macro Design window after the Customer List form was dragged and dropped on it.

Dragging and dropping a table, query, form, report, or module onto the Macro Design window saves you time because all the macro action arguments are automatically filled in for you. Six action arguments are associated with the `OpenForm` action: `Form Name`, `View`, `Filter Name`, `Where Condition`, `Data Mode`, and `Window Mode` (refer to Figure 17.3). Three of the arguments for the `OpenForm` action have been filled in: the name of the form (Customer List), the view (Form), and the window mode (Normal). Macro action arguments are covered more thoroughly in the next section.

Working with Action Arguments

As mentioned, macro action arguments are like command or function parameters; they give Access specific instructions on how to execute the selected macro action. The available arguments differ depending on what macro action has been selected. Some macro action arguments force you to select from a drop-down list of appropriate choices; others enable you to enter a valid Access expression. Macro action arguments are automatically filled in when you click and drag a Table, Query, Form, Report, or Module object to the Macro Design window. In all other situations, you must supply Access with the arguments required to properly execute a macro action. To specify a macro action argument, follow these steps:

1. Select a macro action.

2. If the macro action argument requires selecting from a list of valid choices, click to open the drop-down list of available choices for the first macro action argument associated with the selected macro action. Figure 17.4 shows all the available choices for the **Form Name** argument associated with the **OpenForm** action. Because the selected argument is **Form Name**, the names of all the forms included in the database display in the drop-down list.

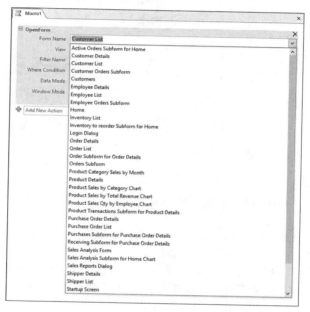

FIGURE 17.4

Available choices for **Form Name** *argument.*

3. If the macro action argument requires entering a valid expression, you can type the argument into the appropriate text box or get help from the Expression Builder. Take a look at the **Where Condition** argument of the **OpenForm** action, for example. After you click in the Where Condition text box, an ellipsis appears. If you click the ellipsis, the Expression Builder dialog box is invoked.

4. To build an appropriate expression, select a database object from the list box on the left, and then select a specific element from the center and right list boxes. Click OK to accept the element into the text box. In Figure 17.5,

the currently selected Expression Element is the Customer List form; the Expression Category is Job Title; and <value> has been double-clicked to add the expression to the top half of the window. The value of Owner is entered in quotes indicating that the Job Title of each record displayed on the form must be Owner. Click OK to close the Expression Builder. The completed expression appears, as shown in Figure 17.5.

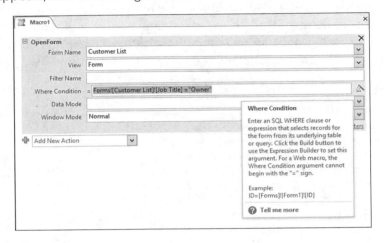

FIGURE 17.5

The completed expression for the `Where` *argument of the* `OpenForm` *action.*

Remember that each macro action has different macro action arguments. Some of the arguments associated with a particular macro action are required, and others are optional. If you need help on a particular macro action argument, click in the argument, and Access provides a tooltip with a short description of that argument. If you need more help, press F1 to see Help for the macro action and all its arguments.

Submacros

Submacros are like subroutines in a programming module; they enable you to place more than one routine in a macro. This means you can create many macro routines without needing to create several separate macros. You should include submacros that perform related functions within one particular macro. For example, you might build a macro that contains all the routines required for form handling and another that has all the routines needed for report handling.

Only two steps are needed to add submacros to a macro:

1. Click and drag a submacro from the Action Catalog onto the macro. A submacro appears.

2. Add macro actions to each submacro. Figure 17.6 shows a macro with three submacros: `OpenCustomers`, `OpenOrders`, and `CloseForm`. The `OpenCustomers` submacro opens the Customer List form, showing all customers. The `OpenOrders` submacro opens the OrderList form displaying only orders placed in March and April 2006, and the `CloseForm` submacro displays a message to the user and then closes the active window.

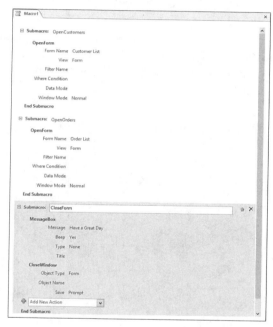

FIGURE 17.6

A macro with three submacros.

Program Flow

At times, you want a macro action to execute only when a certain condition is true. Fortunately, Access enables you to specify the conditions under which a macro action executes:

1. Make sure that the Action Catalog is visible. (If it isn't, click the Action Catalog tool in the Show/Hide group of the Macro Tools Design tab on the Ribbon.)

2. Click and drag the `If` statement to the macro. It appears, as shown in Figure 17.7.

FIGURE 17.7

You can designate the condition under which a macro action executes by selecting If from the Program Flow node of the Action Catalog.

The macro pictured in Figure 17.8 evaluates information entered on a form. The macro evaluates the date entered in the txtBirthDate text box on the frmPersonalInfo form. The Northwind database does not include the frmPersonalInfo form. You must create this form. Here's the expression entered in the first condition:

```
DateDiff("yyyy",[Forms]![frmPersonalInfo]![txtBirthDate],Da
te())Between 25 And 49
```

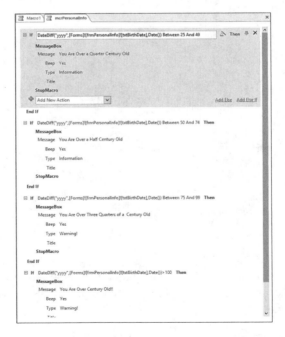

FIGURE 17.8

An example of a macro containing conditions.

This expression uses the `DateDiff` function to determine the difference between the date entered in the txtBirthDate text box and the current date. If the difference between the two dates is between 25 and 49 years, a message box displays indicating that the person is over one-quarter century old.

If the first condition isn't satisfied, the macro continues evaluating each condition. The `CheckBirthDate` subroutine displays an age-specific message for each person 25 years of age and older. If the person is younger than 25, none of the conditions are met, and no message displays.

The `CheckGender` macro works a little differently (see Figure 17.9). It evaluates the value of the `fraGender` option group. One of the first two lines of the subroutine execute, depending on whether the first or second option button is selected. The third line of the subroutine executes regardless of the Option Group value because it is after the End If.

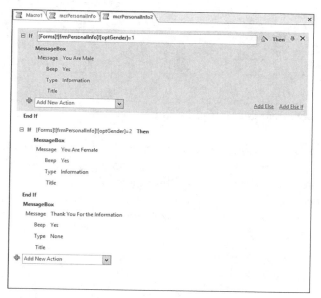

FIGURE 17.9

An example of a macro containing conditions.

Running an Access Macro

You have learned quite a bit about macros but haven't yet learned how to execute them. This process varies depending on what you try to do. You can run a macro from the Macro Design window or by double-clicking the macro in the Macros Group of the Navigation Pane, triggered from a Form or Report event, triggered from a Data Macro, or invoked by selecting a custom Ribbon button.

Running a Macro from the Macro Design Window

A macro can be executed easily from the Macro Design window. Running a macro without groups is simple: Just click Run in the Tools group of the Macro Tools Design tab. Each line of the macro is executed unless conditions have been placed on specific macro actions. After you click the Run button of `mcrOpenCustomerList` (shown in Figure 17.10), the Customer List form opens.

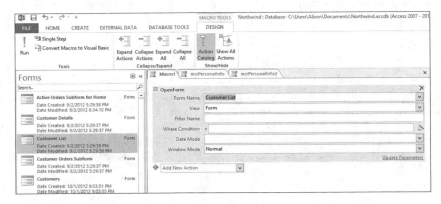

FIGURE 17.10

Running a macro from the Macro Design window.

From Macro Design view, you can run only the first submacro in a macro. To run a macro with submacro, click Run from the Tools group on the Macro Tools Design page to execute the first group in the macro. As soon as the second submacro is encountered, the macro execution terminates. The section "Triggering a Macro from a Form or Report Event" explains how to execute submacros other than the first one in a macro.

Running a Macro from the Macros Group of the Navigation Pane

To run a macro from the Macros group of the Navigation Pane, follow these two steps:

1. Scroll down to the Macros group in the Navigation Pane. If the Macros group does not appear in the Navigation Pane, you need to select All Access Objects from the Navigation Pane drop-down and then expand the Macros group.

2. Double-click the name of the macro you want to execute, or right-click the macro and select Run.

TIP If the macro you execute contains submacros, only the macro actions within the first group are executed.

Triggering a Macro from a Form or Report Event

Sometimes, you execute a macro in response to an event on a form or report. Examples are a form opening, someone clicking a command button, or a form closing. Here, you learn how to associate a macro with a command button.

The form in Figure 17.11 illustrates how to associate a macro with the `Click` event of a form's command button. Four steps are needed to associate a macro with a Form or Report event:

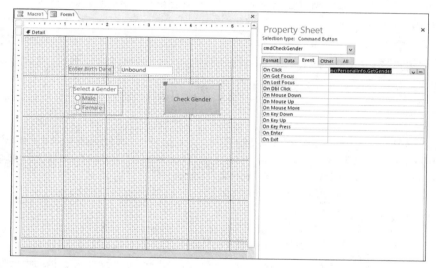

FIGURE 17.11

Associating a macro with a Form or Report event.

1. Select the object you want to associate the event with. In the example, the `cmdCheckGender` command button is selected.

2. Open the Property Sheet and click the Event tab.

3. Click the event you want the macro to execute in response to. In the example, the `Click` event of the command button is selected.

4. Use the drop-down list to select the name of the macro you want to execute. If the macro has submacros, make sure you select the correct submacro subroutine. In the example, the macro `mcrPersonalInfo` and the macro name `GetGender` have been selected. Notice the period between the name of the macro and the name of the macro name submacro. The period is used to differentiate the submacro (`mcrPersonalInfo`, in this case) from the macro name (`GetGender`, in this example).

Modifying an Existing Macro

You have learned how to create a macro, add macro actions and their associated arguments, create macro subroutines by adding submacros, and conditionally execute the actions in the macro by adding macro conditions. However, after you create a macro, you might want to modify it. First, you must enter Design view for the macro:

1. Select the Macros group on the Navigation Pane.

2. Select the macro you want to modify.

3. Right-click and select Design View.

When the design of the macro appears, you're then ready to insert new lines, delete existing lines, move the macro actions around, or copy macro actions to the macro you're modifying or to another macro.

Inserting New Macro Actions

To insert a macro action, follow these steps:

1. Click the line above where you want the macro action to be inserted. An Add New Action macro line appears.

2. Open the drop-down to select the appropriate macro action, click to Add Else, or click to Add Else If.

Deleting Macro Actions

Follow these steps to delete a macro action:

1. Hover your mouse over the macro action, submacro, or If statement that you want to delete.

2. Click the X that appears on the right side of the macro line.

TIP As an alternative, to delete a line within a macro, just right-click that line and select Delete from the context-sensitive menu.

Moving Macro Actions

You can move macro actions in a few ways, including dragging and dropping and cutting and pasting. To move macro actions by dragging and dropping, follow these steps:

1. Hover your mouse pointer over the left side of the macro action you want to move until you see a hand.

2. Click and drag to move the macro action to the wanted location.

3. Release the mouse button.

TIP You can move multiple macro actions as a group by clicking the first action you want to move. You then hold down your Shift key and click the last action you want to move. When you click and drag the hand of the first action, the actions will move as a group.

TIP If you accidentally drag and drop the selected macro actions to an incorrect place, use the Undo button on the Quick Access toolbar to reverse your action.

Copying Macro Actions

Follow these steps to copy macro actions within a macro:

1. Hold down the Ctrl key.

2. Hover your mouse pointer over the macro action you want to copy.

3. When the hand appears, click and drag to copy the macro action to the wanted location.

To copy multiple macro actions simultaneously, complete these steps:

1. Click to select the first action you want to copy.

2. While holding down the Shift key, click the last action you want to copy.

3. Hover your mouse pointer over one of the macro actions in the group.

4. When the hand appears, click and drag to copy the macro action to the wanted location.

Creating an Embedded Macro

Creating an embedded macro is similar to creating a standard macro. The main difference is that the macro is embedded in the object with which it is associated and does not appear in the list of macros in the Navigation Pane. Here's how to create an embedded macro:

1. In Design view, click to select the object to which you want to associate the macro (for example, a command button).

2. Open the Property Sheet, as shown in Figure 17.12.

3. Click the Event tab of the Property Sheet.

4. Click within the event to which you want to associate the embedded macro. In Figure 17.12 the **On Click** event is selected.

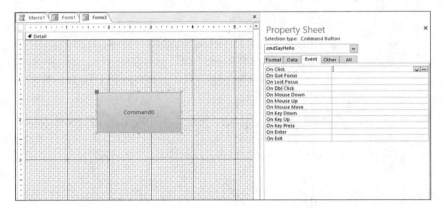

FIGURE 17.12

Use the Property Sheet to associate a macro with the event of an object.

5. Click the build button (the ellipse). The Choose Builder dialog box appears (see Figure 17.13).

6. Select Macro Builder and click OK. A Macro Design window appears, as shown in Figure 17.14. The Macro tab is labeled **cmdSayHello: On Click**, indicating that the macro is associated with the **On Click** event of **cmdSayHello**.

7. Enter the macro commands as you would for any macro, as shown in Figure 17.15.

FIGURE 17.13

The Choose Builder dialog box enables you to specify that you want to build a macro.

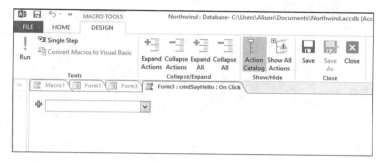

FIGURE 17.14

The macro that you create is associated with the appropriate event of the designated object.

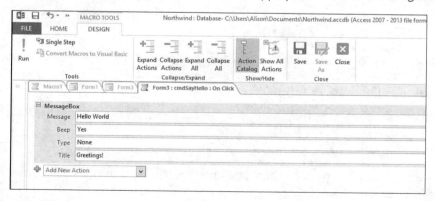

FIGURE 17.15

Your macro commands appear just like macros that are not embedded.

8. Close the Macro Design window. Access prompts you to save changes to the macro and update the property, as in Figure 17.16.

FIGURE 17.16

If you save your changes, Access embeds the macro in the object.

9. Click Yes to save your changes and close the dialog box. You have now created the embedded macro.

 NOTE One advantage of embedded macros is that if you copy the object containing the embedded macro, the macro copies with the object. For example, if you copy a command button from one form to another, the entire embedded macro will be associated with the command button on the second form. If you then change one of the embedded macros, it does not affect the other one.

THE ABSOLUTE MINIMUM

Macros can help you to easily add polish and pizzazz to your application. They can also save time by automating tedious or repetitive tasks. In this chapter you learned all the basics of working with macros.

Macro actions are at the heart of the macros that you build. A macro action instructs Access to perform a task. Macro actions can do everything from opening a form, to displaying a message, to deleting the current record.

After you select a macro action, the appropriate action arguments appear. Each macro action has the appropriate arguments associated with it. These arguments tell the action how to behave. For example, if you select the OpenForm macro action, the arguments that appear all apply to opening a form. If you pick the MessageBox action, the arguments that appear pertain to displaying a message to the user.

If you create a large number of macros, you probably want to use submacros, which enable you to place multiple macros in a main macro. For example, you can place all macros related to opening forms, each as a submacro within a main macro. Each submacro can contain as many macro actions as you need.

Macros would be somewhat limited if you couldn't control the program flow. You introduce logic into a macro by inserting If statements. You can then specify what actions execute in response to different conditions. For example, if the user clicks the Female option button, one set of actions occur. A different set of actions occur if the user clicks the Male option button.

After you create the macros that you want to execute, you must decide how you want to execute them. You can execute a macro from the Macro Design window. This is the least elegant way to execute a macro. Instead, you probably want to trigger a macro from a form or report event. Access exposes a plethora of events that you can choose from. Examples are the Click event of a command button or the Open event of a form.

The chapter completed with a discussion of embedded macros. Unlike macros that appear in the Navigation Pane and can be executed from anywhere in a database, embedded macros are associated with a specific event of an object and are embedded within the object. There are two major advantages of embedded macros. The first is that if you copy the object, the embedded macro follows along with the copied object. The second advantage is that you don't end up with a large number of macros in the Navigation Pane. The main disadvantage of embedded macros is that you cannot call them from multiple objects. In summary, you should use embedded macros when you know that they don't need to be reused and use stand-alone macros when it makes sense to call them from multiple places in your application.

ADVANCED MACRO TECHNIQUES

In this chapter, you learn advanced macro techniques. You learn how to create data macros and Drillthrough macros. You also learn how to add error handling to the macros that you build. You explore the process to include variables in your macros. You then see how you can test the macros that you build. Macros aren't appropriate in all situations. Fortunately, if you decide you want to convert a macro to VBA code, the process is simple. Finally, you explore AutoExec macros and learn why they are important.

Creating Data Macros

Data macros were introduced with Access 2010. They are powerful and take Access macros to a new level.

A Data macro is a macro that executes in response to data changing within a table. The following are the events that you can respond to:

- After data is inserted
- After data is updated
- After data is deleted
- Before data is deleted
- Before data is changed

Respond to Events

Here's how it works:

1. Open the table to which you want to add the Data macros in Design view.

2. Click the Create Data Macros drop-down in the Field, Record & Table Events drop-down on the Table Tools Design tab on the Ribbon. The drop-down appears, as shown in Figure 18.1.

3. Select the event you want to respond to. For the example, select After Insert, which executes after you insert a record into a table.

4. Open the Action drop-down and select the wanted action. For this example I will select LookUpRecord. Access prompts for the table in which to look up the record, the condition under which to perform the action, and the action to perform. The completed event appears in Figure 18.2. It looks up a record in the Users table where the Order ID in the Orders table matches the Order ID of the current record in the Order Details table. It then increments the value of the field NumberOfDetailItems in the Orders table by 1 (to follow along with this example you will need to add the NumberOfDetailItems field to the Northwind Orders table).

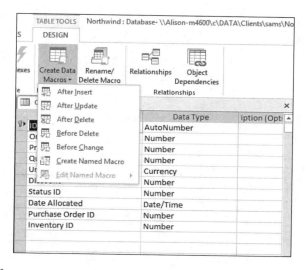

FIGURE 18.1

The Create Data Macros drop-down enables you to select the data event you want to respond to.

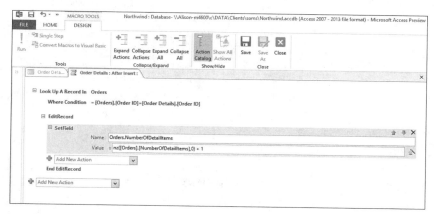

FIGURE 18.2

The LookUpRecord action looks up a record in another table where the specified condition is true.

Creating a Drillthrough Macro

An exciting technique available, also introduced with Access 2010, is the ability to easily create a Drillthrough macro. With a Drillthrough macro, you click an ID on a main form and it takes you to a detail form for the record associated with that ID. Here's how it works:

1. In the list of tables in the Navigation Pane, click to select the parent table. For this example, select the Orders table.

2. In the Forms group on the Create tab on the Ribbon, select Datasheet from the More Forms drop-down. Access creates a datasheet form based on the Orders table (as shown in Figure 18.3).

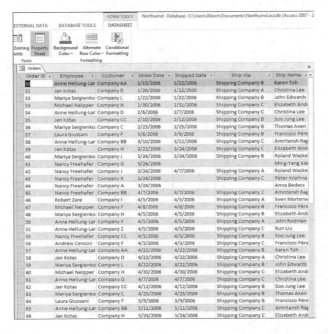

FIGURE 18.3

The datasheet form displays all the table's records in a datasheet.

3. Save the form as **frmOrdersDatasheet**.

4. Select the Order ID column on the form. This may require using the Object drop-down in the Property Sheet.

5. Click the Build button for the On Dbl Click event of the text box. The Choose Builder dialog appears.

6. Select Macro Builder and click OK. The macro appears.

7. Open the Action drop-down, and select If from the list of available actions.

8. Enter the If action to execute only the action that follows it if the Order ID contains a value (see Figure 18.4).

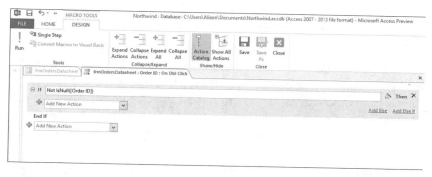

FIGURE 18.4

The If action enables you to determine when the macro statements that follow it execute.

9. Select the OpenForm action as the action you want to execute if the condition entered is true.

10. Fill in the arguments of the OpenForm action to open the Order Details form where the Order ID equals that on the frmOrdersDatasheet form (see Figure 18.5).

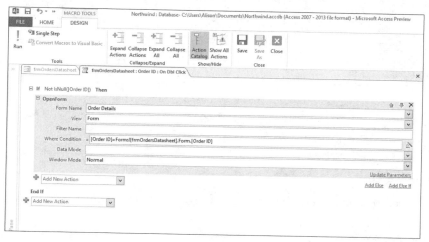

FIGURE 18.5

The completed statement opens the Order Details form, displaying the detail items for the selected order.

11. Save and close the macro.

12. Double-click the OrderID on the navigation form. The Order Details form should open, displaying data for the selected order.

Other New Features Available in Macros

There were two major improvements introduced with Access 2007 macros. The first is the introduction of error handling, and the second is the introduction of variables. Notice the `OnError` macro action in Figure 18.6. The example branches to a macro named `ErrorHandler` in the case of an error. Unlike previous versions of Access, where error handling in macros was virtually nonexistent, the `OnError` macro action provides similar error handling to that of VBA code (the programming language for Microsoft Access).

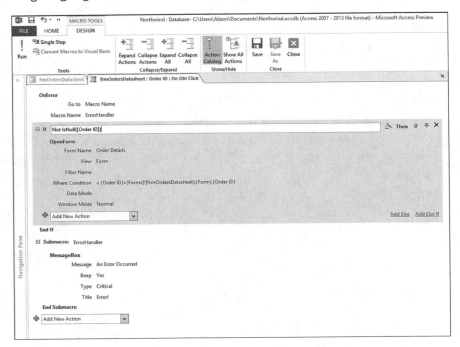

FIGURE 18.6

The `OnError` macro action provides similar error handling to that of VBA code.

Another exciting addition to Access 2007 macros was the introduction of variables. The `SetTempVar` macro action enables you to create a variable and assign it a value. You can then do something with the variable later in the macro. Figure 18.7 provides an example. Notice in the figure that the macro uses the `SetTempVar` action to create a variable called `CurrentDate` and assigns it the value returned from the built-in `Date()` function. The macro then uses TempVars to retrieve the value of the variable and display it in a message box.

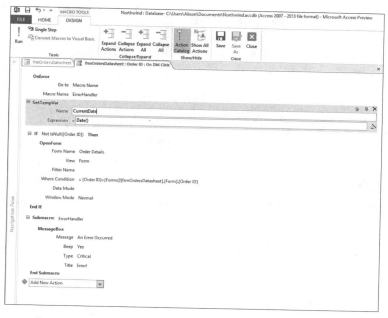

FIGURE 18.7

You use the SetTempVar action to create a temporary variable in a Microsoft Office Access 2013 macro.

Testing a Macro

Although Access doesn't offer sophisticated tools to test and debug your macros, it does give you a method to step through each line of a macro:

1. Open the macro in Design view.

2. Click Single Step in the Tools group on the Design tab.

3. To execute the macro, click Run. The first line of the macro executes, and the Macro Single Step dialog box appears, showing you the Macro Name, Condition, Action Name, and Arguments, as shown in Figure 18.8. In the figure, the macro is the On Dbl Click event of the Order Id, and the condition evaluates to false. The action name and arguments are not available.

4. To continue stepping through the macro, click the Step button in the Macro Single Step dialog box. If you want to halt the execution of the macro without proceeding, click the Stop All Macros button. To continue normal execution of the macro without stepping, click the Continue button.

FIGURE 18.8

In the Macro Single Step dialog box, you can view the macro name, condition, action name, and arguments for the current step of the macro.

 NOTE The Single Step button in the Tools group of the Design tab is a toggle. After you activate Step Mode, it's activated for all macros in the current database and all other databases until you either turn off the toggle or exit Access. This behavior can be quite surprising if you don't expect it. You might have invoked Step mode in another database quite a bit earlier in the day, only to remember that you forgot to click the toggle button when some other macro unexpectedly goes into Step mode.

Determining When You Should Use Macros and When You Shouldn't

Macros aren't always the best tools to create code that controls industrial-strength applications because they're limited in some functionality. Access macros are limited in the following ways:

- You can't create user-defined functions using macros.

- Access macros don't enable you to pass parameters.

- Access macros provide no method to process table records one at a time.

- When using Access macros, you can't use object linking and embedding automation to communicate with other applications.

- Debugging Access macros is more difficult than debugging VBA code.

- Transaction processing can't be done with Access macros.

- You can't call Windows API functions by using Access macros.

- Access macros don't enable you to create database objects at runtime.

Converting a Macro to VBA Code

Sometimes you create a macro and later to discover that you want to convert it to VBA code. Fortunately, Access 2013 comes to the rescue. You can easily convert an Access macro to VBA code. After the macro has been converted to VBA code, the code can be modified just like any VBA module. Follow these four steps to convert an Access macro to VBA code:

1. Open the macro you want to convert in Design view.

2. Select Convert Macros to Visual Basic in the Tools group on the Macro Tools Design tab on the Ribbon. The Convert Macro dialog appears (see Figure 18.9).

FIGURE 18.9

The Convert Macro dialog box enables you to save a macro as a Visual Basic module.

3. Determine where you want to add error handling and comments to the generated code, and then click Convert. Access informs you that the conversion finished and places you in the Visual Basic Editor—VBE (see Figure 18.10).

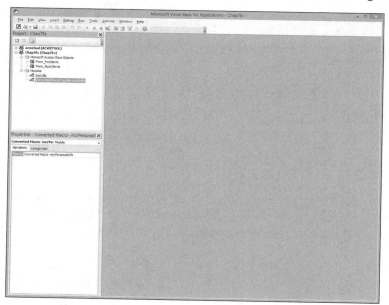

FIGURE 18.10

The Visual Basic Editor enables you to view and modify the programming code that you generated.

4. The converted macro appears under the list of modules with `Converted Macro:` followed by the name of the macro. Click Design to view the results of the conversion.

Figure 18.11 shows a macro that's been converted into distinct subroutines, one for each macro name. The macro is complete with logic, comments, and error handling. All macro conditions are converted into `If...Else...End If` statements, and all the macro comments are converted into VBA comments. Basic error-handling routines are automatically added to the code.

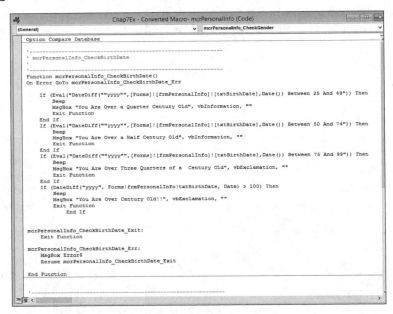

FIGURE 18.11

A converted macro as a module.

Creating an AutoExec Macro

With Access 2013, you can use either an AutoExec macro or Startup options to determine what occurs when a database is opened. Using an AutoExec macro to launch the processing of your application is certainly a viable option.

TIP When you're opening your own database to make changes or additions to the application, you probably won't want the AutoExec macro to execute. To prevent it from executing, hold down your Shift key as you open the database.

Creating an AutoExec macro is simple; it's just a normal macro saved with the name AutoExec. An AutoExec macro usually performs tasks such as hiding or minimizing the Navigation Pane and opening a Startup form or switchboard. The macro shown in Figure 18.12 hides the Navigation Pane, displays a welcome message, and opens the Home form.

FIGURE 18.12

An example of an AutoExec macro.

THE ABSOLUTE MINIMUM

In this chapter, you learned advanced macro techniques. You began with a discussion of Data macros. Data macros are extremely powerful! Using Data macros you can ensure that specific things occur before or after you insert or update data, or after you delete data. The beauty of Data macros is that they execute in response to those events, regardless of how you affect the data. In other words, Data macros execute if you modify data in a table datasheet, query datasheet, form, macro, or programming code. This makes them even more powerful!

Drillthrough macros are also powerful. As their name implies, Drillthrough macros enable you to drill down to the details behind the data on a form. For example, using a Drillthrough macro, the user can double-click an ID on a summary form to open up a form that shows the detail for the record with that ID.

The ability to handle errors in the macros that you build makes them much more powerful. Rather than displaying a generic error message, you can use error handling to determine exactly what happens when an error occurs while your macro executes.

The ability to set and retrieve the value of variables in macros also makes them powerful. You can place values in variables and then retrieve them at a later time.

If you want to test a macro, you can do so with the Single Step feature. After you activate the Single Step feature, your macros execute a line at a time. You can view the value of variables, determine the flow of If statements, and watch exactly what happens as your macro executes. When you solve your problem, you simply turn the Single Step feature off. (It is a toggle.)

You cannot accomplish everything with macros. For this reason, it is a good idea that you know how to convert a macro to VBA programming code. After you convert a macro to VBA code, you must modify your objects to reference the code rather than the macros.

One of the most powerful macros is the AutoExec macro. The actions in an AutoExec macro execute each time the database opens. An AutoExec macro is a great place to control the behavior of the database. Using an AutoExec macro, you can hide the Navigation Pane, display a startup form, and much more!

19

IN THIS CHAPTER

- What is external data, and why do you care?
- What does it mean to import data versus link to data, and when should you use each?
- How can you export access data?
- How can you import data into Access?
- How do you link to data in other Access databases?
- How do you link to data stored in Microsoft SQL Server?

SHARING DATA WITH OTHER APPLICATIONS

Microsoft Access can interface with data from other sources. It can use data from any OLE DB or Open Database Connectivity (ODBC) data source and data from FoxPro, dBASE, Paradox, Lotus, Excel, and many other sources. In this chapter, you learn how to interface with other Access databases, Excel, ASCII text files, and ODBC data sources.

What Is External Data?

External data is data stored outside the current database. External data might be data that you store in another Microsoft Access database, or it might be data that you store in a multitude of other file formats including Indexed Sequential Access Method (ISAM), spreadsheet, ASCII, and more.

Access is an excellent *front-end* product, which means that it provides a powerful and effective means to present data—even data from external sources. You might opt to store data in places other than Access for many reasons. You can most effectively manage large databases, for example, on a back-end database server such as Microsoft SQL Server. You might store data in a FoxPro, dBASE, or Paradox file format because a legacy application written in one of those environments is using the data. You might download text data from a mainframe or midrange computer. Regardless of the reason the data is stored in another format, you must understand how to manipulate this external data in Access applications. With Access' capability to access data from other sources, you can create queries, forms, and reports.

When you access external data, you have two choices: You can import the data into an Access database or you can access the data by linking to it from an Access database. Importing the data is the optimum route (except with ODBC data sources), but it is not always possible. If you can't import external data, you should link to external files because Microsoft Access maintains a lot of information about these linked files. This optimizes performance when manipulating the external files.

Importing, Linking, and Opening Files: When and Why

When you import data into an Access table, Access makes a copy of the data and places it in the Access table. After Access imports the data, it treats the data like the data in any other native Access table. Neither you nor Access has any way to know from where the data came. As a result, imported data offers the same performance and flexibility as any other Access table data.

Linking to external data is quite different from importing data. Linked data remains in its native format. By establishing a link to the external data, you can build queries, forms, and reports that present the data. After you create a link to external data, the link remains permanently established unless you explicitly remove it. The linked table appears in the Navigation Pane just like any other Access table, except that its icon is different. Actually, if the data source permits multiuser access, the users of an application can modify the data as can the users of the applications written in the data source's native database format (such as

FoxPro, dBASE, or Paradox). The main difference between a linked table and a native table is that you cannot modify a linked table's structure from within Access.

Determining Whether to Import or Link

You must understand when to import external data and when to link to external data. You should import external data in either of these circumstances:

- If you migrate an existing system into Access.

- If you want to use external data to run a large volume of queries and reports, and you will not update the data. In this case, you want the added performance that native Access data provides.

When you migrate an existing system to Access and you are ready to permanently migrate test or production data into an application, you import the tables into Access. You might also want to import external data if you convert the data into ASCII format on a regular basis and you want to use the data for reports. Instead of attempting to link to the data and suffering the performance hits associated with such a link, you can import the data each time you download it from the mainframe or midrange computer.

You should link to external data in any of the following circumstances:

- The data is used by a legacy application that requires the native file format.

- The data resides on an ODBC-compliant database server such as Microsoft SQL Server.

- You can access the data on a regular basis, making it prohibitive to keep the data up to date if you do not link to it.

Often, you won't have the time or resources to rewrite an application written in FoxPro, Paradox, or some other language. You might develop additional applications to share data with the legacy application, or you might want to use the strong querying and reporting capabilities of Access rather than develop queries and reports in the native environment.

If you link to the external data, users of existing applications can continue to work with the applications and their data. Access applications can retrieve and modify data without concern for corrupting, or in any other way harming, the data.

If the data resides in an ODBC database such as Microsoft SQL Server, you want to reap the data-retrieval benefits provided by a database server. By linking to the ODBC data source, you can take advantage of Access's ease of use as a front-end tool and also take advantage of client/server technology.

Finally, if you intend to access data on a regular basis, linking to the external table provides you with ease of use and performance benefits. After you create a link, in most cases, Access treats the table just like any other Access table.

Although this chapter covers the process to import external data, this is essentially a one-time process and doesn't require a lot of discussion. After you import data into an Access table, you can no longer use the application in its native format to access the data.

Looking at Supported File Formats

Microsoft Access enables you to import and link to files in these formats:

- Microsoft Access databases (including versions earlier than Access 2010)
- ODBC databases
- HTML (Hypertext Markup Language) documents with `<table>` tags
- eXtensible Markup Language (XML) documents (import and open only)
- Microsoft Exchange and Outlook
- dBASE III, dBASE IV, and dBASE 5.0
- Paradox 3.x, 4.x, and 5.x
- Microsoft Excel spreadsheets, versions 3.0, 4.0, 5.0, and 8.0
- Lotus WKS, WK1, WK3, and WK4 spreadsheets (import and open only)
- ASCII text files stored in a tabular format

Exporting to Another Access Database

You can easily export Access tables and queries to another Access database. The following is the required process:

1. Right-click the object you want to export, and select Export from the context menu. (Alternatively, you can select Access from the Export group on the External Data tab on the Ribbon.) The menu appears as in Figure 19.1.

2. Select Access. The Export – Access Database dialog appears.

3. Select the Access database to which you want to export the object, and then click OK. The Export dialog box appears (see Figure 19.2).

4. In the Export dialog box, select Definition and Data or Definition Only, depending on whether you want to export just the structure or the structure and the data. Click OK.

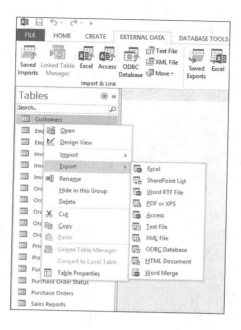

FIGURE 19.1

After selecting Export, you can designate the type of file you want to export to.

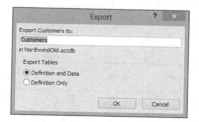

FIGURE 19.2

The Export dialog box enables you to designate whether you want to export the definition and data or the definition only.

 NOTE When you export an object to another database, Access exports a copy of the object. When you choose Definition Only, Access copies just the object's structure (no data) to the receiving database.

Exporting to an Excel Spreadsheet

You might want to export table data or query results to an Excel spreadsheet so that you can use Excel's analytical features. You can accomplish this in many ways. You can export an object by right-clicking it; you can export an object using drag and drop; or you can export it using the External Data tab on the Ribbon.

Exporting to an Excel Spreadsheet Using the Context-Sensitive Menu

To export table data or query results to an Excel spreadsheet, follow these steps:

1. Right-click the object you want to export, and select Export from the context menu. The menu expands to show all the valid Export formats.

2. Select Excel from the menu. The Export – Excel Spreadsheet dialog appears (see Figure 19.3).

3. Designate the filename and file format.

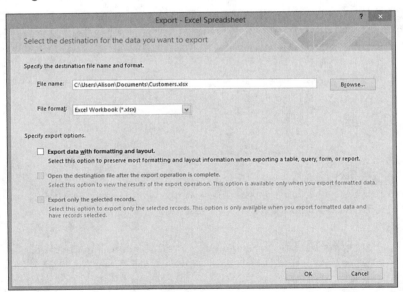

FIGURE 19.3

The Export – Excel Spreadsheet dialog box enables you to designate the specifics for the export process to Excel.

4. Specify the wanted export options (for example, if you want to export the data with formatting and layout and whether you want Excel to launch when the process is complete).

5. Click OK to complete the process.

Exporting to an Excel Spreadsheet Using Drag and Drop

You can export a table or query to Microsoft Excel by dragging and dropping it directly onto an Excel spreadsheet. This whiz-bang technology makes the integration between these two powerful products virtually seamless. Follow these steps:

1. Arrange the Access and Excel application windows so that both are visible.

2. Drag the object (that is, the table or query) from the Access Navigation Pane onto the Excel spreadsheet. The results of dragging and dropping the Customers table from the Access Navigation Pane to Microsoft Excel appear in Figure 19.4.

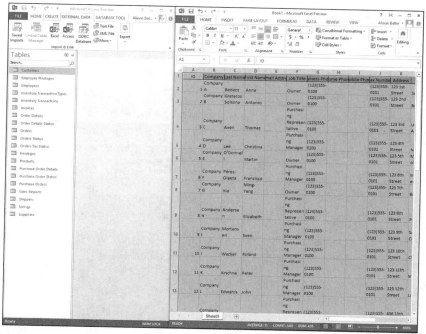

FIGURE 19.4

Dragging and dropping an object directly from the Access Navigation Pane onto an Excel spreadsheet.

Exporting to an Excel Spreadsheet by Using the External Data Tab on the Ribbon

You can use the External Data tab on the Ribbon to export an Access table or query to Microsoft Excel, as follows:

1. Select the object you want to export.

2. Select Excel from the Export group on the External Data tab on the Ribbon. The Export – Excel Spreadsheet dialog appears.

3. Select the destination location and file format and the export options; then click OK. The export process completes.

Exporting to ASCII

ASCII is a standard file format that many programs can work with. Exporting to the ASCII format enables you to make the data in an Access database available to other applications.

Export Tables and Queries to the ASCII File Format

It is easy to export Access tables and queries to the ASCII file format. Here's how it works:

1. Right-click the object you want to export, and select Export from the context menu. (Alternatively, you can select Text File from the Export group on the External Data tab on the Ribbon.) The Export menu expands.

2. Select Text File from the fly-out menu. The Export – Text File dialog appears (see Figure 19.5).

3. Select the destination folder and name for the text file.

4. Designate the export options, and click OK. If you opt to export the data with formatting and layout, the Encode dialog appears.

5. Select the wanted encoding, and click OK. The process completes, and the file appears, as shown in Figure 19.6.

6. If you do not opt to export the data with formatting and layout, the Export Text Wizard appears (see Figure 19.7). This step enables you to select the export format that you want to use. You must select between Delimited and Fixed Width. These are two different text file formats that you may output to. The dialog provides samples of the output to help you make your selection.

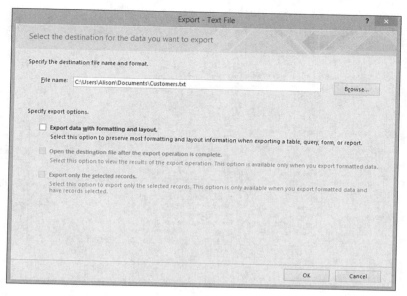

FIGURE 19.5

The Export Text File dialog box.

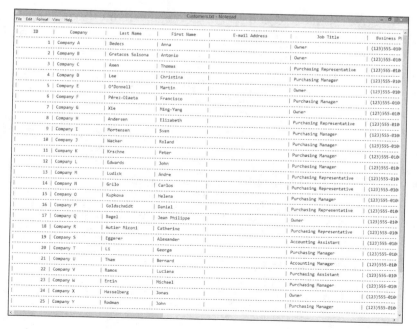

FIGURE 19.6

An exported file when Export the Data with Formatting and Layout is selected.

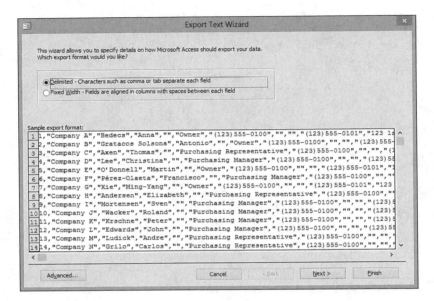

FIGURE 19.7

The Export Text Wizard: step 1.

7. If you select Delimited and then click Advanced, the Text Export Specification dialog box appears (see Figure 19.8). Here you can designate the field delimiter, text qualifier, language, date order, and other specifics about the

FIGURE 19.8

The Text Export Specification dialog box.

file you export. You can modify these options to meet the specifications of the consumer of the file you create.

8. Select the wanted settings, and then click OK.

9. Click Next.

10. Select the delimiter (see Figure 19.9).

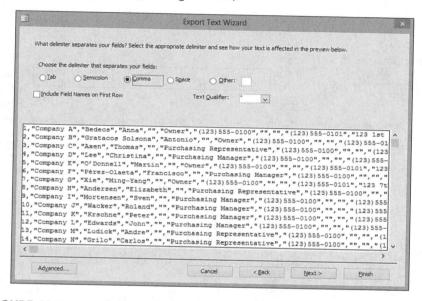

FIGURE 19.9

The Export Text Wizard: step 2.

11. If you select Include Field Names on First Row, the output file includes all the field names in the first row. Click Next. The final step of the Export Text Wizard appears.

12. Type the *appropriate* destination in the Export to File text box.

13. Click Finish to complete the process, and then click Close to close the wizard.

Importing from Another Access Database

You can import objects (for example, tables, queries, and reports) from one Access database into another. When you import an object, you make a copy of the object. Any changes you make to the imported object do not affect the original object.

Import an Access Table

To see how to import an Access table object, follow these steps:

1. Open the database into which you want to import the table.

2. While viewing the list of tables, right-click anywhere within the Navigation Pane, and select Import. (Alternatively, you can select Access from the Import & Link group on the External Data tab on the Ribbon.)

3. Select Access Database from the fly-out menu. The Get External Data – Access Database dialog box appears.

4. Select the folder where the Microsoft Access database you want to import is located.

5. Double-click the database file that contains the object you want to import.

6. Specify how and where you want to store the data in the current database (whether you want to import or link to the table).

7. Click OK. The Import Objects dialog appears.

8. Select the Table tab.

9. Select the table from the list of tables.

10. Click the Options button. The Import Objects dialog appears, as shown in Figure 19.10.

FIGURE 19.10

The Import Objects dialog box after selecting the Options button.

11. Select the wanted options. Options include whether you want to import relationships, menus and toolbars, and import and export specifications. You can also designate whether you want to import just the table definitions, or the table definitions and the data. Finally, you can opt to import the queries as either queries or as tables (the result of executing the queries). Generally, you can leave all these options at their default values; although, you might want to modify them for specific applications.

12. Click OK to complete the process.

Importing Spreadsheet Data

You can easily import an Excel spreadsheet into an Access database. To do so, follow these steps:

1. Open the database into which you want to import the spreadsheet.

2. With Tables selected as the object type, right-click anywhere in the Navigation Pane, and choose Import from the context menu. (Alternatively, you can select Excel from the Import & Link group on the External Data tab on the Ribbon.) The fly-out menu appears.

3. Select Excel from the fly-out menu. The Get External Data – Excel Spreadsheet dialog appears (see Figure 19.11).

4. Use the Browse button to select the Excel file that you want to import.

5. Specify how and where you want to store the data in the current database (for example, Import the Source Data into a New Table in the Current Database).

6. Click OK. The Import Spreadsheet Wizard appears (see Figure 19.12).

7. Select Show Worksheets or Show Named Ranges (Access does not display this step of the wizard if the spreadsheet contains only one worksheet), and then click Next. The Import Spreadsheet Wizard continues.

 NOTE If you plan to import spreadsheet data on a regular basis, it is helpful to define a named range in the Excel spreadsheet, containing the data you wish to import. You can then easily opt to import the named range in step 6 each time that you execute the import process.

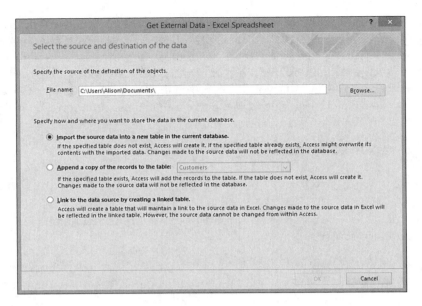

FIGURE 19.11

The Get External Data – Excel Spreadsheet dialog enables you to select the file you want to import.

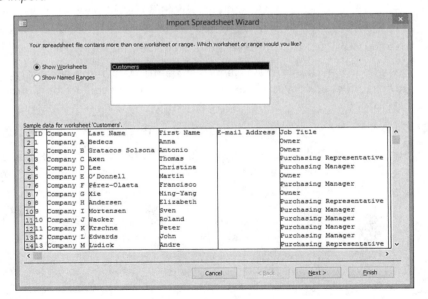

FIGURE 19.12

The Import Spreadsheet Wizard enables you to designate whether you want to import a worksheet or a named range.

NOTE Finally, you shouldn't give a control the same name as its control source. Access gives a bound control the same name as its field, and you need to change this name to avoid problems. If you fail to do so, and you reference the field in a formula for the control, #error# will appear on the report in the place of the data for that field. Following these simple warnings will spare you a lot of grief!

8. Select First Row Contains Column Headings, if appropriate. Notice in the figure that the first row appears as column headings rather than data. Click Next. The wizard appears, as shown in Figure 19.13.

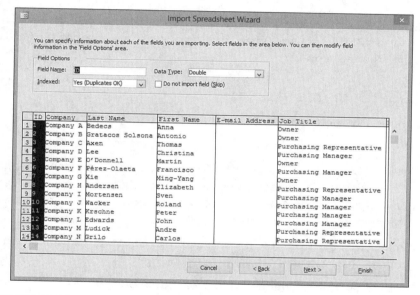

FIGURE 19.13

Designate the specifics of each field that you are importing.

9. Type the field name in the Field Name text box, if necessary.

10. Select whether you want Access to index the field.

11. Indicate whether to import a field by selecting the Do Not Import option for that field, if wanted.

12. Click in the field list to select the next field.

13. Repeat steps 9–12 as appropriate for each field, and then click Next.

14. If your data has a column that is appropriate for the primary key, select Choose My Own Primary Key. Otherwise, select Let Access Add a Primary Key.

15. If you opted to choose your own primary key, select the field from the drop-down box that you want Access to use as the primary key, and then click Next.

16. Type the table name in the Import to Table text box.

17. Click Finish.

18. Click OK.

Importing ASCII Data

Mainframes and minicomputers often export data in the ASCII file format. When you import ASCII data, you often need to make some changes for Access to handle the data properly.

Import ASCII Data into Access

To import ASCII data into Access, follow these steps:

1. Open the database into which you want to import a table.

2. With Tables selected in the list of object types, right-click anywhere in the Navigation Pane, and select Import from the context menu. (Alternatively, you can select Text File from the Import & Link group on the External Data tab on the Ribbon.) A fly-out menu appears.

3. Select Text File from the fly-out menu. The Get External Data – Text File dialog appears (see Figure 19.14).

4. Click Browse to locate the file you want to import.

5. Indicate how and where you want to store the data in the current database, and click OK. This launches the Import Text Wizard (see Figure 19.15).

6. Select Delimited or Fixed Width to designate the format of the file you want to import. Click Next.

7. Indicate the delimiter that separates your fields (for instance, comma), the text qualifier, select or deselect First Row Contains Field Names, as appropriate, and then click Next.

8. Type the field name in the Field Name text box.

9. Select whether you want Access to create an index for the field.

10. Change the data type, if wanted.

11. Repeat steps 8–10, as appropriate.

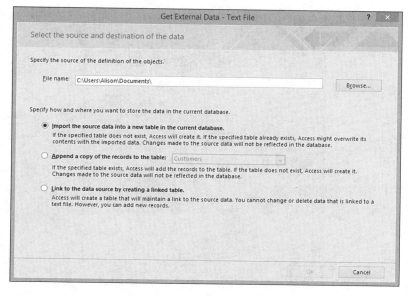

FIGURE 19.14

The Get External Data – Text File dialog enables you to designate the location and name of the file that you want to import.

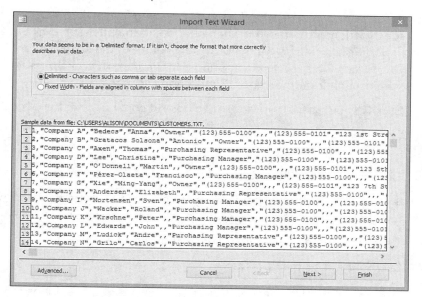

FIGURE 19.15

The Import Text Wizard enables you to designate important information about the format of the file you import.

12. Click Advanced, if wanted, to change the import specifications for each field in one place (see Figure 19.16).

FIGURE 19.16

The Advanced button enables you to change the import specifications for each field.

13. If you plan to import other files with the same format, you can save the import specification and retrieve it when needed. In this situation click Save As in the Import Specifications dialog, provide a name for the specification, and Click OK. To use the specification during a future import, click Specs and Open the specification from the Import/Export Specifications dialog.

14. Click OK to close the advanced dialog and continue with the wizard.

15. Click Next.

16. If your data has a column appropriate for the primary key, select Choose My Own Primary Key. Otherwise, select Let Access Add Primary Key.

17. If you choose your own primary key, select the field from the drop-down box that you want Access to use as the primary key, and then click Next.

18. Type the table name in the Import to Table text box.

19. Click Finish, and then click OK.

When working with ASCII data, you should be aware of a few things that can save you lots of time and effort in working with the imported data, as follows:

• After you import a table, you should open it and view its data. You might want to modify some of the field types to make them the appropriate Access data types. For example, the table you imported from might not have had a currency type.

- You can click the Advanced button anytime in the wizard to change the import specifications for each field (see Figure 19.23).

Linking to Tables in Another Access Database

When you link to data in another database, the data remains in its source location. Access simply creates a pointer to the data. To practice linking to data in different types of databases, follow these steps:

1. Open the database that will contain the link.

2. With Tables selected in the list of object types, right-click within the Navigation Pane, and choose Import and then Access Database from the context menu. (Alternatively, you can select Access from the Import & Link group on the External Data tab on the Ribbon.)

3. Click Browse to locate the database that contains the table that you want to link to.

4. Click Link to the data source by creating a linked table (see Figure 19.17), and then click OK. The Link Tables dialog appears (see Figure 19.18). Only tables actually stored in the database you selected (not linked tables) appear.

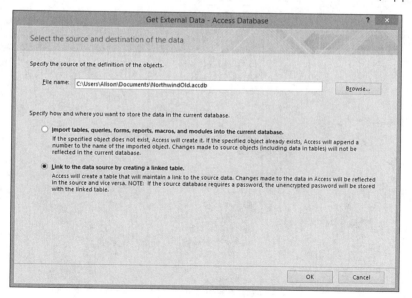

FIGURE 19.17

You must designate that you want to link to the data source.

FIGURE 19.18

The Link Tables dialog box enables you to select the tables you want to link to.

5. Select the tables you want to link to.

6. Click OK. Figure 19.19 shows the results of such an operation.

FIGURE 19.19

The linked tables appear with an arrow.

When working with linked tables in another Access database, you need to remember a few important things, including the following:

- When you link a table to the source, you cannot change some properties in the linked table. The descriptions of these properties appear in red when in Design view of the table.

- If you make a change to any data in a linked table, the change will be reflected in the underlying table.

- Any relationships established between tables in the source are reflected in the linked tables.

- When working with data that needs to be kept on a file server, you should keep the data (that is, the tables) in one database and the other objects (for example, forms, reports) in another database. You then link from the application database to the data database.

Linking to Another Type of Database

Even if you're not ready to actually import data from a database management system (such as FoxPro), you still might want to make changes to it by using Access. You can link to other types of databases and to Excel spreadsheets.

Link to Excel Spreadsheets

Linking to Excel spreadsheets involves the following steps:

1. Open the database that will contain the link.

2. With Tables selected as the object type, right-click in the Navigation Pane, and select Import and then Excel from the context menu. (Alternatively, you can select Excel from the Import & Link group on the External Data tab on the Ribbon.) The Get External Data – Excel Spreadsheet dialog appears.

3. Click Browse to locate the spreadsheet whose data you want to link to.

4. Designate that you want to Link to the data source by creating a linked table.

5. Click OK. The Link Spreadsheet Wizard appears.

6. Select Show Worksheets or Show Named Ranges, as appropriate, and then click Next.

7. Click to select First Row Contains Column Headings, if appropriate.

8. Click Next.

9. Type a name for the linked table.

10. Click Finish, and then click OK. An icon associated with the linked table appears (see Figure 19.20).

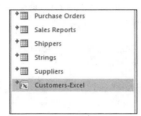

Purchase Orders
Sales Reports
Shippers
Strings
Suppliers
Customers-Excel

FIGURE 19.20

Access associates an Excel icon with the link.

Link to Other Databases

In addition to linking to Access tables and Excel spreadsheets, you might want to link to FoxPro, Paradox, and other database files. Here are the required steps:

1. Open the database that will contain the links.

2. With Tables selected in the object list, right-click in the Navigation Pane, and select Link Tables from the context menu. (Alternatively, you can select the appropriate data type [for example, dBASE] from the More drop-down in the Import & Link group on the External Data tab on the Ribbon.)

3. Click Browse and locate the file containing the data you want to link to.

4. Select Link to the data source by creating a linked table.

5. Click OK. The table appears in the Navigation Pane with the appropriate icon (for example, dBASE).

When working with linked tables in other databases, you need to remember a few important things, including the following:

- When you link a table to the source, there are some properties that you cannot change in the linked table. The descriptions of these properties appear in red while in Design view of the table.

- Any data you change in a linked table changes in the source table too.

Linking to SQL Server Databases

In a system where you store your data solely in Access tables, the Access Database Engine supplies all data retrieval and management functions and handles security, data validation, and enforcement of referential integrity.

In a system where Access acts as a front end to client/server data, the server handles the data management functions. It's responsible for retrieving, protecting, and updating data on the back-end database server. In this scenario, the local copy of Access is responsible only for sending requests and getting either data or pointers to data back from the database server. If you're creating an application in which Access acts as a front end, capitalizing on the strengths of both Access and the server can be a challenging endeavor.

You might ask why you would want to convert your database to a client/server application. The reasons include the following:

- Greater control over data integrity
- Increased control over data security
- Increased fault tolerance
- Reduced network traffic
- Improved performance
- Centralized control and management of data

Scenarios in which you *may* need to upsize include the following:

- Large number of simultaneous users (more than 10–15)
- Large volume of data (tables with more than approximately 100,000 rows)
- Increased need for security (payroll data and such)

Link to SQL Server Data

If you store your data in SQL Server, you must link to it from your Access database. The steps that follow show you how to link from an Access database to a table stored on a SQL Server:

1. Select ODBC Database from the Import & Link group on the External Data tab on the Ribbon. The Get External Data – ODBC Database dialog appears.

2. Select Link to the data source by creating a linked table, and click OK. The Select Data Source dialog appears.

3. Select the Machine Data Source tab. The dialog appears, as shown in Figure 19.21.

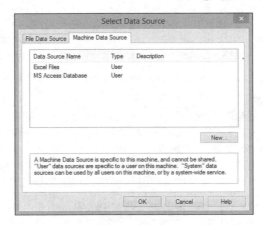

FIGURE 19.21

The Machine Data Source tab of the Select Data Source dialog.

4. Click New. A warning may appear indicating that you cannot create System DSNs. If the warning appears, click OK to dismiss the dialog. The Create New Data Source Wizard appears (see Figure 19.22).

FIGURE 19.22

The first step of the Create New Data Source Wizard.

5. Click Next. The wizard appears as in Figure 19.23.

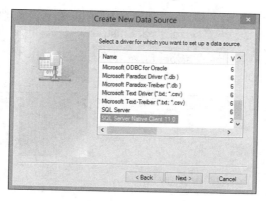

FIGURE 19.23

The second step of the Create New Data Source Wizard.

6. Select SQL Server or SQL Server Native Client 11.0 (depending on which version of SQL Server you are accessing), and then click Next.

7. Click Finish to launch the Create a New Data Source to SQL Server Wizard (see Figure 19.24).

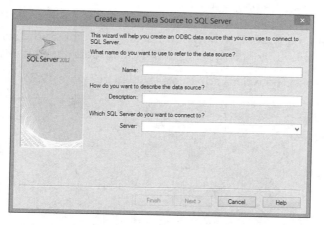

FIGURE 19.24

The first step of the Create a New Data Source to SQL Server Wizard prompts you to name the data source and to designate the source server.

8. Supply a name and optional description for the data source.

9. Designate the name of the SQL Server you want to connect to. (You might need to contact your system administrator to obtain this information.)

10. Click Next. The wizard appears, as shown in Figure 19.25. The wizard may vary based on your network and ODBC configuration.

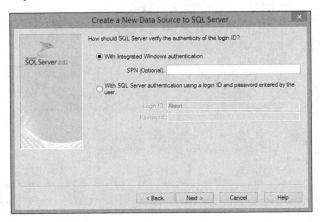

FIGURE 19.25

Indicate the type of security you will use to log on to the server.

11. Indicate the type of security you will use to log on to the server. (Again, you might need to contact your system administrator for this information.)

12. Click Next. The wizard appears as shown in Figure 19.26.

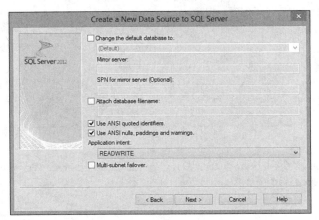

FIGURE 19.26

Designate the default database that you want to connect to.

13. Change the default database to point at the SQL Server database that you want to link to. The database that is selected here by default varies based on your default database defined in SQL Server.

14. Click Next. The final step of the wizard appears. You can generally leave all these settings at their default values.

15. Click Finish. A dialog appears showing you all the settings you have selected.

16. Click Test Data Source to test your connection to the SQL Server database. A dialog appears confirming that the test was successful.

17. Click OK to close the dialog, and click OK again to close the wizard. Your data source appears in the list of available data sources.

18. Click OK to select the new data source, and begin the process to link to the tables within it. The Link Tables dialog appears (see Figure 19.27).

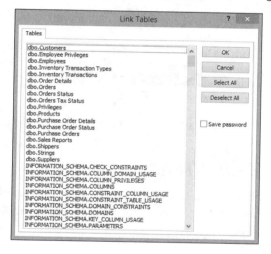

FIGURE 19.27

The Link Tables dialog enables you to designate the tables you want to link to.

19. Select the tables you want to link to, and click OK. The process completes, and the tables appear in the Navigation Pane with globes (see Figure 19.28), indicating that they are using ODBC to connect to the SQL Server. You can now treat the tables like any other linked tables.

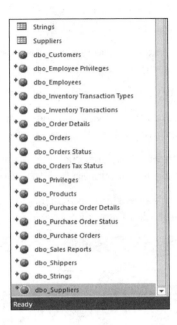

FIGURE 19.28

The tables you selected appear with globes in the Navigation Pane.

The Linked Table Manager

The Linked Table Manager is an important tool to work with linked tables. It enables you to move tables to another folder or another drive and then update the link to that table.

Move and Update Table Links

To move and update table links, follow these steps:

1. Choose Linked Table Manager from the Import & Link group on the External Data tab on the Ribbon. The Linked Table Manager appears (see Figure 19.29).

2. Select the linked tables you want to update.

3. Select the Always Prompt for New Location check box.

4. Click OK.

5. Select the folder or drive to which you have moved the table.

FIGURE 19.29

The Linked Table Manager.

6. Select the table, and then click Open.

7. Click OK.

You might at some time have a link that you no longer need. For example, you might import data because it is no longer necessary to use the legacy system that you have in place. The following are the steps necessary to remove such a link:

1. Select the link you want to remove.

2. Press the Delete key. The dialog box shown in Figure 19.30 appears.

FIGURE 19.30

Access prompts you to remove the link.

3. Click Yes to remove the link. The link is removed.

 CAUTION It is important to note that this process does not remove the linked object. It just removes the link.

THE ABSOLUTE MINIMUM

One of the strong points of Access is its capability to almost seamlessly interact with other types of data. External data refers to data that does not reside in the current database. It can be data in another Access database, data in another file format (such as FoxPro, dBase, or text), or data in an ODBC database such as SQL Server.

When working with external data, you can link to the external data, or you can import the external data. There are times when each is appropriate. You import data if you are permanently moving it into Access, or if you have a large volume of data on which you want to run queries and reports. You link to data that needs to remain in its native format for use with a legacy application. You also link to ODBC data so that you can take advantage of the data processing performance afforded by a client/server database, such as Microsoft SQL Server, while using the awesome capabilities of Access to build forms, queries, reports, macros, and VBA programming code.

The process of importing or linking to data allows you to work with all types of data within Microsoft Access. Sometimes, you need to export Access data to another file format. You can send data to other Access databases, to Excel spreadsheets, to text files, ODBC databases, and to several other file formats. The options available to you vary depending on which type of file format you want to export your data to. For example, if you export data to another Access database, you can opt to export just the structure associated with the data or the structure and data.

The options for importing data into Access are as plentiful as those for exporting. Again the process varies depending on the type of data that you interact with. For example, when importing spreadsheet data, you can designate whether the first row in the Excel spreadsheet contains column headings.

Remember that when you link to data, it remains in its source location. Depending on the type of data that you link to, you may or may not update the data from within Access. For example, you cannot update Excel data from within Access. What you can do is to create powerful and exciting queries, forms, and reports that display the Excel data in a user-friendly format.

The most robust type of data you can interface is that in a SQL Server database. Storing data in SQL Server has many benefits. The main benefit is that queries are processed on the server and SQL Server returns only the results to the user. For example, if you link to a SQL Server database containing 1 million customers, and you create a query in Access to retrieve only the customers in Alaska, the query processes on the server and SQL Server returns only the data for the customers in Alaska. Another major benefit to store data in SQL Server is that you can properly secure the data. You cannot do much to properly secure Access data. To the contrary, SQL Server sports a robust and powerful security model. Using Access as the "front-end" and SQL Server as the "back-end," you can create powerful and high-performing databases.

WORKING WITH WEB DATABASES

Microsoft Access 2013 enables you to create web databases. Using a web database, you can create an application where the database objects can be viewed in a browser. In this chapter, you learn how to create and work with a web database. You learn how to create and use web forms. You also learn how to view your web application in a browser.

Working with Web Databases

As its name implies, a web database is a database whose objects can be published to the web and viewed in a browser. Creating and working with a web database is simple. Here's what's involved:

1. Designate a Blank web database as the type of file you want to create.

2. Create objects that are publishable to the web.

3. Publish the database to Access Services.

4. View your application in a browser.

 CAUTION You must either have access to a SharePoint server or use the version of Office 365 that supports web databases to follow along with this chapter.

Creating a Blank Web Database

The process of creating a web database is similar to that of creating a standard Access database. Here are the steps:

1. Click the File tab on the Ribbon.

2. Select New. Your screen appears as in Figure 20.1.

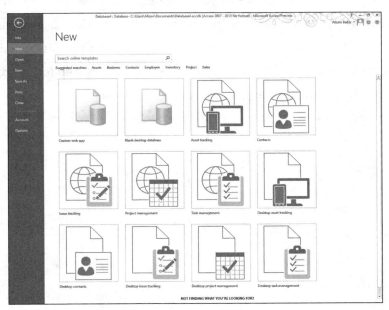

FIGURE 20.1

Use the File tab on the Ribbon to create a blank web database.

3. Select Custom web app from the list of available templates.

4. Supply an app name for the new database.

5. Enter a valid Web Location (see Figure 20.2). You, or someone familiar with Office 365, need to set this up in Office 365 prior to working with this chapter.

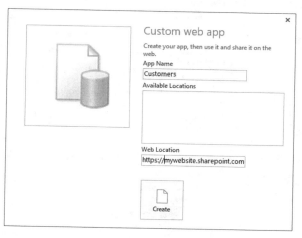

FIGURE 20.2

You must select Custom web app as the available template for your new database.

6. Click Create to complete the process. The new database appears, as shown in Figure 20.3.

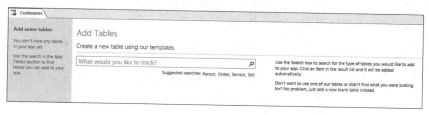

FIGURE 20.3

The web database appears prompting you to add new tables.

7. At this point you can create a table from an existing data source or using a template. To create a table using a template, type a search word in the What Would You Like to Track text box, and click the magnifying glass. Your screen appears, as shown in Figure 20.4.

8. Click the table you want to create. Access creates the table.

9. Continue to click to select other tables you want to add to the database.

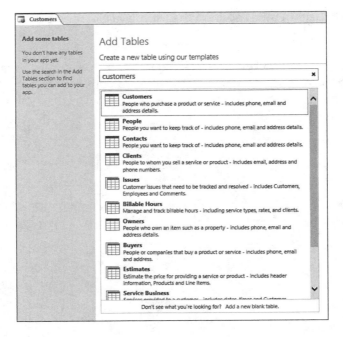

FIGURE 20.4

You can designate what you want to track.

10. Click Add a New Blank Table (a hyperlink on the right-hand side of the Add Tables dialog) to add any tables not available via a template. The table designer appears, as shown in Figure 20.5. Here you can create a table as you do in a standard Access database.

11. To view the Navigation Pane, click Navigation Pane in the Show group on the Home tab on the Ribbon. Your screen appears, as shown in Figure 20.6. Notice that Access created forms to correspond to each table that you created.

Creating a Query

You can create queries based on the tables in your web database. Just like queries in a standard Access database, you use these queries to extract the data that you need from the tables in the database. To create a query:

1. In the Create group of the Home tab on the Ribbon, open the Advanced drop-down.

2. Select Query. The Show Table dialog appears.

3. Click to select each table you want to add, and then click Add. Access adds the table to the query grid.

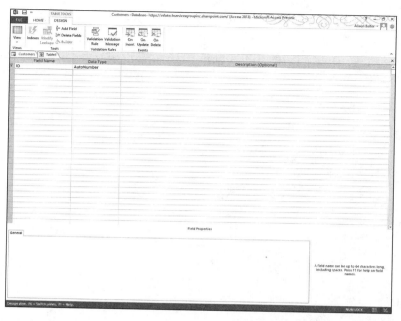

FIGURE 20.5

You can create a blank table without the use of a template.

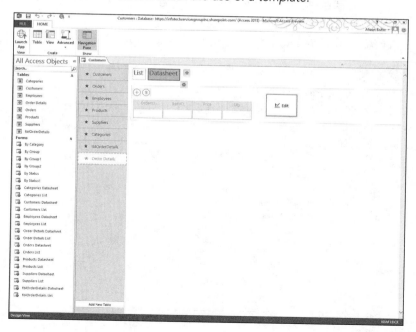

FIGURE 20.6

The Navigation Pane includes tables and corresponding forms.

4. Click Close when you finish adding tables. Access places you in Design view of the query.

5. Add the wanted fields to the query. Figure 20.7 shows the Company, Job Title, Work Phone, Home Phone, and Mobile Phone fields from the Customers table.

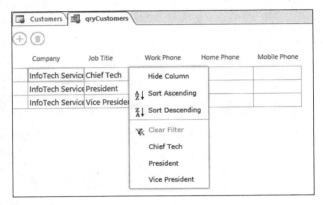

FIGURE 20.7

A query with customer information.

6. From the View drop-down in the Results group of the Design tab, select Datasheet View. Access prompts you to save the query.

7. Click Yes, and then supply a name in the Save As dialog.

8. Click OK to save and run the query.

9. When viewing the results of the query, each field contains a drop-down. Using the drop-down you can hide the column, sort in ascending order by the column, sort in descending order by the column, or filter by data in the column (see Figure 20.8).

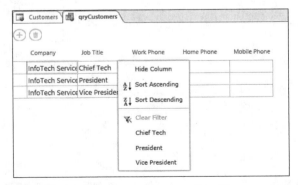

FIGURE 20.8

Each column contains a drop-down.

10. Click Refresh on the Ribbon to refresh the results of the query, or use the View drop-down to return to Design view.

Creating and Working with Forms

When you create tables, Access automatically creates forms associated with those tables. Access automatically creates two forms for each table. The first is a datasheet view of the table data (see Figure 20.9). The second is a list view (see Figure 20.10).

FIGURE 20.9

Datasheet view of the Customers table.

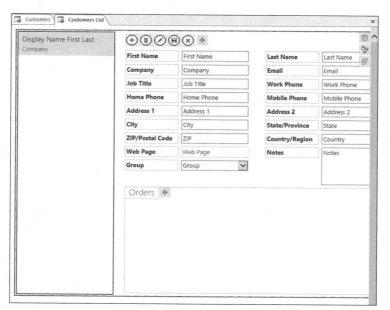

FIGURE 20.10

List view of the Customers table.

You can use these forms as-is, or you can customize them to your liking.

Creating a New Form

You can create a new blank form, a list details form, a datasheet form, or a summary form. All four options are available in the View Type drop-down of the Add New View dialog (see Figure 20.11).

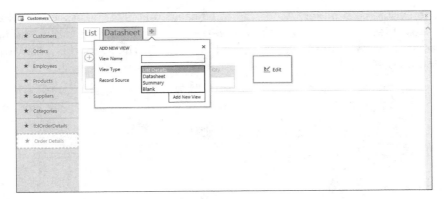

FIGURE 20.11

The View Type drop-down enables you to select the type of form you want to create.

To create a blank form, first select the table on which you want to base the form (for example, Customers). Next click the Add New View button. The Add New View dialog appears (see Figure 20.12). Provide a name for the view. Select Blank from the View Type drop-down. Make sure the Record Source is correct, and click Add New View. A blank form appears. Click Edit. The blank form appears with some standard tools and a Field List that you can use to drag and drop objects on your new form. In Figure 20.13, the ID, First Name, Last Name, Company, Email, Job Title, and phone fields on the form are added. When you click Save, the Save As dialog appears, prompting you to save my work.

After saving the form your were working on, you are ready to create another new form. To create a new form in List Details view, select List Details from the View Type drop-down in the Add New View dialog. As with the Blank View, you must select what data you need associated with the form. You accomplish this by selecting the Record Source in the Add New View dialog. With a List Details form, you can find two Data Tools. One is associated with the list, and the other with the form. You set the data for the form as you did for the Blank View form. When you click the Data tool for the list, it appears, as shown in Figure 20.14. Here you select what appears in the list. For example, you may want the ID and Order Date to appear in the list, and you may want to sort by ID. The completed form appears, as shown in Figure 20.15.

FIGURE 20.12

The Add New View dialog.

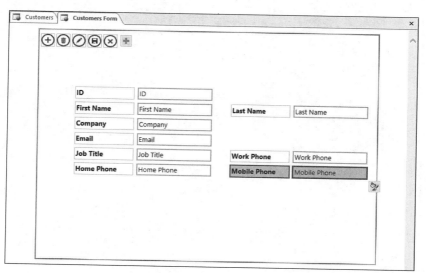

FIGURE 20.13

You can drag and drop fields from the Field List onto your form.

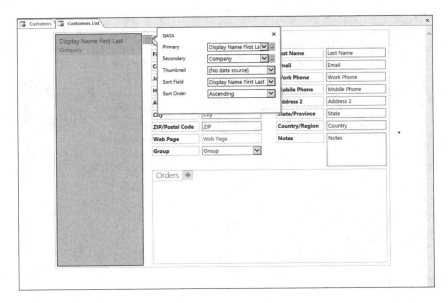

FIGURE 20.14

The Data tool enables you to select what appears in the list.

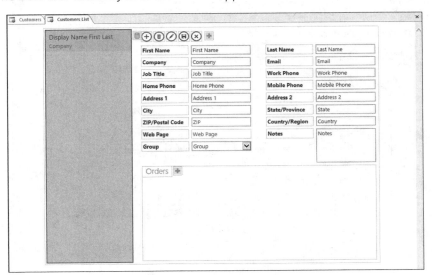

FIGURE 20.15

A completed List Details form.

To create a form in Datasheet view, select Datasheet from the View Type drop-down in the Add New View dialog. Again you must select what data you want to associate with the form. You do this by setting the Record Source in the Add New View dialog. The Datasheet form appears, as shown in Figure 20.16.

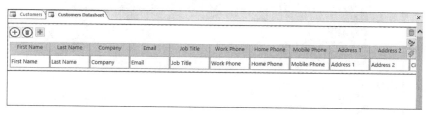

FIGURE 20.16

A completed Datasheet form.

Finally, to create a Summary form, select Summary from the View Type drop-down in the Add New View dialog. Select what data you want to associate with your summary form. A Summary form has three Data tools. You use the tool on the far-right to designate the Record Source for the Summary form. You use the tool associated with the middle section of the form to designate the data for the details associated with the summary (see Figure 20.17). You use the tool on the left for how you want to group and sort the summarized data. An example of a completed summary form appears in Figure 20.18.

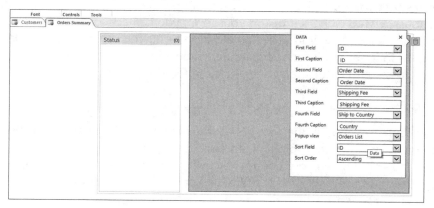

FIGURE 20.17

Designating data associated with the detail portion of the form.

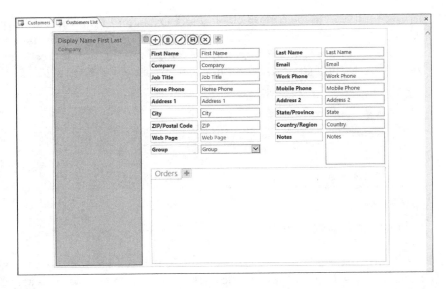

FIGURE 20.18

A completed Summary form.

Customizing an Existing Form

Regardless of the type of form you create, you probably want to customize the forms that you build. Using the Design tab on the Ribbon, you can change the font associated with controls on your form, you can add controls, and you can add existing fields. After you select a field on a form, you can change the data associated with it, format it, or associate an action with it. You can also add buttons to your forms and associate actions with the On Click event of the buttons.

Modifying the Font Associated with a Control

You can easily modify the font associated with a control. First, select the control or controls that you want to affect. To select multiple controls, click the first control, and then hold down your control key while you select subsequent controls. You can then use the Font group of the Design tab on the Ribbon to bold and italicize, and change the font size, alignment, and color.

Adding Controls to Your Form

You may want to add text boxes, command buttons, drop-downs, or other controls to the forms that you build. To do so, first click the control after which you want to add the new control. Then simply click in the Controls group on the Ribbon to select the type of control you want to add. After you add the control, you its Data, Formatting, and Actions properties (see the section "Changing Properties of a Control on a Form").

Changing Properties of a Control on a Form

Form controls have associated properties. These properties include data properties, format properties, and actions. The Data properties vary depending on the type of control you select. For example, the Data properties for a combo box appear in Figure 20.19. Notice you can change the control name, control source, default value, row source type, and row source. A check box, on the other hand, has only a control name, control source, and default value.

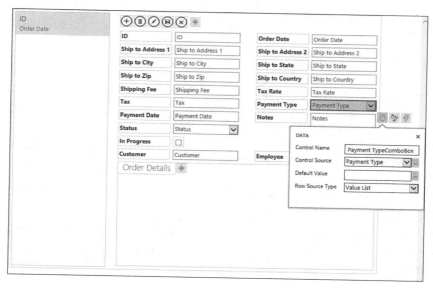

FIGURE 20.19

Data properties associated with a combo box.

The Format properties of a control enables you to provide a tooltip for the control. They also enables you to determine whether the control is visible and whether it is enabled. Text boxes also include a format option and an input hint.

The actions associated with a control vary depending on the type of the control. For example, a check box has only an After Update action, and a textbox has both an On Click action and an After Update action. When you select an action, a macro appears. Figure 20.20 shows the list of macro actions that appear. This list is much more limited than the list you saw in Chapter 17, "Automating Your Database with Macros." You can use all the techniques that you learned in Chapter 17 to build macros for your web forms.

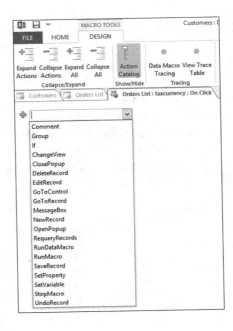

FIGURE 20.20

Macro actions available for a web form.

Adding Existing Fields to Your Form

After you associate a form with data, you can view the field list associated with that data. You can either double-click or else drag and drop fields from the field list onto your form. You simply click a field in the field list and then place it in the wanted position on your form.

Adding Commands to the Action Bar

Every form has an Action Bar associated with it. Using the Action Bar, the user of the form can add, delete, edit, save, and undo changes to form data. You can add your own custom commands to the Action Bar. You can then associate macros with those custom commands. Click the Add Custom Action tool on the right side of the Action Bar (see Figure 20.21). A new button appears. Click the button and then click the Data tool. The Data dialog appears. Here you can designate a control name, tooltip, icon, and On Click event for the button. When you select the On Click event, a macro window appears, enabling you to specify what actions you want to execute in response to someone clicking the button.

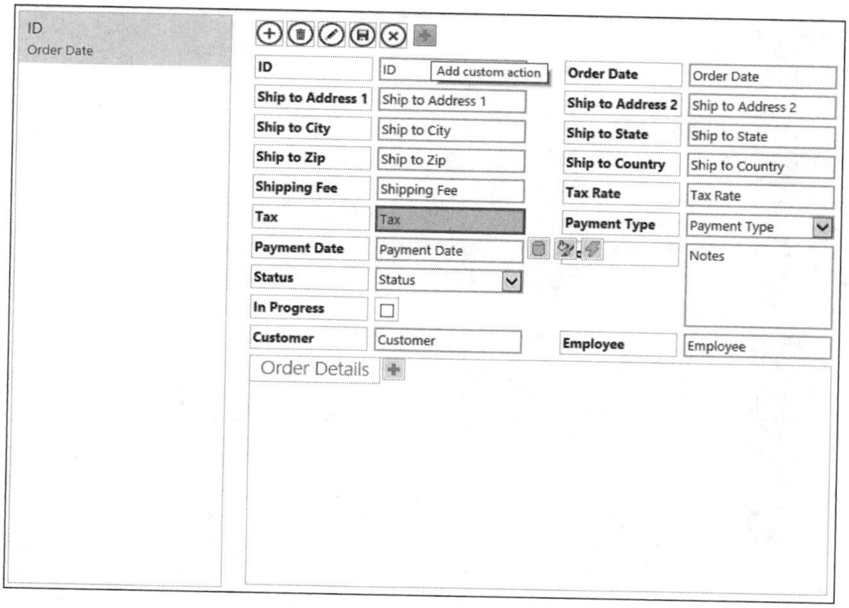

FIGURE 20.21

Click the Add Custom Action tool.

Using a Template to Create a Website

Now that you know how to create a website from scratch, it's time to see how to build a website with a template. After you create a website with a template, you can use all the techniques that you have learned in this chapter to customize the site that you have built. To use a template to create a website, follow these steps:

1. Click the File menu.

2. Click New.

3. Select one of the suggested searches (assets, business, contacts, and so on), or type your search criteria. All the web databases appear with an image of a globe. For example, in Figure 20.22, the Asset Tracking, Contacts, Issue Tracking, Project Management, and Task Management databases are all web databases.

4. Click to select the database template you want to use. The appropriate dialog appears.

5. Click Create. Access creates your new website. The website includes the appropriate tables and forms. Note that you Access may prompt you to log on to SharePoint to gain access to the database.

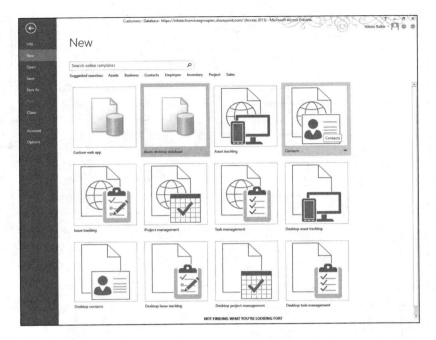

FIGURE 20.22

Web databases appear with an image of a globe.

Viewing Your Website in a Browser

When you finish designing your web application, whether you have built it from scratch or using a template, you need to test it in a browser. First, save all your changes using the Save tool. You can then click the Launch App tool in the View group on the Home tab of the Ribbon. You may be prompted to log on to SharePoint after which your browser launches and your application appears. Your tables appear on the left, and your forms appear across the top (see Figure 20.23). As you click each table name, the forms associated with that table appear. If you click a form name on the top, that form appears in the browser. Figure 20.24 shows a list form for the Orders table. Figure 20.25 shows a datasheet form for the Orders table. Figure 20.26 shows a summary form for the Orders table. The data is grouped by Status, and Shipping Fees are totaled on the left side of the form. The details for each order in the group appear on the right side of the form.

FIGURE 20.23

You can select tables and forms in your web browser.

FIGURE 20.24

The Orders table in List View.

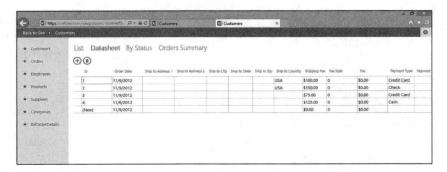

FIGURE 20.25

The Orders table as a Datasheet.

FIGURE 20.26

Orders data summarized by Status.

THE ABSOLUTE MINIMUM

This chapter covered the exciting, yet challenging, world of creating web applications. Web databases are somewhat different than their desktop counterparts. A web database is composed of tables, queries, and forms. When creating a web database, you connect to Office 365 to store your web database. You must configure Office 365 to store your databases prior to creating your first web database. You then use the appropriate location in the New Database dialog.

Just as you can create queries in a standard database, you can create queries in a web database. The queries you create can be based on the data in one or more tables. After you create a query, you can use it as the foundation for the web forms that you build.

When you create tables, Access automatically creates associated forms. You can customize those forms, or you can create your own forms. Access enables you to create four types of web forms: List Details, Datasheet, Summary, and Blank. Each form has a different look and feel. As its name implies, a blank form is a blank slate that you can create to your liking. A List Details form has a list on the left side and detailed data on the right side. When you click an item in the list, the details appear for that item. A Datasheet form displays the data in a datasheet. A Summary form summarizes data based on a key field. When you click the summary data on the left side of the form, the details behind that summary appear on the right side of the form.

Access makes it easy for you to view your web application in a browser. You probably do not want to wait until you complete an application to view it in the browser. Instead, as you make additions and changes to the application, you can periodically view it so that you can see how it looks and behaves in your browser.

IN THIS CHAPTER

- How can you build application tables?
- How can you build application forms?
- How can you design the queries that you need?
- How can you build application reports?
- How can you tie everything together with macros?

21

PUTTING IT ALL TOGETHER

You might have made it through the entire book and are still uncertain how to combine all the skills that you've acquired and create a complete database. This chapter puts everything that you've learned together and shows you how to accomplish the task of creating a complete database application. You build the tables that store your application data, the forms to enter your data, the queries to retrieve the data you need, the reports to display the data that you've entered, and the macros that add polish to your application.

Designing the Tables to Store Your Data

Create a new database and try designing a few of the tables needed by a computer consulting firm's time and billing application. You can build `tblClients` and `tblProjects` tables. The main table for the application, `tblClients`, will be used to track the key information about each client. The second table, `tblProjects`, will hold all the key information users need to store for the projects they're working on for each client. Table 21.1 shows the field names, data types, and sizes for each field in `tblClients`. You should include indexes for all fields except `Notes`. Table 21.2 shows the properties that need to be set for these fields. Table 21.3 shows the fields, data types, and sizes for the fields in `tblProjects`, and Table 21.4 shows the properties that need to be set for these fields. You should include indexes for all fields except `ProjectDescription`.

TABLE 21.1 Field Names, Data Types, and Sizes for the Fields in tblClients

Field Name	Data Type	Size
ClientID	AutoNumber	Long Integer
CompanyName	Short Text	50
ContactFirstName	Short Text	30
ContactLastName	Short Text	50
ContactTitle	Short Text	50
ContactTypeID	Number	Long Integer
ReferredBy	Short Text	82
AssociatedWith	Short Text	82
IntroDate	Date/Time	Stored as 8
DefaultRate	Currency	Stored as 8
Notes	Long Text	–
Miles	Number	Long Integer
TermTypeID	Number	Long Integer
HomePage	Hyperlink	–

TABLE 21.2 Properties That Need to Be Set for the Fields in tblClients

Field Name	Property	Value
ClientID	Caption	Client ID
ClientID	Set as primary key	-
CompanyName	Caption	Company Name
CompanyName	Required	Yes
ContactFirstName	Caption	Contact First Name
ContactLastName	Caption	Contact Last Name
ContactTitle	Caption	Contact Title
ContactTypeID	Caption	Contact Type ID
ReferredBy	Caption	Referred By
AssociatedWith	Caption	Associated With
IntroDate	Input Mask	99/99/0000
IntroDate	Caption Default Value	Intro DateIntroDate=Date()
IntroDate	Validation Rule	<=Date()
IntroDate	Validation Text	Date Entered Must Be On or Before Today
IntroDate	Required	Yes
DefaultRate	Caption	Default Rate
DefaultRate	Default Value	125
DefaultRate	Validation Rule	Between 75 and 150
DefaultRate	Validation Text	Rate Must Be Between 75 and 150
DefaultRate	Format	Currency
Miles	Validation Rule	>=0
Miles	Validation Text	Miles Must Be Greater Than or Equal to Zero
TermTypeID	Caption	Term Type ID
HomePage	Caption	Home Page

TABLE 21.3 Field Names, Data Types, and Sizes for the Fields in tblProjects

Field Name	Data Type	Size
ProjectID	AutoNumber	Long Integer
ProjectName	Short Text	50
ProjectDescription	Long Text	–
ClientID	Number	Long Integer
PurchaseOrderNumber	Short Text	30
ProjectTotalEstimate	Currency	8
EmployeeID	Number	Long Integer
ProjectBeginDate	Date/Time	Stored as 8
ProjectEndDate	Date/Time	Stored as 8

TABLE 21.4 Properties That Need to Be Set for the Fields in tblProjects

Field Name	Property	Value
ProjectID	Caption	Project ID
ProjectID	Set as primary key	–
ProjectName	Caption	Project Name
ProjectName	Required	Yes
ProjectDescription	Caption	Project Description
ClientID	Caption	Client ID
ClientID	Default Value	Remove default value of 0
ClientID	Required	Yes
PurchaseOrderNumber	Caption	Purchase Order Number
ProjectTotalEstimate	Caption	Project Total Estimate
ProjectTotalEstimate	Format	Currency
EmployeeID	Caption	Employee ID
ProjectBeginDate	Input Mask	99/99/0000
ProjectBeginDate	Caption	Project Begin Date
ProjectBeginDate	Input Mask	99/99/0000
ProjectEndDate	Caption	Project End Date

You need to relate `tblClients` and `tblProjects` in a one-to-many relationship based on the `ClientID` field. You must enforce referential integrity to ensure that the user cannot add projects for nonexistent clients. There is no need to set Cascade Update Related Fields because the client ID that relates the two tables is an `AutoNumber` field in `tblClients`. You do not want to enable Cascade Delete Related Records because you do not want any billing information to change if the user deletes a client. Instead, you want to prohibit the deletion of clients who have projects by establishing referential integrity between the two tables.

You also need three supporting tables, which are tblContactType, tblTerms, and tblEmployees, as shown in Tables 21.5, 21.6, and 21.7.

The tblContactType table stores the valid contact types. It relates to the tblClients table and is a lookup table for the ContactTypeID stored in the tblClients table. Make sure you set the primary key of the tblContactType table to the ContactTypeID field. Add some records to the table.

TABLE 21.5   The tblContactType Table

Field Name	Type	Size (Bytes)
ContactTypeID	AutoNumber	Long Integer
ContactType	Short Text	50

The `tblTerms` table stores the valid term types. It relates to the tblClients table and is a lookup table for the TermTypeID stored in the tblClients table. Make sure you set the primary key of the table to the TermTypeID field. Add some records to the table.

TABLE 21.6   The tblTerms Table

Field Name	Type	Size (Bytes)
TermTypeID	AutoNumber	Long Integer
TermType	Short Text	50

The tblEmployees table includes relevant employee information, such as name, address, and billing rate. The EmployeeID will be the primary key of the tblEmployees table. Add some employees to the table.

TABLE 21.7 The tblEmployees Table

Field Name	Type	Size (Bytes)
EmployeeID	AutoNumber	Long Integer
FirstName	Short Text	50
LastName	Short Text	50
Title	Short Text	50
EmailName	Short Text	50
Extension	Short Text	30
Address	Short Text	255
City	Short Text	50
StateOrProvince	Short Text	20
PostalCode	Short Text	20
Country	Short Text	50
HomePhone	Short Text	30
WorkPhone	Short Text	30
BillingRate	Currency	8

The tables, and all their relationships, appear in Figure 21.1.

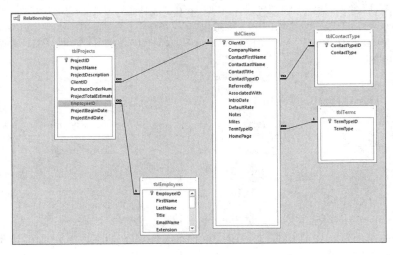

FIGURE 21.1

The Time and Billing tables and relationships.

Building the Forms to Edit Your Data

Your application will consist of two forms: the Clients form and the Projects form. You can open the Projects form from the Clients form. The following sections contain the steps necessary to build the required forms.

Designing the Clients Form

Here are the steps involved in creating the Clients form:

1. Click the Create tab, and then click Form Design.

2. Activate the Data tab of the property sheet. Select the `Record Source` property, and select `tblClients` as the Record Source.

3. Click to select the Add Existing Fields tool in the Tools group on the Design tab.

4. Select the `ClientID`, `CompanyName`, `ContactFirstName`, `ContactLastName`, `ContactTitle`, `ReferredBy`, `AssociatedWith`, `DefaultRate`, `Notes`, `Miles`, and `HomePage` fields from the field list. Drag and drop them to the form so that they appear as shown in Figure 21.2.

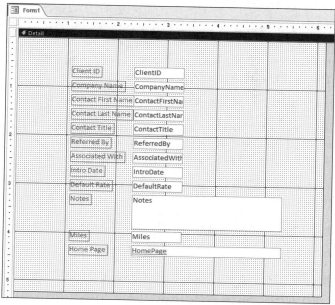

FIGURE 21.2

The frmClients form enables you to select and work with a particular client.

The next step is to add a combo box that allows the user to select the appropriate contact type for the client. The easiest way to accomplish the task is to use the Control Wizards:

1. Make sure that the Control Wizards tool is selected.

2. Click to select a combo box from the Controls group. Then click and drag to add the combo box to the appropriate location in the detail section of the form. The Combo Box Wizard launches.

3. Select I Want the Combo Box to Look Up the Values in a Table or Query. Click Next.

4. Select the `tblContactType` table from the list of available tables, and click Next.

5. Select both the `ContactTypeID` and the `ContactType` fields, and click Next.

6. Indicate that you want to sort by `ContactType`. Click Next.

7. Leave the Key column hidden, and size the `ContactType` column, if wanted. Click Next.

8. Select Store That Value In This Field. Select `ContactTypeID` from the combo box, and click Next.

9. Enter `Contact Type` as the text to appear within the label, and click Finish.

You can add another combo box to the form, allowing the user to designate the terms for the client, with the following steps:

1. Make sure that the Control Wizards tool is selected.

2. Click to select a combo box from the Controls group on the Design tab on the Ribbon; then click and drag to add it to the appropriate location in the detail section of the form. The Combo Box Wizard launches.

3. Select I Want the Combo Box to Look Up the Values in a Table or Query. Click Next.

4. Select the `tblTerms` table from the list of available tables, and click Next.

5. Select both the `TermTypeID` and the `TermType` fields, and click Next.

6. Indicate that you want to sort the records by `TermType` and click Next.

7. Hide the key column and click Next.

8. Store the value in the `TermTypeID` field, and click Next.

9. Enter `Term Type` as the text to appear within the label, and click Finish.

Take the following steps to refine the look and feel of the form:

1. Use the appropriate tools to size and align the objects.

2. Set the `Dividing Line` and `Record Selector` properties of the form to `No`. Set the `Auto Center` property to `Yes`.

3. Select Tab Order from the Controls Layout group on the Arrange tab, and set the tab order of the controls as appropriate.

4. Set the `Caption` property of the form to `Client Data Entry`.

You have now built the foundation for the form.

The next step is to add a combo box to the form that allows the user to select the client whose data she wants to view:

1. Right-click the form, and select Form Header/Footer.

2. Expand the header to make it large enough to hold the combo box and a command button that navigates to the `frmProjects` form.

3. Make sure that the Control Wizards tool is selected.

4. Click to select a combo box from the Controls group on the Design tab; then click and drag to add it to the header section of the form. The Combo Box Wizard launches.

5. Select Find a Record on My Form Based on a Value I Selected in My Combo Box. Click Next.

6. Select the `ClientID`, `CompanyName`, `ContactFirstName`, and `ContactLastName` fields as the Selected fields, and click Next.

7. Size the columns as appropriate (keeping the Key column hidden) and click Next.

8. Type `Select a Company` as the text for the label, and click Finish.

9. Click the Data tab of the property sheet. Select the `Row Source` property, and click the ellipsis to launch the Query Builder.

10. Change the Sort Order to sort the combo box entries by `CompanyName`, `ContactFirstName`, and `ContactLastName`.

11. Close the Query Builder window, and choose Yes; you want to save changes made to the SQL statement and update the property.

12. Run the form and make sure that it functions properly. It should appear as in Figure 21.3. Save the form again. Use the completed form to add some clients to the table.

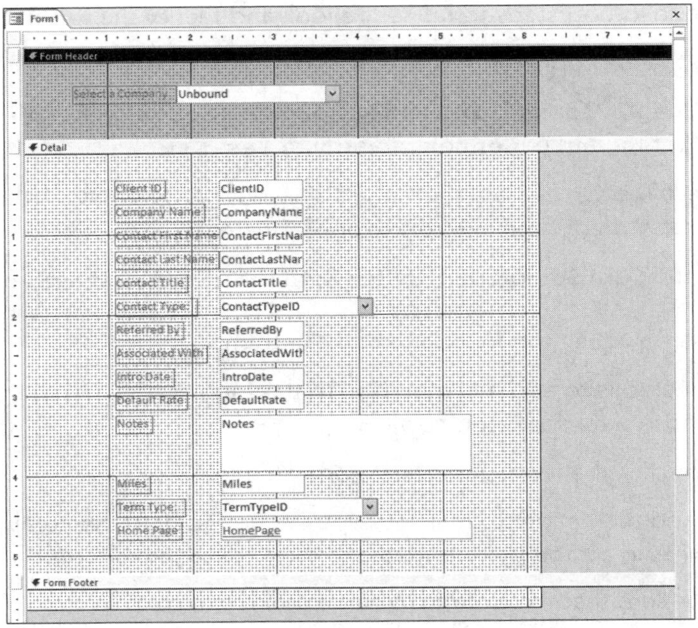

FIGURE 21.3

The frmClients form enables you to select and work with clients.

Designing the Projects Form

The next step is to design the Projects form, which is shown in Figure 21.4. The form is easily created with the Form Wizard and then customized. Here are the steps involved:

1. Select the Create tab.

2. Select Form Wizard.

3. Select `tblProjects` from the Tables/Queries drop-down.

4. Click to select all fields and click Next.

5. Select Columnar from the list of layouts and click Next.

6. Title the form `frmProjects` and click Finish.

7. Switch to the Form Design view. Delete the `ProjectID, EmployeeID, and ClientID` text boxes. Move and size the form objects so that the form appears as shown in Figure 21.4.

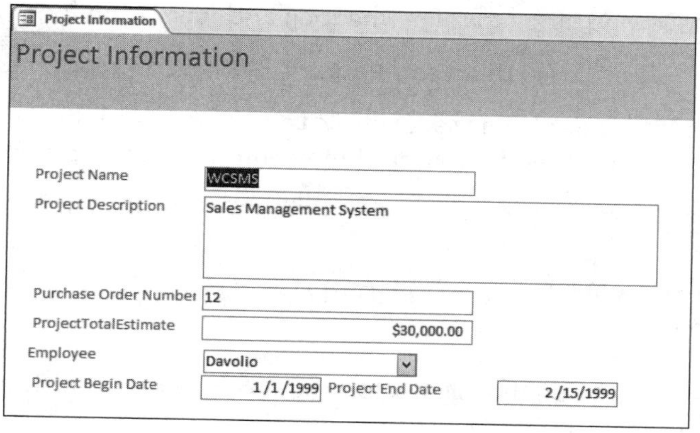

FIGURE 21.4

The completed frmProjects from.

A combo box must be added for the `EmployeeID`:

1. Make sure that the Control Wizards tool is selected.

2. Click to select a combo box from the Controls tab of the Design tab on the Ribbon; then click and drag to add it to the appropriate location in the detail section of the form. The Combo Box Wizard launches.

3. Select I Want the Combo Box to Look Up the Values in a Table or Query. Click Next.

4. Select the `tblEmployees` table from the list of available tables, and click Next.

5. Select the `EmployeeID`, `LastName`, and `FirstName` fields, and click Next.

6. Indicate that you want the data sorted by Last Name and then First Name, and click Next.

7. Leave the Key column hidden, and size the `LastName` and `FirstName` columns, if wanted. Click Next.

8. Select Store That Value in This Field. Select `EmployeeID` from the combo box, and click Next.

9. Enter `Employee` as the text to appear within the label, and click Finish.

Take the following steps to refine the look and feel of the form:

1. Set the `Dividing Line` and `Record Selector` properties of the form to **No**.

2. Select Tab Order from the Controls Layout group on the Arrange tab on the Ribbon, and set the tab order of the controls as appropriate.

3. Set the `Caption` property of the form to **Project Information**.

Adding a Command Button That Links the Clients and Projects Forms

The final step is to tie the Clients form to the Projects form. The Command Wizard helps to accomplish the task:

1. Return to the `frmClients` form in Design view.

2. Make sure the Control Wizards toolbar button is active.

3. Click to select a command button, and then click and drag to place it within the Header section of the `frmClients` form. The Command Button Wizard launches.

4. Click Form Operations within the list of categories.

5. Click Open Form within the list of Actions, and click Next.

6. Select `frmProjects` as the name of the form you would like the command button to open. Click Next.

7. Click Open Form and Find Specific Data to Display. Click Next.

8. Click to select the `ClientID` field from the `frmClients` form and the `ClientID` field from the `frmProjects` form. Click the <-> button to designate that the fields are joined. Click Next to continue.

9. Select a picture or enter text for the caption of the command button.

10. Enter the name for the command button. Don't forget to use proper naming conventions (for example, `cmdShowProjects`). Click Finish.

11. Switch from Design view to Form view, and test the command button. The `frmProjects` form should load, displaying projects for the currently selected client. Add projects associated with the clients that you added previously.

Building the Queries to Extract the Data You Need

You are going to build two queries to support the Time and Billing application. The first query will be used by the rptClientListing report. The second will be used by the rptProjectsByEmployee report. The first query is called qryClientListing. The query includes the `CompanyName`, `IntroDate`, and `DefaultRate` fields from the `tblClients` table. It joins the `tblClients` table to the `tblContactType` table to obtain the `ContactType` field from `tblContactType` and joins the `tblClients` table to the `tblTerms` table to obtain the `TermType` field from the `tblTerms` table. It also includes an expression called `ContactName` that concatenates the `ContactFirstName` and `ContactLastName` fields. The expression looks like this:

```
ContactName: [ContactFirstName] & " " & [ContactLastName]
```

To create `qryClientListing`:

1. Select Query Design from the Queries group on the Create tab on the Ribbon. The Show Table dialog appears.

2. Add the tblClients, tblContactType, and tblTerms tables to the query.

3. Click Close to close the Show Table dialog.

4. Add the CompanyName, IntroDate, and DefaultRate fields from tblClient, the ContactType field from tblContactType, and the TermType field from tblTerms, all to the query grid.

5. Add the expression ContactName: [ContactFirstName] & " " & [ContactLastName] to the query grid between the CompanyName and IntroDate fields.

6. Save the query as qryClientListing.

The second query is called qryProjectsByEmployee. It groups by employee, totaling the ProjectTotalEstimate for each employee for all records within a specified date range. The date range is based on parameters entered when the user runs the query.

To create `qryProjectsByEmployee` pictured in Figure 21.5:

1. Select Query Design from the Queries group on the Create tab on the Ribbon. The Show Table dialog appears.

2. Add the tblProjects and tblEmployees tables to the query.

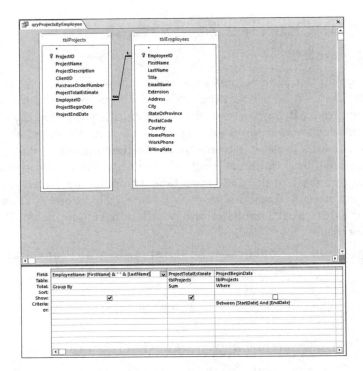

FIGURE 21.5

The `qryProjectsByEmployee` *query is grouped by employee and totals the ProjectTotalEstimate for a date range.*

3. Click Close to close the Show Table dialog.

4. Click the Totals tool in the Show/Hide group on the Design tab on the Ribbon.

5. Add the expression EmployeeName: [FirstName] & " " & [LastName] to the query grid. You will be grouping by that expression.

6. Add ProjectTotalEstimate from tblProjects to the query grid. Specify that you want to sum ProjectTotalEstimate.

7. Add ProjectBeginDate to the query grid. Specify that ProjectBeginDate will be your Where clause.

8. Enter the following in the criteria: Between [StartDate] and [EndDate].

9. Click the Parameters tool in the Show/Hide Group of the Design tab on the Ribbon.

10. Add StartDate and EndDate as Date With Time parameters. Close the Parameters dialog.

11. Save the query as qryProjectsByEmployee. The completed query appears as in Figure 21.5. When run with data in the tables, the query appears as in Figure 21.6.

EmployeeName	SumOfProjectTotalEstimate
Andrew Fuller	$2,000.00
Dan Balter	$267,000.00
Janet Leverling	$3,000.00
Laura Callahan	$2,500.00
Margaret Peacock	$1,000.00
Nancy Davolio	$11,700.00

FIGURE 21.6

The results of running qryProjectsByEmployee.

Designing the Reports to Display Your Data

The sample application requires several reports. A couple of the simpler ones are built here.

Designing the rptClientListing Report

The `rptClientListing` report lists all the clients in the `tblClients` table. The report includes the company name, contact name, intro date, default rate, and term type of each customer. The report is grouped by contact type and sorted by company name. It provides the average default rate by contact type and overall.

The `rptClientListing` report is based on a query called `qryClientListing`, which you created earlier in the chapter.

To build the report, follow these steps:

1. Click the Report Wizard tool in the Reports group on the Create tab.

2. Use the drop-down list to select the `qryClientListing` query.

3. Click the >> button to designate that you want to include all the fields in the query within the report. Click Next.

4. Indicate that you want to view your data by `tblContactType`. Click Next.

5. Do not add any grouping to the report. Click Next.

6. Use the drop-down list to select `CompanyName` as the sort field.

7. Click Summary Options and click the Avg check box to add the average default rate to the report. Click OK to close the Summary Options dialog box, and click Next to proceed to the next step of the wizard.

8. Select Landscape for the Orientation, and click Next.

9. Give the report the title `rptClientListing`; then click Finish.

10. The completed report should look like Figure 21.7. Click Design to open the report in Design view. Notice that both the name and title of the report are `rptClientListing` (see Figure 21.8). Modify the title of the report so that it reads `Client Listing by Contact Type and Company Name`.

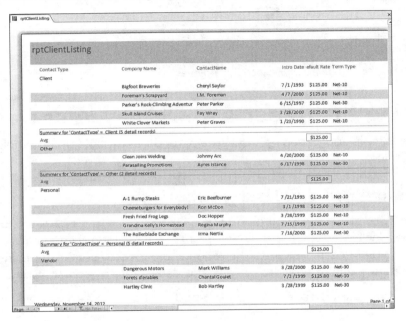

FIGURE 21.7

A preview of the completed report.

The second report is based on `qryProjectsByEmployee`. To build the report:

1. Click Report Wizard in the Reports group of the Create tab on the Ribbon.

2. Select qryProjectsByEmployee in the Tables/Queries drop-down.

3. Add both query fields to the query. Click Next.

4. Don't add any grouping to the report. Click Next.

5. Sort in Descending order by the SumOfProjectTotalEstimate field. Click Next.

6. Keep the default layout and orientation, and click Next.

7. Call the report rptProjectsByEmployee, and click Finish.

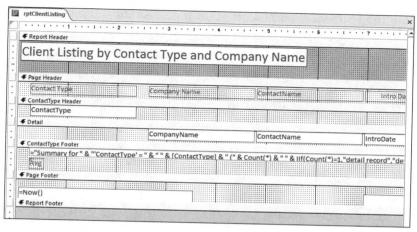

FIGURE 21.8

Changing the report title.

8. You will be prompted to add the parameter values for the query. The completed report appears in Figure 21.9.

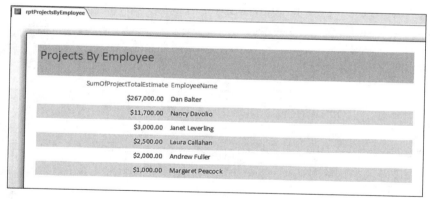

FIGURE 21.9

A preview of the completed report.

9. Switch to the design of the query.

10. Change the label in the report header to read **Projects by Employee.**

11. Click and drag to expand the report footer.

12. Copy the SumOfProjectTotalEstimate expression into the report footer.

13. Modify the expression to read

    =Sum(SumOfProjectTotalEstimate).

14. Set the Format property of the control to Currency. The report should appear as in Figure 21.10.

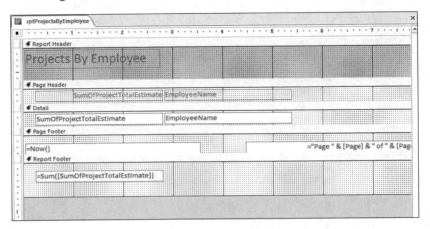

FIGURE 21.10

Design view of the report after adding the total project estimate.

15. Preview the report. It should appear as in Figure 21.11.

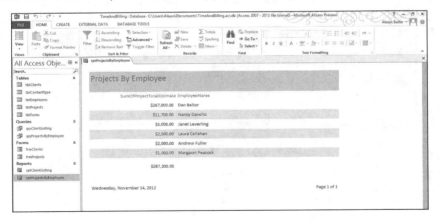

FIGURE 21.11

Preview of the report after adding the total project estimate.

Building the Macros Necessary to Automate Your Application

Build the macro shown in Figure 21.12. Start by opening a new macro in Design view. Set the first action of the macro to `RunMenuCommand` and then set the `Command` argument to `WindowHide`. This will hide the Navigation Pane when it's run. Set the second action of the macro to `MessageBox` and set the message to `Welcome to the Client Billing Application`. Set Beep to `No`, the Type to `Information`, and the Title to `Welcome`. The final action of the macro opens the `frmClients` form. Set the action to `OpenForm` and set the FormName to `frmClients`. Leave the rest of the arguments at their default values. Save and name the macro AutoExec.

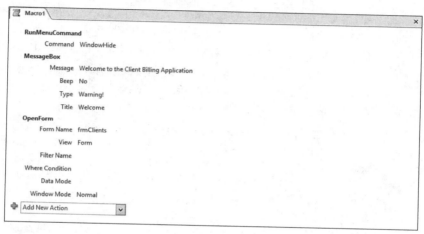

FIGURE 21.12

The completed macro.

Close and reopen the database. The AutoExec macro should automatically execute when the database is opened. Close the database and open it again, holding down the Shift key to prevent the macro from executing.

THE ABSOLUTE MINIMUM

This chapter showed you how to design a complete database application in Microsoft Access. You started as you would start with any database application, by building the tables that lie at the foundation of the database. You then related those tables. Remember that without a sound database structure, it is difficult to build the queries, forms, reports, and macros that make your database meaningful and useful.

You built two forms, adding functionality to open the projects form based on the selected client in the clients form. In this way, only projects associated with the current client appear in the projects form.

You then built two queries so that they could be used by your application reports. The first query contained client data, as well as an expression that concatenated the contact first name and contact last name. It is a good idea to build queries that contain expressions that you want to use on a regular basis so that you don't need to build those expressions again and again. The second query was a totals query and a parameter query. It summarized information by employee, totaling the project total estimate for a date range. By designing the queries properly, it made it extremely easy to build the necessary reports.

After using wizards to create the reports, you modified the design of the completed reports to customize them to your liking. Finally, you built a macro that runs each time that the user opens the database. The macro hides the Navigation Pane and displays the Clients form.

With all this information under your belt, you should now be ready to build your own complete database applications. I hope that you enjoy building databases with Microsoft Access as much as I do.

Index

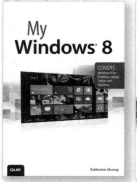

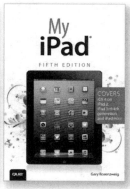

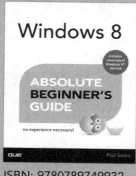

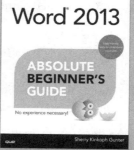

 ® quepublishing.com

Browse by Topic ▼ | Browse by Format ▼ | USING | More ▼

Store | Safari Books Online

QUEPUBLISHING.COM
Your Publisher for Home & Office Computing

Quepublishing.com includes all your favorite— and some new—Que series and authors to help you learn about computers and technology for the home, office, and business.

Looking for tips and tricks, video tutorials, articles and interviews, podcasts, and resources to make your life easier? Visit **quepublishing.com**.

- **Read the latest articles and sample chapters** by Que's expert authors

- **Free podcasts** provide information on the hottest tech topics

- **Register your Que products** and receive updates, supplemental content, and a coupon to be used on your next purchase

- **Check out promotions and special offers** available from Que and our retail partners

- **Join the site** and receive members-only offers and benefits

Business Management
Finance and Investing
Graphics, Pictures & Video
Gadgets & Hardware
General Computing
Entertainment & Gaming
Internet & Web Apps
Computer Software
Operating Systems
Web Design & Development

QUE NEWSLETTER
quepublishing.com/newsletter

 twitter.com/ quepublishing

 facebook.com/ quepublishing

 youtube.com/ quepublishing

 quepublishing.com/ rss

 ®   Que Publishing is a publishing imprint of Pearson